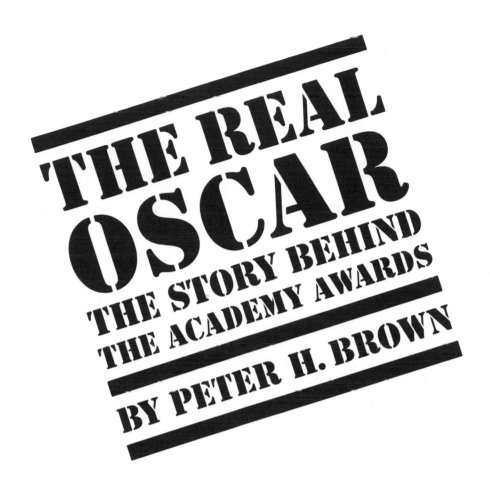

THE REAL OSCAR
THE STORY BEHIND THE ACADEMY AWARDS
BY PETER H. BROWN

ARLINGTON HOUSE
WESTPORT, CONNECTICUT

This book was produced for Arlington House/Publishers by

Rosebud Books
1777 Vine Street
Los Angeles, California 90028

Design by Laura LiPuma

Library of Congress Cataloging in Publication Data

Brown, Peter H.
The Real Oscar

1. Academy awards (Moving pictures) I. Title.
PN1993.U6B9   791.43'079   80-26101
ISBN 0-87000-498-0

First printing January, 1981
Printed in the United States of America

Acknowledgements

The Academy of Motion Picture Arts and Sciences is, itself, an incredible survivor in a city where even yesterday's stars are quickly discarded. The heart and soul of the Academy—its officers and staffs through the decades—have always been above reproach, dedicated to film preservation, research, and the healthy state of the art. This heart has been assaulted by the producers, victimized by actors and writers, twice drained of its financial lifeblood, and left out in the sun to die numerous times. Still it has survived, saving—along with itself—hundreds of rare films, the entire history of the medium, and a million still photographs. No book on film history has ever been published without the help of the monumental Margaret Herrick Library. And the Academy's Oscar show, for better or worse, has spread the word of the movies to an audience of three hundred million. The Academy of Motion Picture Arts and Sciences is NOT the Oscar race and, in a perverse way, the Oscar race is not the Academy. The voters, the economic marketplace, and the force of greed control the Oscars; the Academy only serves as the vessel in which the ceremony is carried.

This book is not the story of the Academy but is rather an examination of the Oscars as people in the industry seem to have viewed them—believing, as they do, that the Academy Awards are the movies' ultimate publicity stunt. The original founders established them as a glorified voice to the world. They remain that today. This book is also not a history of the Academy Awards—only select years and winners-losers are covered. Fine statistical histories of the Oscars have been done recently by Robert Osborne in *50 Golden Years of Oscar: The Official History of the Academy of Motion Picture Arts and Sciences,* published by ESE California in 1979, and by Richard Shale in *Academy Awards: An Ungar Reference Index,* Frederick Ungar Publishing Co., New York, 1978. Both authors, in different ways, have made order and interest out of the Academy Awards' disjointed history. Together, they form a unique whole. In a way, those books made this one possible. Before these two volumes, the only works on the Academy were little more than glorified depictions of the Academy's own P.R. line.

Most of this book relies on original interviews by the few people willing to discuss the "other side" of the Oscars. For that, I thank: Lee Grant, film writer for the *Los Angeles Times;* scriptwriter Philip Dunne; Joan Fontaine; Rod Steiger; Estelle Parsons; Cliff Robertson; agent Martin Baum; Elaine Young, ex-wife of Gig Young; Gale Sondergaard; Kim Hunter; George C. Scott; Trish Van Devere; George Cukor; Lana Turner; Debbie Reynolds; Ann Miller; actress and director Lee Grant; Dore Freeman, MGM archivist and MGM still director for three decades; Marc Wanamaker, founder of Bison Archives in Beverly Hills; Jet Fore, publicity director for Twentieth Century-Fox; actor George Kennedy; publicist Henry Rogers, founder of Rogers and Cowan and author of *Walking the Tightrope: The Private Confessions of a Public Relations Man;* and Howard Suber, Ph.D., film professor at UCLA and an expert in the Hollywood blacklist and the Academy Awards. For research help I thank Carole Epstein, a research director at the Academy's Margaret Herrick Library; Terri Roach, director of research, Margaret Herrick Library; and Anthony Slide, Academy official in charge of special film programs. For stills, I thank Eddie Brandt's Movie Matinee, the Margaret Herrick Library, Larry Edmunds Book Shop, Paul Hunt Books, and Hollywood Book City. I am also grateful to Hal Ashby, Pola Negri, Lillian Gish, Carl Foreman, and actor-coach Jeff Corey for earlier interviews that were used in part. And especially to Irv Letofsky, editor of *Calendar* magazine, the *Los Angeles Times,* for helping me start entertainment writing in the first place.

CONTENTS

PROLOGUE

"The way I see it, there's only one place that does it right. Every year in Barcelona they give awards for poetry. The third prize is a silver rose. The second prize is a gold one. The first prize, the one for the best poem of all, is a real rose." Peter Bogdanovich.

Vivien Leigh accepting her Oscar before a live radio remote broadcast as best actress of 1939. Miss Leigh, an unknown to American audiences, leaped to prominence for her portrayal of Scarlett O'Hara in *Gone With the Wind*.

There's something slightly desperate about it. It's even a bit coy—a scene too cute for words.

Dustin Hoffman has just come down from Hollywood's Valhalla. Just a knight and his Oscar ready to take on the world.

Two minutes earlier, Dustin Hoffman had bought Hollywood. All of it, from the zircon hemline on Cher's dress to the last inch of cement in front of Grauman's Chinese Theatre. There are others in that rarified light, of course. Sally Field, for instance. And Meryl Streep. But that was only for a few seconds.

Hollywood is still a chauvinistic empire. Man rules; the actor, not the actress. So Hoffman has a fraction of time to himself—at the top of a billion dollar hill. It's dizzy up there—a heady atmosphere that still has a hint of Gable and Bogie. And it's slippery—slick from the tracks of yesterday's kings on their way back down: Voight, Dreyfuss, Nicholson.

Plenty of time. It's not midnight yet. And Hoffman's won himself a few extra minutes by lustily dedicating his Oscar to all those nameless and faceless actors out in the smog. The ones who won't make it; quickly aging waiters and carhops smiling vainly at a town on the make.

Hoffman tugs at his beautifully cut tuxedo. His face turns up at the corners in a little boy smile. His friends hardly recognize it. But no matter; this isn't a smile for intimates. It's a smile for Brazil, and Soho. A smile for the faceless fans in Kankakee, Illinois, and Midlothian, Texas.

Finally the last flashbulb has popped and even the gossip columnists are getting bored. Oscar in hand, Hoffman glides over to the ice lady of all Hollywood journalists, Rona Barrett, sits down next to her, and lowers his handsome head into her lap. "Well," he says, "the soap opera won." Rona's smile doesn't vary a millimeter.

She probably knows—as does everyone else in the room—that this is a new Dustin Hoffman, a "born again" Hoffman; the Dustin Hoffman of *Kramer vs. Kramer*—not the same man of *Straw Dogs* or even of *Lenny*. For he has crossed over into Hollywood's twilight zone, the inner-sanctum of the establishment. And if he looks in the mirror and says, "Hey, who's this guy?" he doesn't show it. It's been far less than a decade since Hoffman, at that time still the angry young man of *The Graduate*, lashed out at the cruel realities of the Oscar rites. Then he cried out, as if in pain, about the pointless, gross charade of the Academy Awards—an institution that honors the cotton candy of the box office instead of artistic integrity.

Well, Dustin Hoffman has some cotton candy of his own now. This year's winner. The larger world knows it as *Kramer vs. Kramer*, but the guys and dolls on Rodeo Drive know it as "Dustin's film"—many miles of celluloid that have carried him over the top. Only six months ago they had sat in their Puccis and Guccis and chatted cattily about whether or not Dustin would be able to overcome a couple of weighty turkeys known as *Straight Time* and *Agatha.* Now they all laugh bravely into their Perrier water and chortle that they "knew it all along." Then they rush back to their sleek executive towers to call Dustin's agent: Perhaps, they coo, he could do a little *Kramer vs. Kramer* for them. They'd been planning to call him all along, of course. Isn't it funny about timing. This town is just one long coincidence.

The same guys who whispered that he was through when *Lenny* bombed now smile and wave bravely from their Alfas. Hoffman just continues jogging up the hill in Westwood. The Cheshire cat smile is back. He's forty-three, and this is Act Two.

Who can blame him for the momentary lapse. The Oscar is a pagan rite after all; a night when the tribe comes out to bay at the moon and drink the heady waters of fame. The young ones come to nurse at the nipple of glamour; the old ones come to bathe in the golden light and reaffirm their manufactured identities. See, I'm still there—just look at the monitor if you don't believe it. The most realistic of them see it for what it is. Coming off the Oscar stage in the fifties, Joan Crawford heard a fellow star murmur, "You looked wonderful up there on the screen." Crawford pulled at her diamonds and hissed: "That's not me; that's Joan Crawford."

And so it was.

If there was anyone left in town who doubted the paganism of the Academy Awards, the last five years have made converts out of them.

First there was Susan Hayward, almost carried onstage by a pair of strong arms, wearing a $2,000 dress and her old, gutsy smile. There was a pause before she started speaking which sent a frozen dagger out into the heart of Hollywood. Everyone knew Susan Hayward was dying—bad news gets around Beverly Hills and bounces back in less than an hour. Indeed, the world knew. The *National Enquirer* had dished up all the blunt details to eighty million readers. Up in a sterile medical tower at 9000 Sunset Boulevard two doctors and a nurse held their breath, hoping that Hayward would make it those few last steps—her last in the soothing spotlight of mass love. One of them dug his fist into a steel counter and wondered at a world willing to put a girl that sick through a dog and pony show.

The Oscars, though, bear no resemblance to the real world of supermarkets and family cars. This is *Brigadoon.* Here for three hours and gone. Ever since the Academy dragged D.W. Griffith out of cold storage in 1936, one of Oscar's three rings has been reserved for fading or dying stars. "When they sign you up for one of those so-called 'special awards,'" remarked Joan Crawford, "you know it's time to cash it in."

No sacrifice is too great for the voracious appetites of the three hundred million out in the world television arena.

But when they offered up Mary Pickford in 1976 there was no lower to go. As usual, the Academy softened the blow with that balmy term,

Dustin Hoffman reads last-minute script changes on the set of *Kramer vs. Kramer*, the movie that finally brought him the Oscar after years of supressed bitterness. Hoffman, whose finest performances in *Straw Dogs* and *Papillon* failed to bring even nominations, carefully played the Oscar game with a rare virtuosity— appearing at the secondary award ceremonies with an All-American smile.

Susan Hayward, in a hot red dress, holding aloft the Oscar she won for *I Want to Live!* It had been a long haul to the top for the former Edith Marriner whose face first appeared among those screen testing for the Scarlett O'Hara role in *Gone With the Wind*. Pushing her way through a series of exploitive film roles, Susan finally got her teeth into a decent script in 1947 with *Smash-up: The Story of a Woman*. Other nominations followed for *My Foolish Heart*, *With a Song in My Heart*, and *I'll Cry Tomorrow*. Then *I Want to Live!* The actress couldn't know on Oscar night that her high point was over. In usual fifties post-Oscar tradition, Hayward was pushed into one overblown production after another—all designed to cash in on her status as an Oscar winner. Her big movie exit was in the tawdry *Valley of the Dolls* where she fumed, to an equally obnoxious Patty Duke, "Get your butt outta my dressin' room."

© A.M.P.A.S.

Mary Pickford as she appeared to the world for the last time on Oscar's fiftieth birthday. It was exploitive to be sure. But there were defenders. Such as columnist Mike Royko who said: "Many of those say they would rather remember her as she once was. Why? She's not dead. She may be old but she is a living, breathing human being. She has thoughts and emotions, and, I'm sure, experiences happiness. That's what I thought I saw on her face when the camera came in close. There was even a tiny teardrop in her eye."

"special award." They had promised no fuss, no invasion of privacy for the first superstar—a lady who had exited gracefully from the hurricane of mass hysteria. "A couple of people. One camera," they told the man who ran the vast Pickford empire.

Mary agreed. Four people! And they'd hardly be noticed in her own living room. The day came, Mary Pickford came down from the distant upper-reaches of Pickfair, the castle she'd shared with Douglas Fairbanks when movies were silent and they were king and queen. She rounded the corner into a blaze of lights that blanked out the room's soft curtains. The network had squeezed about forty people in there—a restless, poking crowd. It would have frightened Streisand, let alone Pickford.

Still, she lifted her chin and broke into the fading Pollyanna grin. "Thank you so much," she said, tears forming at the edges of her eyes. On the Oscar show the boys in charge let this tape run its full, devastating course, tracing the camera over her Victorian face as if it were the surface of the moon and Oscar an astronaut.

The jig was suddenly up. It became clear that the Academy and its TV henchmen would root up any part or all of its ravaged past in the ratings game—in much the same way that a dashing and handsome streaker materialized from the wings in the 1974 ceremony. What's one more publicity stunt in the biggest Hollywood publicity stunt of them all—the Academy Awards?

Ratings translate into millions of viewers; millions of viewers translate into ticket buyers, which only mean money. Money; profits; movie grosses—this is the essence of Oscar.

Some say it wasn't always that way—a claim that's hard to judge. One thing's for sure, it *was* that way in 1948 when all the studios pulled their money out of the Oscar show after it became obvious that a British

Jack Nicholson, who was finally triumphant in 1975's *One Flew Over the Cuckoo's Nest* and became well-known all over the world as one of the finest actors in film today. But it was a long and twisted road to the top for Nicholson. A trick of fate, in fact, pulled Nicholson out of the shade when Rip Torn backed out of Peter Fonda's and Dennis Hopper's *Easy Rider* and Nicholson was given the part—really just a cameo—as a drop-out lawyer. He was nominated for the Oscar and went into a string of acting victories perhaps unequaled in the past twenty years—*Five Easy Pieces, Chinatown, The Last Detail*, and finally playing R.P. McMurphy in *One Flew Over the Cuckoo's Nest*. But he'd been in Hollywood for ten years with little success until Rip Torn turned down a good part. As Dustin Hoffman said, "How many other Oscar-calibre actors are out there—undiscovered?"

film, *Hamlet,* and a British actor, Olivier, were going to be the big winners. "Jeez," said some of the moguls. "We didn't go to ALL THIS trouble to publicize foreign pictures."

The big boys weren't worrying about artistic integrity. They were worried about ticket sales. That is Oscar's overriding purpose today.

There used to be a big glass case over at MGM which held the studio's Oscars—all stacked up neatly in a row: by movie and by year. Tour guides used to point out the case to tourists, quoting prices up and down the box office scale. "Now this here's the ten million dollar Oscar," he would say, pointing to the little gold man won by *Ben-Hur.*"And over here is the five million dollar Oscar for *An American in Paris.*"

Those tour guides aren't there anymore, and there's a rumor that the Oscars have all been moved to the MGM Grand Hotel in Las Vegas—closer to the money.

The same thing happens to the Oscars of today. Only inflation has hit. Boy, has it hit! Now they call them "the twenty-five million dollar Oscars." Some of them are worth a lot more than that. *One Flew Over the Cuckoo's Nest*, the first film to win all top five Oscars since *It Happened One Night*, cashed in on its Academy Awards and added more than forty million dollars to its worldwide ticket sales. The film would have made additional dough anyway. But it's hard to separate fact from Oscar fiction. The studio bosses of today might be mildly interested in what a film would do without ANY Oscar exposure, but they sure wouldn't want to risk finding out.

The result is inevitable and unfortunate—an Oscar that can literally create financial empires overnight will never be free of meddling and blatant attempts to buy or coerce the award out of the Academy's voters.

Adding to the problem is the failure of the Academy's own physical

Two of the biggest reasons why the list of the un-Oscared often seems more illustrious than the winner's circle—Cary Grant and Irene Dunne—in *The Awful Truth*. It's hard to believe that Dunne and Grant—on almost anybody's list of Hollywood's finest actors—never won the big one. Irene Dunne was nominated for *Cimarron, Theodora Goes Wild, The Awful Truth, Love Affair,* and *I Remember Mama*. Her work in *Anna and the King of Siam* and *The Mudlark* was ignored by Oscar voters. Cary Grant was nominated only twice—for *Penny Serenade* and *None But the Lonely Heart*—and his ignored triumphs are too numerous to mention. In 1969 the Academy finally honored him with an honorary statue for "unique mastery of the art of acting."

Cary Grant and Rosalind Russell in *His Girl Friday*.

strength to keep up with the vast growth of the crafts and specialties. The industry now has a central core of at least 40,000 actors, writers, cinematographers, etc. The Academy has 4,000. And only about fifty to sixty percent of those can be counted on to vote. This means the single most important decision is made by only one-twentieth of the industry. And there is little chance that it will ever change.

A few of the wiser winners and nominees have seen through the desperation and avarice that surround the Oscar.

Rosalind Russell, four times nominated and never a winner, came to view the city's barbaric rite with increasing dismay. "In 1942, I'd got my first Academy Award nomination for *My Sister Eileen*. Glad as I was about it, the honor put me under heavy pressure. It means too much to the studios to have their people win," said Russell in the seventies. "I still can't bear to think about the tension surrounding those races without breaking into a sweat."

Charles Champlin, entertainment editor of the *Los Angeles Times*, now calls the Oscar "the tail that wags the Academy." And it's true; nobody truly cares that the Academy is at the forefront of the drive to restore and save old films, or that its archives now contain the largest single historic collections of stills and movie clips—a library that has rescued many chapters of film history.

Likewise its research, scholarship programs, festivals, and technical publications get little or no media attention from the howling mob of reporters that storms the gates each year to report on the bacchanal that crowns Hollywood's king and queen of the May.

Only a stalwart few have been able to resist the sweet screams of this Lorelei and her seductive promises of wealth, instant fame, and ego elixir.

Many have tried and failed—like Dustin Hoffman who kicked out in rage at the Oscars when it seemed hopeless to him, but came back to the fold when Oscar's honeyed words were whispering his song.

Two men stand above the pack—an almost forgotten screenwriter named Dudley Nichols and George C. Scott.

Nichols was first. He entered Academy history in 1936 by refusing to show up Oscar night for his prize. (He'd already been told that he had won.) At that time the Academy was still being used by the studio establishment to halt the spread of labor unions. The 3,000-member Screen Actors Guild, the 500-member Writers Guild, and the fledgling Directors Guild of America had all asked their members, winners included, to boycott the ceremony.

Only Nichols and director John Ford kept their word. Bette Davis, Victor McLaglen, and others dutifully showed up to take their statues home.

Twenty-five years later, when even a best supporting actor Oscar added two million dollars to a career, George C. Scott was caught up in the annual Oscar lust before he consulted his own conscience. Scott, already a legend on the stage, made his film debut in *The Hanging Tree*, 1959. Six months later Otto Preminger picked him to play the driven, vicious prosecuting attorney in *Anatomy of a Murder*.

Even up against Lee Remick, James Stewart, and Ben Gazzara, Scott walked away covered with glory. As his biographer, W.A. Harbison, said, "He never had to worry about getting a film once *Anatomy of a Murder* was released."

Hedda Hopper predicted an Oscar for him and he was easily nominated—along with Arthur O'Connell from the same film, Hugh Griffith in *Ben-Hur*, Robert Vaughn in *The Young Philadelphians*, and Ed Wynn in *The Diary of Anne Frank*.

Karl Malden and George C. Scott in *Patton,* which brought the Oscar gold to Scott—a grand touch of justice for an underhonored actor. But the lure of patriotism was, once again, a Siren call that far finer films such as *M*A*S*H* and *Five Easy Pieces* could not compete with. So *Patton* was named best picture and brought the best director Oscar to Franklin J. Schaffner which was a crime because the work of Robert Altman, for *M*A*S*H,* Federico Fellini, for *Satyricon,* and Ken Russell, for *Women in Love,* was better. David Lean wasn't nominated for *Ryan's Daughter.* Injustices like these caused George C. Scott to refuse the Oscar and vow never to discuss the subject again.

Scott was the new face in town. He stood a good chance to win. And he wanted the Oscar. Friends said he wanted the Academy Award as much as he'd wanted anything in his career. Newcomers to the factories of mediocrity are often dazzled by the Oscar's reflected golden light. And Scott may have been one of them.

Years later, in a reflective moment, he told his wife, actress Trish Van Devere, that he learned a valuable lesson on Oscar night, 1960 (for the 1959 awards). "He said he wanted it so badly that he became almost completely wrapped up in it. When he didn't win, he took a hard look, and came to believe it wasn't healthy to want something so much."

Trish Van Devere, who became her husband's co-star in a half dozen films and on Broadway, says Scott first looked at himself and his own morbid fascination with the Oscar, and then at the larger picture.

1960 was a good year to do it.

Old-style studio greed still had the Academy Awards in a vice. Whether the Oscar went to a good film or merely an expensive film was decided at the whim of potentates—Darryl Zanuck, Dore Schary, and Jack Warner. Nominations were easy to control—the finals were more difficult but still "buyable" in one way or another.

Nominations were decided by a slippery "sliding scale" where Academy members listed or voted their five choices as first, second, third, fourth, and fifth. But the studios, viewing the Oscars in much the same way as a college sorority views the election for homecoming queen, perfected a system that kept out many good films and included many, many turkeys. If you were a studio insider in 1959, you knew that you could put your guy first, and then list four completely hopeless choices as two through five. Your man got five votes instead of one.

MGM, the studio which founded the Academy, used the weighted

Charlton Heston, one of the most popular Oscar winners in history, has given a touching, indelible portrait of what it feels like to win. Writing in his diary at 5 a.m. the next day, Heston said: "Just before Susan Hayward read it off, something popped into my head. 'I'm going to get it.' And I did. I kissed my wife and walked to the stage dripping wet, except for a pepper-dry mouth: classic stage fright. I'll never forget the moment, or the night. Backstage, posing with Willy (William Wyler, director of *Ben-Hur*), I said, 'I guess this is old hat to you.' 'Chuck,' he said, 'it never gets old hat.' "

scale beautifully in 1959. The men from the executive washrooms played the system as if it were a fine violin. A man who was truly loyal to his studio, for instance, would list Charlton Heston as his first choice, perhaps followed by Dean Martin and Jerry Lewis, Rock Hudson for *Pillow Talk*, and Tab Hunter. This cinched a nomination for Heston without bringing in a heavyweight to spar against him in the finals.

Of course the system backfired occasionally, depending on an individual's definition of a silly performance. In 1959, Universal-International may have listed Doris Day tops for *Pillow Talk*, while over at MGM "April Fool" voters put her on THEIR lists as a fairly hopeless choice. In any case, Doris Day was nominated for best actress on the flimsy strength of *Pillow Talk*.

Ben-Hur, a super-expensive chariot soap opera, went into the finals with more nominations than any film since *Gone With the Wind*. This headwind carried the film, Heston, Hugh Griffith, and director William Wyler to victory. In their respective races, the Heston and Griffith performances were the weakest in their classes. Today, Heston's stint as the dashing charioteer is completely overshadowed by the work of his competitors: Laurence Harvey in *Room at the Top*, Jack Lemmon in *Some Like It Hot*, Paul Muni in *The Last Angry Man*, and James Stewart in *Anatomy of a Murder*.

George C. Scott may not have been aware of these cruel Oscar realities in 1959—but he knew what he disliked, the fawning, dizzy "meat contest" staged every spring. "The process was not something I could live comfortably with," says Scott. "I still can't."

Scott had to face up to Oscar barbarism two years later when he was nominated again for his performance in *The Hustler*. Scott told the Academy, by telegram, to take his name the hell off the Oscar list. The Academy refused, stating tersely that it was "George C. Scott's work in *The Hustler* and not Scott himself which was nominated."

Scott, in turn, replied to the Academy, saying that the campaigning by the actors and their agents degraded the whole process. "It encourages the public to think that the award is more important to the actor than the work for which he was nominated," Scott told a writer for the *New York Times*. A close friend told the same writer: "He dislikes that whole Hollywood, back-patting atmosphere. For the Oscar, you have to throw a few cocktail parties yourself and get people to screenings so they can take a look at you and all that sort of thing." The friend said the Oscar facade was against Scott's own philosophy of life: "He told me that the Oscars were just a way for the motion picture companies to make more money on the pictures and had little other value."

The Oscar voters caught the cue this time. (It usually takes more than a gallant gesture to get through these crowned heads. (Despite his work in *Dr. Strangelove or: How I Learned to Stop Worrying and Love the Bomb*; *The Flim-Flam Man*, and *Petulia*, he wasn't again knighted by the swift Oscar sword until 1970 when *Patton* burst onto the scene.

Scott had immersed himself into Patton's character; he ordered up old newsreels from World War II, running them dozens of times. The introspection showed in the film—the actor covered himself completely in the Patton facade. There was no doubt that he'd be nominated for the Oscar. The question was: What would he do about it?

"The Academy Award show is a 'meat parade,' " Scott told the Associated Press. "Life isn't a race. It's a war of survival and there are many who get crippled and injured on the way. And because it's not a race, I don't consider myself in competition with my fellow actors for rewards or recognition. That is why I have rejected the nomination for playing Patton."

This furor secretly delighted the Academy voters who like nothing better than to give an award to a self-styled maverick. Many of them saw Scott's Oscar for *Patton* as a glorious sign that the Academy Awards— once and for all—were free of arbitrary favoritism, a strange claim for an organization which, a year later, gave the Oscar to *The French Connection* instead of *The Last Picture Show* or *A Clockwork Orange*.

So Scott decided to shut up about it. And he got his chance the year after *Patton* when the Academy again listed him for his work in *Hospital* (which many feel to be, along with *Hardcore*, his finest screen performance).

George C. Scott has seen nothing in Oscar's more recent history that would make him change his mind. "I fully expect that I'll never get another nomination," he says. "But if I did, I wouldn't talk about it."

His is the weariness adopted by many others tired of Hollywood's incessant worship of the dollar.

Liz Taylor, on the morning after her second Oscar for *Who's Afraid of Virginia Woolf?*, smiled tiredly and said, "It's nice to win, but the edge is certainly taken off because Richard didn't win. And he WAS the best actor of the year." (Also for *Who's Afraid of Virginia Woolf?*)

These dissenting voices have, however, been weak and few. The first half-century of the awards has wrapped the Oscar in Wagnerian-like myth and legend; the statue is truly a "golden idol," an international symbol of glamour and excellence.

George C. Scott before the flag—the scene that undoubtedly won the Oscar for Scott and the film which bagged seven awards from ten nominations. Scott turned down that Oscar on principle—believing then and now that choosing a best actor is a farce. But the rejection brought him and the Oscar more publicity than he would have received by merely picking up the prize, adding layers to Academy Award lore. "When I was nominated for *Hospital* a year later, I just kept my mouth shut—didn't say a word. Now that worked. I'd do it again if I were nominated in the future—which I doubt."

The Oscar was the first thing shown to U.S. Army intelligence officers when they visited the home of Nazi actor (and fat cat) Emil Jannings in Bavaria. Jannings, the first best actor for *The Way of All Flesh*, had long before returned with his trophy to Germany, becoming powerful and wealthy as Hitler's "first actor."

Jannings, then fatally ill with cancer, invited international journalists and photographers to his home on the shores of Lake St. Wolfgang and leaned on his Oscar for help. In halting English he explained, as would others, that he was forced to "go along with Hitler or be sent to a concentration camp." With the Oscar near his fingertips, the heavy, aged actor explained, "I've only made one propaganda film, *Ohm Kreuger*—and that I did under pressure. When Goebbels first offered me the leading role in that anti-British picture, I refused. And he ordered it." It would later come out that Jannings was not only popular but favored economically by being declared tax-exempt by Nazi Finance Minister Fritz Reinhardt.

This led Peter Bogdanovich to predict: "Who knows—if there's life on some distant planet, as the movies would have us emphatically believe, and if we're invaded, an Oscar for *Star Wars* could someday stop a ray gun."

This reality would be funny if the industry, and now the world, didn't take the publicity stunt so seriously. And that's what it is still—a gilded publicity stunt foisted off on the planet.

Many of Oscar's earliest generation wonder how it became so serious. It didn't start that way.

To quote Cary Grant: "It was a private affair—no television, of course, no radio even—just a group of friends giving each other a party. Because, you know, there is something embarrassing about all these wealthy people publicly congratulating each other. When it all began, we kidded ourselves and said: 'All right, Freddie March,' we'd say, 'we know you're making a million dollars—now come on up and get your little medal for it."

By the late thirties it had veered too far out of control; Oscar was becoming a monster.

A quite famous director of mysteries was so worried about an Oscar race in 1941 that he could not bear to attend the ceremony. He just paced up and down the silent hall of his Beverly Hills house.

"Turn on the radio!" he yelled to his wife. The first pearly-toned sounds of the Oscar's orchestra began to waft through the house. But the director decided that made it worse. "No, no," he yelled, "turn it off."

He picked up a tennis racket and dashed out to his private court. One ball. Two. Then he was back in, stepping into his tuxedo. "Maybe if we just went on down." His wife had finally had it.

"For Chrissakes don't take it so seriously. Just remember, this is a group that gave an Oscar to Luise Rainer. Twice!"

That did it. A smile formed at the corners of his mouth. The very famous director never mentioned the Oscar again. He never got one either. But he didn't care—or so he said.

In this same era—the early forties—mystery writer Raymond Chandler braved an Oscar ceremony and didn't come away unscathed.

"If you can go past those awful idiot faces on the bleachers outside the theater without a sense of the collapse of human intelligence; and if you can go out into the night and see half the police force of Los Angeles gathered to protect the golden ones from the mob in the free seats, but not from the awful moaning sound they give out, like destiny whistling through a hollow shell; if you can do these things and still feel the next morning that the picture business is worth the attention of one single, intelligent, artistic mind, then in the picture business you certainly belong

Inger Stevens in Oscar's first miniskirt and Shirley MacLaine with brother Warren Beatty "making an entrance" on one of the many years in which she lost. These trappings have only added to Oscar's reputation as a glittery stunt—much on the order of skywriting and arc lights. Oscar-winning writer Dalton Trumbo called it "the intellectual rutting season from January 2 to May. The skin reddens, the eye whites curdle, the interior organs swell sometimes to twice their normal size. A peach-flavored mist settles over the hills and horrible things are done in the night. It is the season of the graven image— the time of Oscars, plaques, cups, figurines, globes, medals, badges, scrolls, certificates, citations, ribbons, medallions, memorials, testimonials, and other symbols of esteem . . . a thoroughly awful and debasing time."

because this sort of vulgarity, the very vulgarity from which the Oscars are made, is the inevitable price Hollywood exacts from each of its serfs."

Chandler wrote those words for a Los Angeles newspaper. The newspaper didn't dare print them. Finally, they found a home in the *Atlantic Monthly*, which was on the East Coast, safe from Oscar's revenge.

Is there hope for Oscar?

Probably not. Oscar salvation may come only through laughter at the impossibility of even trying to choose a best film or a best performance.

So often the nominees are basically cultural apples and oranges. Can one truly say, for instance, that Sally Field's touch of genius in *Norma Rae* is artistically better than Bette Midler's raw gutsiness in *The Rose*?

Humphrey Bogart was probably right when he suggested: "Let each of the five nominees do the soliloquy from *Hamlet* before an audience of voters."

Picture the scene as it would have been that year, when Bogie won for *The African Queen*. He would have competed against Montgomery Clift, Marlon Brando, Arthur Kennedy, and Fredric March. Incendiary!

"Of course," said Bogie, "I wouldn't have proposed that if Larry Olivier had been up."

WINNERS AND LOSERS

1

"Having been forced by its own celebrity to take itself seriously, Oscar's trouble is that it now takes itself too seriously. The voting rules and bylaws are now longer than the U.S. Constitution and harder to understand. Occasionally the bylaws seem intended to function like protective tariffs, keeping out imports and modernist tendencies." Charles Champlin, 1980.

April 14, 1980—A line of black limousines glistens in the smog and is hopelessly snarled at a downtown off ramp of the Hollywood Freeway.

The Cadillacs are backed up for blocks—stalled in a gaunt and deserted canyon of concrete. The bankers in vested suits and the secretaries in Gloria Vanderbilt jeans have all disappeared into the suburban maze.

Here in downtown Los Angeles there's hardly a sound—the occasional hacking cough of a derelict wino, an army of cleaning ladies chattering in Spanish, a far off siren.

The engines of the limos purr in unison. A sandy-haired transient looks out from his bed of newspapers and raises a bottle of Tokay wine toward the cars. "Have a nice day!" he yells. The chauffeurs don't turn their heads; they can't hear him—encased as they are in an air-conditioned, perfumed world. In the back seats—all sign of life is safely hidden behind glass of midnight blue. Sometimes a window or two will roll down, revealing the flash of a Halston gown or the sensuous fabric of a Calvin Klein dinner jacket.

The line of sleek cars stretches up an asphalt hill and ends at a blaze of strobe lights on the concrete terrace of the Los Angeles Music Center—an icy and impersonal monument to pretentious architecture. A fleet of helicopters hovers overhead—shooting down on the crowd with banks of video cameras. Chauffeurs click their heels, jerk open the doors, and the Hollywood of today spills out in a garish puddle of plastic chic.

Two old women in dirty sweaters and ripped polyester pants barely glance up from the standing ashtrays they are clawing at for used cigarettes. One shrugs; the other stares ahead. Up above their heads soars the sign that explains it all—"Welcome," it says, "to the Fifty-second Academy Awards."

The Oscars. They now play out their story of envy and greed in a palace of cement, surrounded by the empty skyscrapers and dirty streets of downtown Los Angeles—only five miles from where they started (in the Hollywood Roosevelt Hotel) but light-years away in time and style.

Shirley Temple, a powerful actress even as a little nipper, receives her toy Oscar from Irvin Cobb. It was all too darling. Shirley was awakened from a nap offstage, her hair was fluffed, and she tottered onstage. Years later, Shirley Temple said she viewed the Oscar as a toy. "I took it home and dressed it just like a little doll," she said.

Many of the superstars now drive anonymous family cars to the Oscars, park them down in the bowels of the earth, and then ride the elevator up to the auditorium. Some of them even come in car pools: from far away in the San Fernando Valley, or from the stucco and swimming pool forests out in Orange County. Because this is where the so-called new Hollywood lives.

It's all sedate, a shopping center sort of thing. Even the applause seems muffled. And when the show starts, the doors are shut and locked—returning the city to its sterile quiet.

But this severe setting is uniquely appropriate for the Oscars of the seventies and eighties—an era that has finally swept clear the baroque ghosts of Hollywood past and ushered in the new Hollywood, a kingdom ruled by Jane Fonda's generation. It's a world where a director (such as Steven Spielberg or George Lucas) or a super exec (such as Alan Ladd, Jr., or Richard Zanuck) is more likely to be a celebrity than the actors who work for him.

And it's an era of machines and grotesque novelties: the biggest stars at the 1978 Oscars were a whining robot (Artoo-Detoo) and a golden tin man with a stutter (See-Three-Pe-Oh).

Well into their sixth decade, the Academy Awards more closely resemble the annual banquet of Chrysler-Plymouth dealers than the gathering of movie royalty they are supposed to be. Most of the men in finely cut dinner jackets are glorified accountants . . . and the movie reporters backstage ask the winners questions about camera angles or the intricacies of scripting.

There's an up-front honesty about the Oscars now that would have been impossible in the old Hollywood. For instance, Jane Fonda, when asked about her Oscar chances in 1980, shook her head decisively, "No, I think Sally Field will win—she gave the best performance."

There are also brave changes in the ceremony itself. In 1980, when the acting nominations were announced, the traditional scenes from the performance were deleted, replaced by clips showing the entire panorama of an actor's career. The bits of film for Al Pacino, for example, traced his work from *The Godfather* to *Dog Day Afternoon*, concluding with . . . *And Justice for All*, 1980. A subtle change on the surface. But it's a clear sign that the Academy is finally facing up to the unfortunate reality of its voting patterns—where an actor is almost always rewarded for a total career rather than for any single performance.

Even the new style brought by Johnny Carson has given the awards a new objectivity and a sense of humor about Oscar's highly dubious past—riddled as it is by unscrupulous politics, inappropriate winners, and pure Hollywood silliness.

In a sense, the Academy of Motion Picture Arts and Sciences is haunted by its past; it has to gracefully live with the fact that it never gave Garbo an Oscar; or Cary Grant; or Alfred Hitchcock. What else can it do but joke about a best picture list that honored *Mrs. Miniver* and *The Greatest Show on Earth* but not *Citizen Kane* or *A Streetcar Named Desire*.

Everyone involved is now comfortable with the reality that Oscar's story IS the story of Hollywood—its pitiless avarice; its fatal disregard for the integrity of its actors; and its shameless worship of a golden idol—the box office.

When they passed out the first statues at the Hollywood Roosevelt Hotel on May 16, 1929, Hollywood was still in the high noon of its gothic period. Gloria Swanson came to the Oscars in a chauffeured car whose puce tones matched the embroidery on her gown; Harlow was still an extra

Martin Ritt coaches Sally Field on the set of *Norma Rae*, which brought Sally an Oscar in 1980 and immediately launched her into superstar status. The actress had journeyed to the top from her nonsensical roles as television's *Gidget* and *The Flying Nun*, and she reminded an audience at the Golden Globes of her indignities on the way. "The last time I was up here I came down on a wire to present one of the awards," she said. "And I didn't fight it. The only thing I refused to do was to wear a nun's habit while I was doing it."

Why didn't Alfred Hitchcock win an Oscar? The very question dogs at the Academy's heels. In his first decade, as an import from Britain, Hitchcock's film *Rebecca* easily took the best picture award, but John Ford took the best director Oscar for *The Grapes of Wrath*. He was not nominated again until 1944 for the breakthrough movie *Lifeboat* in which all the action occurred in a cramped rescue boat. Perhaps that film was simply too dazzling, since Oscar voters tossed the prize to Leo McCarey's maudlin film *Going My Way*. Later, Billy Wilder's direction of *The Apartment* bested Hitchcock's masterpiece *Psycho*, which wasn't even nominated for best picture.

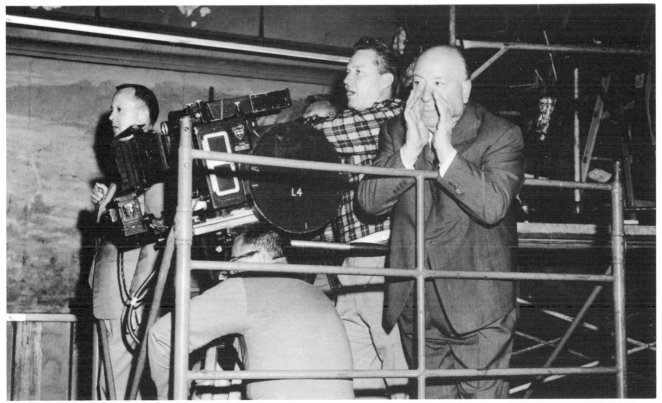

Doug Fairbanks, Sr., and Janet Gaynor with the first Oscar. The Academy had decided to keep the affair private until an MGM publicity man talked Louis B. Mayer into letting him grind it up into hype. Gaynor was always amazed at the legend of glory that came to surround the Oscars. In the beginning nobody took it that seriously. This picture with Fairbanks and Gaynor had to be posed five years after the Oscar ceremony, since Hollywood didn't think it was important enough to assign a photographer.

John Barrymore as Don Juan, by his artist friend John Decker. The painting was used as a prop in the film *The Great Profile,* made toward the end of the actor's stormy career. Acclaimed as one of America's greatest actors, Barrymore was never nominated for an Oscar.

player; and the voters couldn't decide whether or not they should allow talkies into the competition.

The first best actress was Janet Gaynor, a girl all the Academy members knew personally and the best actor was Emil Jannings, a man none of them knew and who had already fled back to Germany in fatal fear of sound cameras.

But Oscar's deadly flaw had already appeared. It was an unspoken guest at the head table. These were awards BY the establishment TO the establishment: it was the way you played the game that got you an Oscar: not how WELL you played it. Scriptwriter Frances Marion, who later won an Oscar for gamesmanship, said you could walk down Hollywood Boulevard the day before the voting and tell then and there who was going to win. Actors who toed the studio line got Oscars—the rest didn't. The studio brass in charge of the early Academy conceived of a foolproof way to torpedo any hint of prejudiced voting.

If an actor, no matter how fine, refuses to play the studio game, then just don't nominate him. What can folks say about that? Not much—and Louis B. Mayer and the boys knew it.

Oscar's history is littered with the artistic skeletons of those frozen out by the establishment before round one: Marilyn Monroe, George Raft, Alan Ladd, Errol Flynn, and the most haunting of them all—John Barrymore.

John Barrymore was probably the best screen actor of the early thirties—certainly he was the best actor in 1932 when his work in *Grand Hotel*, *Bill of Divorcement*, and *The Mad Genius* was on the screen. Greta Garbo, after working with Barrymore for only one day, called the cast together, took Barrymore's hand, kissed it, and said, "It's such a great pleasure to work with so perfect an artist."

In the Victorian parlors of the Hollywood Hills, Barrymore had two counts against him. First, he was the great offscreen lover of the twenties. Rudolph Valentino and Ramon Novarro got the girls on the set, but Barrymore took them into his own, real bed. The studio bosses—most of them great lechers—fumed at Barrymore's easy conquests. And second, he refused to play by the rules—drank too much, snickered at Hollywood's pretensions, and spurned the invitations to their dull weekend parties.

Louis B. Mayer and others soothed their feelings of shame by nodding and agreeing that Barrymore wouldn't be all that interested in the Oscar anyway; he'd already possessed all the adulation of Broadway and London. But Barrymore wanted an Oscar—desperately. Frances Marion was only one of many who sensed "his hurt, his denials, the shame of becoming an object of ridicule but most of all, his frustration at never once being recognized as a great artist by Hollywood circles. He always insisted he would toss that 'phony Oscar' into the ocean if he won it," said Miss Marion. "But that was only a small boy whistling into the dark—he really wanted an Oscar above any honor he had ever received."

Just before Barrymore died, he told his biographer, Gene Fowler, that he had spent sleepless nights puzzling over his failure to even get a nomination. "You know, Gene, I think they were afraid I'd come into the banquet drunk, embarrassing myself and them. But I wouldn't have, you know."

The establishment, particularly Mayer, also shut John Gilbert out in the cold. A matinee lover of the late silent period, Gilbert barely hung onto his career after his disastrous talking debut, *His Glorious Night*. His fortunes and the quality of his films dropped lower each year. But Garbo made a last-ditch stand to save him in her film *Queen Christina*. He was good

enough to attract attention from both the New York and London critics. A brave coterie of Gilbert's cronies—with help from Joan Crawford—approached Mayer about getting John an Oscar nomination. "Mayer just laughed at us," one of the group said later. "He'd already counted Gilbert out."

Mayer was a person whose whims could come true in the Academy—if he didn't want an MGM player nominated, no force in Hollywood could override his veto. For that matter, the head of any major studio had Oscar veto power in the first decade. "They all got together and passed those awards around—you were either on the list or off it; it didn't matter how good you were," said Joan Crawford—long after she'd won her hard-fought Oscar (in 1946 for *Mildred Pierce*).

This fact alone accounts for whole decades full of so-so Oscar winners that clutter up Academy history. An entire generation of Oscar holders bagged their awards for moderately good service for the home studio. The Oscars held by Ginger Rogers, Loretta Young, Bing Crosby, Spencer Tracy, Norma Shearer, and Marie Dressler are best excused by those conditions. (Have you ever tried to watch *Kitty Foyle* or *The Divorcee*?)

Hollywood mavericks didn't begin taking home the gold statues in any numbers until George C. Scott and Jane Fonda broke the spell in 1970 and 1971.

The forty years before that are crowded with oversights—not the least of which were Alan Ladd and Marilyn Monroe. Confusion about Marilyn's Oscarless status is obvious: The decades following her death have seen her elevated to hallowed places on every critic's list of good performances. Her artistic status was somewhat fuzzy at the time. And she'd been preceded by a long tradition concerning comediennes and bombshells: they

Cukor and Marilyn—a delicate balance but dynamite when it worked. Privately, Cukor said that Marilyn deserved an Oscar—if they gave them for comedy. Marilyn's home studio, fattened from her box office, insured her exclusion from the nominees (for *Bus Stop*) by deliberately throwing their votes to Deborah Kerr for *The King and I*. Still later, after her brilliant work in Billy Wilder's *Some Like It Hot*, Fox executives hinted to their Oscar voters that since *Some Like It Hot* was a United Artists film, it would be better to slight Marilyn again. Sheila Graham would later depict publicly Marilyn's heartache over her failure to gain a nomination.

Gable, Monroe, and Clift on the set of *The Misfits*, a self-conscious film so obviously written to gain Marilyn an Oscar that even Hollywood audiences saw through it. There was no doubt that Marilyn could have qualified for an Oscar for any one of three roles: *Some Like It Hot, The Seven Year Itch,* or *Bus Stop.* During the same time period, Fox was able to wangle a nomination for Lana Turner in *Peyton Place.* So, in the final analysis, it's obvious that Monroe was never nominated because her studio, Fox, didn't want her to be . . . in fact, never thought of her as anything more than a blonde sexpot who made money.

Eli Wallach and John Huston (rear) pose on the set of *The Misfits* with Montgomery Clift, Marilyn Monroe, and Clark Gable. Sadly, *The Misfits* was to be the last film for both Monroe and Gable.

didn't get nominated (including Mae West and Jean Harlow). On the other hand, everyone in Hollywood knew she wanted a nomination which she, if nobody else, felt she would get for *Bus Stop* in 1956.

Her work in the film was praised universally by the critics. And the gossip factory in Hollywood buzzed with stories of her painstaking study of the tawdry Cherie. The first day on the set, Monroe threw out the costumes designed for her and drove to used clothing stores in the run-down parts of Los Angeles to replace them. Her director Joshua Logan fed the gossip columns with a steady drivel of praise.

But when the nominations were announced the afternoon of February 18, her exclusion from the list was heartrending. "She was bitterly disappointed when she heard about the list," says gossip columnist Sheila Graham. "The two things she wanted most during that era—an Oscar and a baby—were to just escape her grasp. To her, it meant they felt she 'wasn't good enough.'"

But studio politics doomed her work in *Bus Stop.* Her studio, Twentieth Century-Fox, put on a massive campaign to get a nomination for Deborah Kerr in *The King and I,* which was an expensive picture and needed all the help it could get from the Oscars. In those days, the studios still divided up the Academy Award pie (no matter how many times the Academy denies it). They let word get around that Kerr was to get the nomination— NOT Marilyn. A good indication of the fury with which they campaigned is evident in the ease with which Yul Brynner won the best actor prize— over James Dean, Laurence Olivier, Kirk Douglas, and Rock Hudson. Hedda Hopper always said that a shaved head "is a strange reason for giving somebody an Oscar." (Hedda was for Dean in *Giant.*)

(Of course, Marilyn Monroe had a second Oscar taboo working for

Richard Burton and Elizabeth Taylor in *Who's Afraid of Virginia Woolf?* As a person savvy to the convoluted Hollywood psychology of winning and losing, Taylor frequently said she won her first Oscar because she nearly died and her second because of the performance Richard Burton gave opposite her in *Who's Afraid of Virginia Woolf?* Her first Oscar, for *Butterfield 8*, came only days after she rallied from near death in a London hospital. When she won for the second time, she flatly told reporters, "I'm always glad to win, but Richard's loss (to Paul Scofield in *A Man for All Seasons*) is very disappointing and dampens my own joy."

her—her rapidly expanding temperament and unreliability.)

But Alan Ladd, another casualty of the studio system, had none of these problems. In fact, Ladd had already turned in several Oscar-caliber performances (including *The Blue Dahlia*) by the time he got his once-in-a-lifetime part, *Shane*. The Academy voters rated the film highly, giving it nominations for best picture, best direction (George Stevens), and two best supporting actor bids, Brandon DeWilde, a juvenile, and the film's heavy, Jack Palance. The voters turned a cold shoulder to Ladd, who was the strongest acting force in the film. Ladd's wife, the former silent star and then agent Sue Carroll, used her considerable influence in Hollywood's drawing rooms to launch a grass-roots campaign. She forgot about Paramount's considerable clout with the Academy, and Paramount, in this case, was the studio scorned. Ladd, long under contract there, had not renewed his contract. It was an unwritten law that a star, once off the payroll, was immediately jettisoned, and denied the considerable fringe benefits of a studio contract—including publicity and help in the Oscar sweepstakes. Paramount, therefore, gave all its votes to contractee William Holden, who won for the studio's *Stalag 17*. There was certainly room for Ladd on the 1953 acting list, since the performance in *Shane* far outshone Richard Burton, in the biblical extravaganza *The Robe*, and Marlon Brando in the embarrassing *Julius Caesar*.

As Hollywood from 1920 until 1960 was a dictatorship of moguls, all these Oscar voting patterns were subject to change at the drop of a memo. Which means there are no true patterns or trends in a half century of Oscar balloting.

Some seasons maudlin emotion ruled. It was surely that, and nothing but, that got Liz Taylor her first Academy Award for the miserable *Butterfield 8* in 1960. The week voting started in March of 1961, Hollywood

Montgomery Clift and Elizabeth Taylor from Edward Dmytryk's 1957 film *Raintree County*. Her performance won a best actress nomination.

Judy Garland never won an Oscar—that's legend. But in 1939's *Wizard of Oz*, above, she won a toy statue for her work on the yellow brick road gang. MGM had chances to nominate the grown-up Judy for *Meet Me in St. Louis* and *The Clock*, but the front office vetoed it. Her next and only other chance came in 1954 when she was nominated for her comeback in *A Star Is Born* with James Mason. Below, Judy, Greer Garson, and Jane Wyman . . . all show signs of age at the disastrous 1954 nominations party. This was the year that Hollywood tried to televise the nominations as well as the finals . . . an idea which was quickly dropped when the audience failed to turn up. The nominations just didn't have the "horse race" atmosphere so beloved by the American public.

Elizabeth Taylor and Rock Hudson in a publicity still taken during the filming of George Stevens's sprawling production based on Edna Ferber's bestselling novel, *Giant*.

tabloids carried the headline "LIZ DYING." And she was, given up for gone in a London hospital. Her second-by-second battle for life dominated the front pages right up until the last voting day when the headlines crowed, "LIZ RALLIES." The most jaded Oscar voter would have needed a heart of lead to withstand the publicity from Taylor's brush with death. In February, Taylor, who'd just stolen Eddie Fisher from the town darling Debbie Reynolds, didn't have a prayer to win the Oscar. By late March it was a foregone conclusion. "Hell, I even voted for her," said Debbie years later. Any of the four actresses up against Liz should have gotten it over her (if the Academy enforced its own term, best actress of the year). Her competition: Greer Garson in *Sunrise at Campobello*, Shirley MacLaine in *The Apartment*, Deborah Kerr in *The Sundowners*, and Melina Mercouri in *Never on Sunday*.

Greatly to her credit, Taylor said then, and repeated it hundreds of times, "I won the Oscar because I almost died—pure and simple." The irony of it is that she deserved the Oscar in 1959 for *Suddenly Last Summer* or even the year before that for *Cat on a Hot Tin Roof*.

Even emotion, however, will go only so far. It didn't do Judy Garland a bit of good when she was up in 1954 for *A Star Is Born*. Garland had been driven out of MGM four years earlier after an all-too-public battle with booze, pills, and her own emotions. At one point she was literally thrown off the lot. Less than eighteen months later, Garland had clawed her way back up, culminating in a new deal husband Sid Luft got for her at Warner Brothers—four films in four years starting with *A Star Is Born*. The filming was a long one, punctuated here and there by temperament and Judy's yo-yo weight problems. But when George Cukor called it a wrap, he viewed the final rough cut, calling it a masterpiece. Jack Warner didn't think so. First he cut about an hour from Cukor's footage, substituting a mediocre production number which was eventually called "Born in a Trunk." Both Judy and Cukor hated the result.

The reception was thunderous, hoisting Judy easily into a best actress nomination.

Rumor in Tinseltown predicted Garland as an easy victory. The producers of the Oscar show (and many Academy officers) were so certain she would win that a bank of cameras were jammed into her Los Angeles hospital room. (She had had a baby several days earlier.) There was a letdown and bizarre quiet after the envelope was opened and Grace Kelly was named best actress for *The Country Girl*.

Several things probably happened to the headwind Garland had when she entered the race. Warner Brothers politely let it be known that they weren't officially backing her. (The Garland deal had collapsed under the weight of the expensive musical.) Plus, Paramount campaigned heavily for Kelly. Rumor has persisted that the Kelly-Garland race was the closest race that didn't end in a tie. Hedda Hopper, who had pried bits and pieces from accountants in earlier races, always said that Kelly beat Garland by seven votes. "And you know where those seven votes were, don't you? They belonged to those bastards in the front office at MGM."

Occasionally Oscar's maudlin side emerges as guilt. It was surely that which threw the Oscar to Ingrid Bergman in 1956 for *Anastasia*. The Swedish star had been hounded by both the press and the Hollywood establishment after she left her physician husband and moved to Italy with her lover and later her husband Roberto Rossellini. The whole incident might never have happened if her first Hollywood boss, David O. Selznick, hadn't shaped an image for her that fell somewhere between Joan of Lorraine, which she played and the Virgin of the Roses, a role planned for her but never made. Bergman was pilloried to such an extent that she began fighting back with a series of interviews of her own—in Rome.

Garbo never really said, "I want to be alone," but Bergman did—in a fiery press conference at the New York airport. It came to a head when Ed Sullivan, in a maudlin moment of his own, announced that Bergman would appear on a future show and to welcome her back he would sponsor a public opinion poll to see if Ingrid should be forgiven and welcomed home. Everybody perceived the silliness of that, and the furor about her Rossellini years evaporated in a hail of humor. Thus the Oscar for *Anastasia*.

A hint of that same "we forgive you" sentiment operated in Jane Fonda's favor in 1971 when she won her first Oscar for *Klute*. A perverse form of Oscar-oriented radical chic was adrift during those years also. The wilder an actor's politics and the more angry his put-down of the Academy, the more likely he was to get a nomination—and to win. It worked for George C. Scott in 1970's *Patton*. He refused the nomination, and he refused the Oscar. (It's still in the Academy's overstock.) The Oscar voters took that on the chin and turned the other ballot, nominating him again the very next year for *Hospital*, a mostly forgettable exercise. It was more of the same with Brando, who had a sometime Indian maiden refuse his statue for *The Godfather*. Next year, the miniskirted and blue-jeaned Oscar electors tossed him a bouquet for *Last Tango in Paris*, for a performance which, quite privately, scared Academy officers out of their leather seats.

Fonda's *Klute* Oscar is tinged with more of the same, and the actress told Charles Champlin, during a Theta Cable interview, that her post-Oscar benefits in 1972 hardly counted because of the political atmosphere. Which leads directly to her 1978 triumph for *Coming Home*. The awards to Fonda and Voight are viewed by many as a definite sign of Oscar's newly found maturity. Fonda had fought the Hollywood establishment for six

Jane Fonda, shown here during her sixties goddess period, has seen Oscar from all angles: disappointed loser (for *They Shoot Horses, Don't They?*), uneasy winner (for *Klute*), and as a triumphant winner-take-all (for *Coming Home*). It has given her a healthy outlook. Arriving at the 1980 ceremony, Fonda answered a reporter, "No, I don't think I'll win. Sally Field will win. She gave the best performance." Such a comment would have been unheard of a decade earlier. Part of Hollywood is growing up. The victories of Diane Keaton, Faye Dunaway, Sally Field, Richard Dreyfuss, and Dustin Hoffman are all signs that Oscar may be shedding its bias against mavericks and politically undesirables. The victory of Vanessa Redgrave for *Julia* was more . . . in an organization afraid of its own shadow, that was a milestone. "There's hopefully no going back now," commented Charles Champlin.

Peter Sellers, here in one of the *Pink Panther* films, and Shirley MacLaine, here in *Irma La Douce,* have perhaps been too subtle, too consummately skilled for their own good.

Another look at Garbo . . . the face that haunts the Academy's dreams of objectivity.

years to launch the withering picture of life after the Vietnam War. In the past, the voters have grudgingly given awards to projects that were made "in spite of" the film establishment.

Only a decade earlier the voters gave the Oscar to Cliff Robertson for *Charly*, a property he had been forced to buy himself and carry from bank to bank seeking financing. They tossed him the Oscar almost as a grudging trophy. But they sure as hell weren't going to do him any other favors. His parts were, mostly, few and unimaginative.

These erratic patterns have made (and continue to make) the Oscar voting seem like an overgrown election for prom queen, at worst, and a contest for the "most likely to succeed" at best.

Some members of the Hollywood elite say openly that the roll call of the Oscarless has become more exclusive and illustrious than the winners' circle itself.

Just the cream of "the unawarded," as Burgess Meredith calls them, includes Greta Garbo, John Garfield, Paul Newman, Rosalind Russell, Charles Boyer, Leslie Howard, Merle Oberon, Edward G. Robinson, Franchot Tone, Montgomery Clift, Marlene Dietrich, Fred Astaire, Peter Sellers, James Mason, Kirk Douglas, Danny Kaye, Peter O'Toole, Richard Burton, Robert Mitchum, Cary Grant, Irene Dunne, Liv Ullmann, Warren Beatty, Shirley MacLaine, Kim Stanley, Robert Redford, Tyrone Power, Tony Curtis, Charles Bickford, John Gielgud, Sylvester Stallone, . . . and, undoubtedly, more in the future.

It takes a long time for a message to sink into the Hollywood consciousness.

But the Oscar people looked a second time when Ingrid Bergman, taking a third Oscar for *Murder on the Orient Express*, held the genderless statue upside down and recognized another nominee, Valentina Cortese, "who should have won," said Bergman, "for *Day for Night*." But of course, "It's always nice to get one of these."

2 LITTLE ORPHAN OSCAR

"The Academy began its existence as a guild-busting company union dominated for many years by the massive resources of Metro-Goldwyn-Mayer." Andrew Sarris.

D.W. Griffith looked ghastly. His skin had an ashen, almost dead look; his stomach jutted out as a memorial to many boozy nights in two-bit bars. His hair was pillow-slip white, and his dinner jacket was not of the best cut.

They sent a limousine to get him—a Hollywood courtesy he hadn't known in more than a decade. At sixty-one, the "father of the movies" was washed up; had been for ten years. His two greatest movies, *The Birth of a Nation* and *Intolerence*, were made twenty years earlier. And twenty years is a lifetime in Hollywood. The studio bosses had closed the gates to him: Louis B. Mayer didn't even return his calls, while Cecil B. DeMille was conveniently "on location" when Griffith dropped by the Paramount lot.

His 500 films wouldn't even buy him a bowl of soup in the Warner Brothers commissary. Hollywood only asks one question: What did you do last week? Last year was too far back in history and next year may never come. Has-beens like Griffith, John Gilbert, and Jesse Lasky, Sr.,—no matter how great—were treated like lepers. Failure, after all, can rub off, can't it?

But the limo that picked up D.W. Griffith late on the afternoon of March 5, 1936, was to drop him back into the arms of the Hollywood establishment. When the long, sleek car pulled up to the red carpet at the Biltmore Hotel, boy genius Irving Thalberg was there to greet him; so was the city's hottest new director, Frank Capra. And Walt Disney. Their dinner jackets were cut better than his; they had smooth tans from afternoons on private tennis courts. Diamond bracelets dripped from the arms of their wives. Their smiles said, "Welcome home . . . why'd you stay away so long?"

They greeted him like a retired Roman senator, coming in for tribute from his country villa. He was actually more like Banquo's ghost, emerging from the shadows and living death of forced retirement and seedy apartment-hotels.

One hopes Griffith didn't see the forced warmth and icy chill that lay beneath the glassy smiles of the movie moguls. Because forced it was. They had pulled Griffith out of the pasture in a last-minute publicity stunt designed to save the 1936 Oscars and, therefore, to save the collapsing Academy of Motion Picture Arts and Sciences, which was down to only a few

Joan Crawford, her husband Douglas Fairbanks, Jr., and director Frank Lloyd, three members of Hollywood's royalty arriving at the 1930 Oscars. The Academy Awards were a family affair in those days. They didn't even call it Oscar then, and the award had no effect on box office—not that anyone could tell.

hundred members and sinking fast.

Oscar was finally reaping the bitter harvest from almost ten years of misuse by Louis B. Mayer, Jack Warner, and their cronies. These men (particularly Mayer) founded the Academy to serve as a vast company union designed to keep all the unions, and therefore decent wages, out of Hollywood. In 1935 the name directors, actors, and writers all abandoned the Academy for the fairness and safety of their own guilds. When the moguls still clung to the Academy in its disguise as a company union, the movie stars blew the whistle on Oscar.

Paul Muni, James Cagney, and Gary Cooper, suddenly big men in the new Screen Actors Guild, sent out telegrams on March 3—two days before the Oscar ceremony. The messages, which differed according to star, told virtually every name actor in Hollywood to boycott the Oscar ceremony. "It was either that or give the group some tacit recognition," said Cagney years later. "They were hoping that respect for the Oscar awards would help them keep the Academy in the labor business as a company guild."

The studio bosses countered with telegrams of their own—politely ordering their studio artists to show up at the Oscar show. Or else! "It was like the iron fist in a velvet glove," said Jeanette MacDonald. "It's unnerving to ignore a telegram from your boss, Louis B. Mayer, telling you to show yourself at the Oscars."

But the guilds went management one better. A network of phone calls was initiated the very afternoon of the 1936 Oscar show: Jeanette Mac-Donald called Nelson Eddy; Joan Crawford called Harlow and Gable; Cagney called Blondell.

But before that, Frank Capra, new president of the Academy, had dropped his own bombshell. The Academy had suddenly found it in its collective little heart to give recognition at long last to the "father of the movies," D.W. Griffith.

"We had to do something," Capra said later. "The Academy was dying. And I was sure the upcoming Academy Awards banquet loomed dark and discouraging. So, to spur attendance, we countered the boycott by persuading Griffith to come out of his retired oblivion and accept a special statuette for his past achievements."

It worked, says Capra. "The boycott fizzled." Hardly! Capra is looking at the thirties through rose-colored glasses. Bette Davis finally agreed to come (but probably because she knew she would win for *Dangerous*), Norma Shearer came on the arm of her husband, MGM chief Irving Thalberg, Victor McLaglen came (to pick up his acting award for *The Informer*), but almost all the other name stars in Hollywood stayed firmly inside their Hollywood hill homes. "It was so bad I didn't find but four people worth taking pictures of," says Darryl Warren, a photographer for three fan magazines. "I got a shot of Davis, but she looked like hell—and Shearer must have come in the back door. One thing we had though—plenty of Frank Capra shots—plenty of 'em."

So D.W. Griffith became the first of a long parade of old and ailing stars used by the Academy for one reason or another (usually to relieve Hollywood's collective conscience).

They paraded him out like a champion horse with a lame leg. "It was a moment I could hardly bear," said Oscar winning scriptwriter Frances Marion, who was discovered by Griffith before World War I. "How had the industry honored this man who had contributed so much to all our lives? By presenting him with an Oscar for 'PAST achievements.' No studio in the last fifteen years had given him a directorial job when he needed it financially—and what was more important to him—to preserve his dignity."

It was the lowest point for the Academy.

Jean Harlow knew the score way back in 1932 when she shot to fame. "Awards? Those are for the hoities. What'll they buy?—nothin'!" Hollywood body language was more simple back then. The blonde bombshell wore no underwear and washed her tresses in a fortune in platinum: the world of shop girls and secretaries from Munich to Kansas City followed her lead.

Louis B. Mayer presenting the Oscar for best picture to Carl Laemmle for Universal's *All Quiet on the Western Front*.

It's ironic that the Griffith charade was engineered by Frank Capra—one of the few truly feeling men in the Hollywood hierarchy. He had said, after five years in Hollywood, "The city is brutal to has-beens. Those pushed off the top are rolled into the valley of oblivion. Often they are mired in degradation. I saw it all around me: D.W. Griffith, a forgotten man; Mack Sennett, walking unnoticed in the city where he had reigned as a King of Comedy; old stars pleading for jobs on the extra line. It's a stern warning."

Over the long haul, however, Frank Capra was probably right about one thing—D.W. Griffith was the only man who still had enough respect in Hollywood to fill the vast empty tables of the Biltmore Bowl. The stars didn't come; the directors didn't come; but 1,200 of the movies' middle ranks showed up, paid for tickets, and got Oscar through one more year.

That was all Capra counted on. The day after the 1936 Oscar ceremony, Capra laid down the law to the Academy board. He slammed his fist down on the oak table and ordered fellow officers to vote the Academy of Motion Picture Arts and Sciences OUT of the labor union business. Eight shameful years were over for the Academy; years during which it had served, more or less, as a big studio stool pigeon, stalling the winds of unionism, fair wages, and decent standards swirling around the movie industry—the fourth largest industry in America.

It had all started quietly (but not innocently) over Cuban cigars and Napoleon brandy in the "company" parlor of Louis B. Mayer's luxurious home. The year was 1927—before the depression and before talking pictures. But not, as Mayer knew, before the unnerving labor movement gathering at the studio gates.

"Why shouldn't there be an organization of the creative elite of Hollywood?" asked Mayer, looking out over his badger nose at the headtops of two of his serfs, Conrad Nagel and director Fred Niblo. And Mayer smiled inscrutably: "And of course, the organization could serve as a convenient mediator and harmonizer in any disputes involving the crafts." Just how convenient would only appear later. What Mayer left unsaid was that "the members will be by invitation only—the cream of Hollywood actors, writers, directors, cinematographers, and, of course, the cream of Hollywood producers." But the cream of the crop by whose definition? At first it was by Mayer's definition alone. He set out to form the Academy in his image. And he succeeded—down to paying for the first dinner at the Ambassador Hotel, January 11, 1927. Why, that good soul even paid and supplied his own personal attorney to draft the constitution and by-laws. (As hard to believe as it is now, Academy Awards came only as an afterthought on the Academy's agenda. It was an easy way to throw each of the creative groups a bone once a year, insuring their goodwill during the labor squabbles.)

So thirty-six of Hollywood's "best people" came to Mayer's little gathering. And those people invited their friends; and their friends. . . . Soon there were two-hundred and thirty-one members, all organized into ranks and categories. (It's interesting to note that awards were not even listed in a statement of aims adopted that night.)

"Those jerks in charge wanted it to seem like a labor union but to function as a company trust. Then it would seem like everything was done kosher. In other words they could freeze the guilds and labor unions out of Hollywood," said Zelda Cini, a correspondent in Hollywood for *Life* and *Time*. "The early Academy was so controlled by the bosses it was a wonder it survived."

"Everybody sat back and waited to see when the studios would call the Academy into action," said Cini, who once wrote a history of the Academy for *Life*'s Golden Decade series.

It wasn't long. Four months after the Academy's organizational banquet, Louis B. Mayer came before it hat in hand. Things were going tough in the East, boys, real tough! The money men back East were out for blood. It was a bad rap, said Mayer. But those bankers just don't know how we do things out here in Tinseltown. They think we're irresponsible and wasteful. So just for the moment, perhaps a little ten percent cut in everybody's wages would solve the problem temporarily. All the Academy had to do, according to Mayer and the other brass, was to take up the proposal with the other branches.

Mayer knew that the other branches had already threatened to strike if the ten percent cut was put into effect. To the great credit of the Academy, its leaders were not docile. They told Mayer to take back the ten percent slash. And the warning spread to the other studios.

Joan Crawford describes Mayer as being "mad as hell" when he found out the organization he'd created in his image had somebody else's brain.

Okay, boys, no pay cut. The producer's branch of the Academy decided to officially withdraw the proposed cut at the Academy's July 28 banquet. And they worded their withdrawal so that the other branches were blamed for the "rampant extravagance and cost overruns of our industry."

Then the Academy quickly polished off an attempt by Actors Equity to organize. Why join that "eastern stage union" when you can get everything you want through the Academy, said the producers. We'll even give you a contract.

And they did—the first contract of any kind between artists and producers. "Most actors were unconcerned as to which organization represented them as long as they had their way," said author Murray Ross in *Stars and Strikes*. "If the Academy would help them, they saw no reason for clinging to Equity."

Erich Von Stroheim and silent lover John Gilbert—fast friends on the set of 1925's *The Merry Widow*. Von Stroheim, who had made *Greed*, probably one of the five finest American films, had been kicked off every lot in town for wasteful extravagance by the time of the first Oscars. They did finally nominate him in the fifties for his self-parody in Billy Wilder's *Sunset Boulevard*. As for Gilbert, they only laughed when his friend and lover Greta Garbo suggested he might get an Oscar for his performance in *Queen Christina*. It was an award that might have saved his career. But he had somehow slighted Louis B. Mayer, who made sure that Garbo was the only person on the MGM lot who voted for him.

In the East, spokesmen for Equity claimed the Academy was a "company union" bound to cause trouble sooner or later. It was true. The producer's branch held the destinies of Academy members in an iron fist. "An examination of the Academy's first three years shows that a small number of influential 'foundation members' guided the Academy," said Ross. "The 'foundation members' were charter members and a select few who were elected to the inner circle. Other Academy members were not eligible for election to the board of directors and could not amend the bylaws."

Ross concluded: "The Academy was obviously never meant to be a thoroughly democratic organization."

The dictators who controlled the Academy had given just enough to make the actor and writer peons happy. But not enough to lose their iron control. By 1932, the Academy of Motion Picture Arts and Sciences had become the perfect company union, presenting no danger at all to the studios while making it seem as if Hollywood workers actually had a working labor union. Even founding members of the Academy such as Douglas Fairbanks, Sr., wondered when reality would intervene and demolish the house of cards.

The inevitable happened in 1933. Depression had finally hit the balmy shores of Hollywood, but it had taken a national bank holiday (1933) to make even a dent on film profits. Overnight, Paramount officially went bankrupt; movie financiers were ruined by bank failures across America. Only the earthquake of the same year made as big a dent in Beverly Hills.

Louis B. Mayer's gruff bark suddenly became a whine; the Warner brothers admitted that they didn't know where their next ten million was coming from; and Paramount's Adolph Zukor began eating at home instead of at his swanky club.

Mayer, one of the highest paid men in America, called together his fellow producers and said he had just the ticket. Boys, he said, we'll all just take a fifty percent cut in pay. He spread his chubby arms and offered to take the first official cut—pledging the thousands of others at MGM with a sweeping executive order. And you boys, he said, will get your studios to do the same. Presto! No depression.

Mayer and the boys ran for their cars and headed in one direction—east to the downtown Hollywood offices of the Academy of Motion Picture Arts and Sciences. They had all been saving the Academy for just such a situation anyway. The timing was perfect.

The fat cats explained to the Academy's board that a fifty percent cut for everybody—across the board—would surely be better than no paychecks at all. And that's what would happen if the Academy didn't act. And fast!

After all, weren't the big boys themselves taking pay cuts right along with the grips and the hairdressers? Sure they were. That's the spirit, Mayer told the Academy officers.

Then somebody remembered just how much guys like Mayer and Warner were taking home—and just how little everybody else took out of the pot. Mayer would still have $335,000 per year after his cut. Warner would have a little more. And Gable would still be stinking rich. But thousands earned fifty dollars a week—even less; seventy-five percent of all actors (and there were 30,000 of them including free-lancers) pocketed less than $2,000 a year.

The Academy called a halt until it could work out a better formula. What say the cuts only last for eight weeks—with graduated reductions according to income? And what about exempting guys who make less than fifty bucks a week? The producers, in the glow of putting over their charade, answered a quick, "Sure." The Hollywood workers could even choose

between the waiver of half pay for eight weeks or give up full salary for four weeks. The Academy even demanded and received the right to audit all the studios' books so that the waivers could be canceled as soon as each studio recovered.

A month later the waiver committee said Warner Brothers was in good enough shape to put all its employees back on full pay. Your move, said the Academy to Jack Warner. Go to hell said Warner. "It's my studio."

The executive suite at Warner Brothers quickly turned into a political mine field. Darryl F. Zanuck, the Warner executive who had signed the agreement with the Academy, stormed into Warner's office and told him to pay up. No dice, said Warner. If you don't, I quit, said Zanuck. There's the door! said Warner. And Zanuck walked out on Warners and drifted over to Twentieth Century-Fox which he made great with his leadership.

Then the waiver committee discovered that Samuel Goldwyn Studios

A cozy little group—Janet Gaynor, the first Oscar winner, gathers with Douglas Fairbanks, Sr., and a gaggle of the producers, accountants, and directors who founded the Academy of Motion Picture Arts and Sciences. The Academy was formed as a glorified publicity stunt to add a note of the highbrow to the scandal-ridden movie industry. "It honestly wasn't that big a deal at first," said Gaynor decades later. "It was just a small group getting together for a pat on the back."

was solid enough to pay up in full. Go to hell, said Sam Goldwyn.

Murray Ross, in his *Stars and Strikes*, says that these two actions were the first and probably the greatest blow to the Academy's prestige. When the dictators who ran the Academy said no, the Academy had nowhere to turn. Pierre Norman Sands, in his study of the Academy for the University of Southern California, believes that "the Academy only relied on a spirit of cooperation and lacked any enforcement mechanism." He also feels that the producers themselves may have scuttled the Academy's labor function in 1933. "It's quite possible that the unions themselves looked better to western management of the studios since they could be bargained with at arms length rather than having their books opened up and audited by the Academy and therefore by their employees."

For the actors, the rat had eaten the cheese. The Screen Actors Guild was formed in October of 1933. Within twelve months there were 3,000

Darryl Zanuck, the producer who brought Twentieth Century-Fox out of the dark ages, became one of the few moguls who sided with the Academy in its battle against being misused as a guild-busting company union. In the mid-thirties he resigned as Warner Brothers production head when the studio refused to restore salary cuts which had been approved by the Academy as an emergency measure. It became clear to Zanuck and to others that the studios were merely using the Academy to force artists to take pay cuts which the moguls had no intention of restoring. Outraged, Academy members deserted in droves.

Louis B. Mayer himself with actor Conrad Nagel who Mayer later handpicked for president of the Academy. Legend has it that Nagel looked up over his shrimp cocktail one evening and suggested how fine it would be for the industry to have an organization of the "crème de la crème" of moviedom. Mayer stopped—his fork poised over a juicy gulf shrimp, and beamed in agreement. Then it all came up roses. This, of course, was only the dream of some MGM publicist.

members. Soon to follow was the Directors Guild, which was literally founded outside the Academy offices—on the steps. "We finally realized how the producers were using the Academy and us," says director King Vidor, a founding member of the Directors Guild of America. "What a lot of people didn't know was the fact that many producers and executives were subtracting the cuts from their employees' checks but not from their own."

Actor Conrad Nagel, the man Louis B. Mayer handpicked to found the Academy, resigned both as president and as a member, telling friends that he could not remain as an officer of an organization that was so basely used. Thousands followed his action. The Academy's membership was cut in half overnight.

Still, the producers insisted on using it. The labor guys in Washington D.C. were busy all across America, drafting new codes and regulations for labor unions and employee groups. Mayer, Warner, and Thalberg cashed in on old debts and had the Academy of Motion Picture Arts and Sciences named as the official studio-labor spokesman for the crucial hearings of the National Recovery Administration (a fancy way of describing total reorganization of labor).

Mayer and the other brass forced the Academy to forward the studio demands to Washington and therefore into the new federal code. The studios asked for—and got—a code forcing all artists' agents to register and receive a license (a measure that would have put the agents directly under the thumb of political and industry-wide management). The studios asked for—and got—provisions limiting high salaries of actors, directors, and writers. (But no limits for executives.) All these provisions were quickly written into the code, and the studio bosses sat back and waited to pull the rug out from under the artists.

They hadn't reckoned on Eddie Cantor. The singer with the banjo eyes wangled an invitation to spend Thanksgiving, 1933, with President and Mrs. Franklin D. Roosevelt in Warm Springs, Georgia. Cantor, who was also the new president of the Screen Actors Guild, convinced the President, once and for all, that the Academy represented only the producers. F.D.R. got on the hotline to D.C. and stopped, by executive order at the last second, the anti-labor provisions of the code.

The executives were shocked into silence. Mayer was so confident of the final victory that he scurried about Hollywood openly discussing the soothing balms of the salary-fixing board that would soon be put into effect.

Finally, it was too much even for the toadying Academy. They yelled for a halt and got the government to okay a series of producer-artist committees to again draft a set of fair standards for the film industry. But Mayer and the others never got around to naming their delegates to the study groups. It was the last act in a pageant of bad faith: the Academy had played its last card.

Bosley Crowther, Louis B. Mayer's biographer, believes that Mayer had intended all along for the Academy to stave off the march of labor in Hollywood. "Finally, the Academy was exposed for what it was," wrote the New York Times film critic. "It was a 'company union' in a nice, refined, dignified way.

"Mayer's maneuvering during the 'bank holiday' period led to a spirit of rebellion toward the Academy that led to the genesis and strengthening of the guilds. Then there was the inevitable collapse of Mayer's company union."

Crowther blames Mayer directly for the collapse of the Academy in the mid-thirties. "Certainly Mayer's cute maneuver to raise the organization as a device for controlling actors and writers and his encouragement of it

Norma Shearer and Tyrone Power arriving at the première of *Marie Antoinette* in 1938. Shearer played the title role that William Randolph Hearst wanted for Marion Davies.

to play a hand in the obvious interests of the producers contributed to the end result. Mayer was often shortsighted and naive."

And the Academy needn't look backward fondly at its founder. When Marie Dressler and Norma Shearer warned him that the backstabbing might destroy the Oscar ceremony, he looked up glassy-eyed and said, "So what?" Still later, when his attorney warned him he should give a nice chunk to the Academy for tax purposes (after all, Mayer did found it), Mayer looked up and said, "Are you crazy?"

It was into this cauldron that Frank Capra dropped in 1934. For the next six years the story of the Academy Awards is Frank Capra's story. He saved them. Indeed, he was the first to really believe there was something worth saving.

Capra had been in and around Hollywood for twelve years before he finally acquired the right patina and pedigree to qualify for the Academy. The son of an orange picker just off the boat from Sicily, Frank Capra played the banjo in a Los Angeles honky-tonk, worked his way through the California Institute of Technology to become a chemical engineer, and sold stocks door to door before he bluffed his way into a job as a director. A San Francisco producer, in an unhinged moment, let Capra direct a one reeler entitled *Fultah Fisher's Boarding House*. That was enough for Frank. He didn't know A THING about films. And it showed. So he went underground as a film cutter in a back-door Los Angeles sweat shop—jumping from there to an assistant director and on to full director status on Harry Langdon comedies. Harry Cohn hired him for Columbia pictures, making him king of that lot within five years.

They called Columbia "the pauper" in those days—just a small-timer looking in at the show windows of the big boys—MGM, Paramount, Warner Brothers. Then he released a film that became an instant hit—*Ladies*

Director Frank Capra during his tenure as Academy president. Some claim that Capra was responsible for saving the institution from total collapse during his six-year term.

of Leisure, which made a star of Barbara Stanwyck.

The MGM brass got word that the movie was being sneak previewed in a neighborhood theater in distant San Bernardino—a city at the end of L.A.'s old red trolley line. Mayer sent one of his yes men up with a round-trip ticket and one order: find out if this movie's any good and if it is, find out if we can hire that Capra guy away from Columbia. The answer to the former was yes. But it was no dice on Capra. Cohn had him sewn up for a decade.

This should have been flattering for the new director in town. But Capra had caught the near fatal Oscar mania. He told Stanwyck he'd get one for himself, get one for Harry Cohn, and one for her. Ordinarily he would have had a good chance since, to quote Louella Parsons, "Everybody—and I mean EVERYBODY—is talking about Frank Capra and his film." The day nominations were announced Capra sent an office boy out in a limo to get *Daily Variety,* which reported minute-by-minute news of Hollywood to a captive audience. Capra paced back and forth on the Columbia sound stage. "I hope to hell he gets nominated," said Cohn. "Otherwise we'll never get any work out of him." The page finally made it back from Sunset Boulevard, and Capra knew from the look on his face that he (Capra) wasn't nominated. "But I thought Stanwyck would get a nomination for sure," said the director. "It opened my eyes immediately to the truth about the Oscars."

"That was the disadvantage of working at Columbia—nobody there could get the Oscar. It galled my ego. The major studios had the votes. I had my 'freedom,' so to speak, but all the honors went to those who worked for the big, establishment studios."

Capra threw down his copy of *Variety* and became a celluloid crusader—jousting after his personal "Holy Grail"—the Oscar. Only four others would match the ferocity of his Oscar campaigns: Irving Thalberg seeking a second Oscar for his wife Norma Shearer; William Randolph Hearst trying to get even a nomination for his mistress, Marion Davies; John Wayne seeking to bag the award for his epic *The Alamo*; and David O. Selznick who was obsessed with a second Oscar for his wife, Jennifer Jones.

The Academy was especially vulnerable, Capra deduced, because of its perverse control by eight or ten bosses. So be it—stick them in their Achilles' heel. The director used his considerable writing techniques to attack the Academy in a letter that dripped with fury. "The Academy is unfair to the creativity of the films." Next Capra whispered in Harry Cohn's ear that the men in control of the Oscar were robbing him of his due. At first, Cohn told him to forget it. "Capra, don't worry about those awards— they only give them to that arty junk."

Capra knew Cohn's weak spot—cash. And he used it. "Harry, they may give Oscars for 'arty junk' but a bunch of Oscars can add a million bucks to the ticket sales." Cohn's face brightened immediately. He was on the phone to Academy member Jack Warner the next day.

It's easy to imagine the panic Capra's letter caused in the founder's circle of the Academy. The organization was particularly vulnerable in 1930—frazzled with the toils of being a labor union and awards monitor at the same time.

A special delivery letter reached Capra's front door a couple of weeks later. It was from MGM director Fred Niblo—one of the men Mayer had handpicked to found his "company union." "The Board of Governors *cordially* invites you to Academy membership." This was better than Capra had dared hope. Usually, one Academy member nominates another with a long process of screening and voting. Capra was being invited to join by the entire board—voted, sealed, and delivered. A week later he found himself the "unanimous nominee" for the Academy of Motion Picture Arts and Sciences board of directors. His letter had really hit the Oscar people where they hurt; they could afford not one more public slap at their dubious integrity.

Once inside, Capra found the final voting to be quite kosher. It was the nomination process that was rotten. Then as now the nomination process favored box office hits over artistic achievement, gave emotion the edge over acting ability, and was dominated by cliques within the branches. "By secret vote each branch selected five nominees for their respective Oscar," Capra said. "For example, only directors who were Academy members voted to select the 'best' five directors. The trick was to get *nominated* by the clique of major studio directors who had achieved membership. And those brahmins were not about to doff their caps to the 'untouchables' of Poverty Row."

He decided he'd have to direct at least one picture for a big studio, such as MGM, to even get his first nomination. "Making good pictures was not good enough—unless you had the correct pedigree." Harry Cohn got his enemy Louis Mayer to make a trade, but Capra turned out to be too innovative for MGM. Mayer bounced him back like an India rubber ball. Back to square one.

Why not make one of those super-real "Depression" films as King Vidor had done in *The Crowd*, which was nominated? Thus came Capra's *American Madness*, one of the first films to grapple directly with the fear and panic of the Depression. To rescue his film from the turgid pace of realistic melodramas, Capra stayed in the editing lab for a month, creating a new form of fast cutting from one bit of action to the other. "I speeded up the pace of the scenes to about one-third of a normal scene. If a scene played normally in sixty seconds, I increased the actors' pace until it played in forty seconds. When *American Madness* opened, there was a sense of

This thoroughly unfamiliar face belongs to Warner Baxter, winner of the second best actor Oscar for playing the Cisco Kid in the film *In Old Arizona*. Baxter got the part and the Oscar because Raoul Walsh, a much more popular actor, lost an eye and could not take the role. In those days the award brought precious little other than twelve dollars worth of metal and a gratis dinner, however lukewarm. Baxter found that Oscar fame was a fleeting thing; he was down to playing second leads a couple of years later and eventually descended to "B" movies such as *Slave Ship* and *Crime Doctor*. His career rebounded, however, and he is probably best remembered in the role of Julian Marsh in the classic musical *Forty-Second Street*.

Edward Arnold and Barbara Stanwyck in Frank Capra's *Meet John Doe*, which Stanwyck dominated in spite of Gary Cooper's fine performance. Capra said many years later that Stanwyck was the finest actress he ever worked with, but her agents and studios steadfastly refused to take her Oscar bids seriously.

The "King and Queen of Hollywood," Tyrone Power and Jeanette MacDonald at their coronation (with crowns made and annointed in the Metro-Goldwyn-Mayer costume department). Few took either of these two seriously—Power was too good-looking and MacDonald was told, firmly and politely, that she was Metro's reigning soprano, which did not include acting. As the Oscar men tried to wash their petticoats and regain their seriousness, the Academy Award choices were monopolized by heavy, theatrical performers such as Greer Garson and Robert Donat. In these contests Power's looks couldn't help him. He showed a rare virtuosity in *Johnny Apollo*, *The Razor's Edge*, and *Blood and Sand*, but his studio, Twentieth Century-Fox, kept cramming him into tights and Hussar costumes and forcing him to prance around such beauties as Linda Darnell and Loretta Young.

urgency, a new interest, at work. The audience loved it."

Here, surely, was an Oscar for Capra. The Hollywood critics quickly killed his chances. They didn't like it. "They said it was not 'Academy material.' Although critical appraisals were light reading for the public, they were gospels for highbrow Academy voters." (This is still true today. Films that are universally panned by Charles Champlin of the *Los Angeles Times*, Stephen Farber of *Los Angeles* magazine, and Rona Barrett stand little chance of taking home the big awards. Fortunately the carefully weighted criticism of Champlin, the major force, has moved the Oscar voters light-years ahead in time.)

Capra decided to make "the artiest film of them all. How about miscengenation. That ought to get 'em." The film was *The Bitter Tea of General Yen*, about the gothic affair between a Chinese warlord and an American missionary (played by Stanwyck, Capra's preferred actress). The finished film was of rare quality and, according to European directors, was thirty years ahead of its time. Not everyone agreed. Certainly not the Academy which quickly passed it over completely.

"There was and is a mystique about Academy voters that confounds trends, predictions, and logic," said Capra. "But those who grabbed off the little statuettes didn't give a hang how they got them. They just knew an Oscar tripled their salaries and zoomed them to world fame. Salary increases didn't whet my appetite. But world fame—wow!" There was only one more road open to the director—corn. Oscar voters loved maudlin emotion and belly laughs more than the gold on their statues. Capra had just the formula: a Damon Runyon story about an "Apple Annie" who becomes a "lady for a day." So let's just call it that, said Capra, *Lady for a Day*. Tears and sappy dialogue worked. The film was nominated in four major categories, including best picture and best director.

In his own words, Frank Capra became impossible to live with. "I kept telling myself that I would win 'four awards.' No other picture had ever won four awards. I would set a record. Hot damn! I wrote and threw away dozens of acceptance speeches. I ordered my first tuxedo. Rented a plush home in Beverly Hills. All to be 'seen' by the few hundred Oscar voters." (To everyone's chagrin, these things are still done today.)

He went to the Oscars with his speech tucked carefully into the pocket of his $600 tux.

Things started going wrong ten minutes into the ceremony. The writing award went to RKO's *Little Women*. Then Will Rogers came out with the sealed envelope for best achievement by a director. Roger's honeyed words described the profession of directing. Then he opened the card: Well, well, well, what do you know. I've watched this young man come up from the bottom—and I mean the bottom."

Frank Capra stirred in his seat. It was him. It *had* to be him. Nobody else had worked up from the sawdust floor of a honky-tonk. At last, at last . . . it was "my turn." Rogers drawled out his words, "It couldn't happen to a nicer guy. . . . Come on up and get it—Frank."

Capra's table exploded, and Capra rose slowly with dignity—as befitted Hollywood's newly knighted. It was a long way up to the dance floor. Capra dodged around Norma Shearer, bumped into Robert Taylor, squeezed by Ginger Rogers, and headed toward the spotlight—which was searching through the dark to find the winner. "Right here," Capra waved. "Right over here." All those people in the dark were confused, but the man on the spot was not. The lighting director already knew who'd won . . . gotten the word when he came in to work. Frank Lloyd it was. He located the MGM table and threw the glare onto the best director of 1933, Frank Lloyd.

"I stood petrified in the dark, in utter disbelief. 'Down in front!' somebody yelled, and I began the longest, saddest, most shattering walk of my life. I wanted to crawl under the rug. All my friends at the table were crying." Capra's humiliation was complete. "I decided that if they ever did give me one, I wouldn't be there to accept. Not me . . . never again."

He didn't keep his pledge. A year later the Oscar voters did give his film *It Happened One Night* all four of the major Oscars (best picture; best actor, Clark Gable; best actress, Claudette Colbert and . . . best director). At the end of the same year the Academy turned to him in a last-ditch attempt to save the fast sinking Academy.

They elected him president. "It was a dubious honor," Capra said. "I say 'dubious' because it would be presiding at a deathwatch. The Academy had become the favorite whipping boy of Hollywood; its membership down from six hundred to forty; its officers dedicated but discouraged; its staff reduced to one loyal, underpaid executive secretary Margaret Herrick—who was the Academy's alter ego. With few dollars in its treasury—and fewer in sight—the odds were ten to one the Academy would fold and Oscar would acquire the patina of a collector's item. (The major source of Academy funding—help from the big studios—was swiftly curtailed once the brass could no longer "use" the organization as a guild buster.)

But the Academy was also under siege by the guilds representing actors, directors, and writers. "The producing companies did everything short of asking for the National Guard to prevent guild organization. Then the talent decided to wreck the Academy in order to deny the studios the promotional value of the Oscars. Oddly enough," Capra said, "the shortsighted company heads couldn't have cared less—the Academy had failed them as an instrument of salary cuts so they (the studios) withdrew their memberships and financial support. The organization was beached—left

Laurence Olivier first appeared on American screens as Heathcliff in Samuel Goldwyn's *Wuthering Heights*. He is shown here with Merle Oberon in a scene from that film. His performance won him a best actor nomination.

in the care of a very few staunch Academy-oriented visionaries dedicated to the cultural recognition and preservation that has become the Academy's strong card."

How few? Capra says that only seventeen people were left as truly active members. "The recognition should go to them. Nobody else helped."

"I don't think most people know how close we came to dissolving," Capra said. "Board members had to put up their own money to pay the people who made the Oscars, and I had to do some fancy pleading for cash to pay the phone bill and buy stationery. Then I had to plead with the officers of the talent guilds to allow me to mail Academy ballots to their guild members."

It was four long years, but it worked. By 1939, new blood began flooding in. Then the war; it literally was the cavalry to the rescue. Nobody had time for Oscar politics during World War II. The studio bosses, however, decided to put their dough back in to support the Oscar shows—which were fast becoming the best publicity stunt in Hollywood history. The Oscars were once again smiled on by Mayer, Warner, and the other money gods; all was right in the Academy's world.

The truce was, sadly, a false one. The studios would make one last attempt to sink the Oscars—this time in the name of false patriotism.

And it all started with Laurence Olivier—a man Hollywood turned down on his first go-round. Olivier, as handsome as dawn itself, was brought to America in 1933 to star with Garbo in *Queen Christina*. He barely got inside the gates when Garbo, apparently trying to save lover Jack Gilbert's career, said she would not make the film with Olivier; it had to be Gilbert or nobody. It was a bitter blow to the British actor, who fled back to England as a reject. Sam Goldwyn, however, had seen his tests for

the MGM picture and decided, the same day, to cast Olivier as Heathcliff in *Wuthering Heights,* and when he strode onto the screen in his suffocatingly snug riding habit there were collective sighs from lady moviegoers around the world. He was rushed into a dizzying list of movies—*Rebecca, Pride and Prejudice,* and *That Hamilton Woman.* On one of his trips to Hollywood in 1939, Vivien Leigh, his lover but not yet his wife, tagged along; agent Myron Selznick saw her, took her to his brother David, and signed her up as Scarlett O'Hara. The lovers were suddenly the hottest stars on this or that side of the Atlantic.

A year later Britain was engulfed in war, and Olivier talked himself into a flying commission in the Royal Navy Air Corps for the duration. Hollywood forgot him. He mustered out of the air corps and immersed himself in his first love, Shakespeare. They say he produced the monumental *Henry V* on a budget so tight it wouldn't pay for a decent newsreel in expensive Hollywood. One thing was certain; the ad budget was zero, and the film opened to no fanfare in Los Angeles. Ticket buyers came in trickles; David O. Selznick dropped by for a matinee and found the theater playing to half a dozen patrons. Backfence gossip in movieland fixed that. Hedda Hopper referred to the movie capital as the "biggest small town in the world." For instance Joan Crawford rushed into the sprawling Los Angeles Farmers Market one noon and ran out with an armful of kiwi fruit. "A friend wrote me from Paris—telling me that a paste from this mixed with egg whites and ice water took off wrinkles and frownies in five minutes," said Crawford to Jeanette MacDonald. The movies' top soprano had dropped in at the market to pick up a gift—a fact she quickly forgot as she drove out with the last of the kiwi fruit. By late afternoon the fruitsellers in the open air shops had been driven nearly mad with calls for kiwi. Telegrams were sent to Mexico ordering bushels of the seedy little pods. By then it was too late; Crawford had tried it; scraped it off her face and phoned a couple of friends to say: "That junk didn't do one Goddamned thing. And today I could have used it."

It was this network that turned Olivier's *Henry V* into a sleeper; the movie folk went in theater parties, ordered private screenings, and filled gossip columns with descriptions of Larry. As a result, the film was nominated for best picture; best performance by an actor; color, music, etc., etc.

The studio bosses were horrified. The British were coming and threatening to engulf their cozy little relationship with the Oscar. The Oscar voters, lured to the theater to see one British film, started shopping around for others. British acting, British costumes, British cinematography, and British accents were Oscar-vogue. *Brief Encounter, The Seventh Veil,* and *Caesar and Cleopatra* were all nominated in one category or another. Louis B. Mayer fumed. And other studio bosses talked as if the British nominations were outright treason!

The Academy pulled an emergency rabbit out of the hat. Laurence Olivier, they decided would receive a "special" Oscar, lauding him for his guts. (I mean, who else would film a dull Shakespeare historical play when *The Jolson Story, The Yearling,* and other nice themes were around for the picking?) A special award it was, and he could just keep his sticky English fingers off the regulation Oscars. That was 1946, and the British only got two minor awards—the special effects prize for *Blithe Spirit* and the writing Oscar given to *The Seventh Veil.* That was that.

But 1947 was worse. *Great Expectations,* a film by David Lean, was nominated for five Oscars—including best picture. This time the fat cats couldn't dismiss it as a tribute to William Shakespeare; this film could have been made right here in Hollywood. To top it off, some normally patriotic American directors like George Cukor and King Vidor were spreading it

David Lean's *Great Expectations* was so superior to Hollywood products that it took five nominations—including best picture. It won for best cinematography and best art direction.

around town that David Lean was a pretty fair director—fair enough for them to give him a personal nomination for best director.

Peter O'Toole and Richard Burton on the set of *Becket*.

The disease was also catching. The Academy had nominated an Italian film, *Shoeshine*, for best screenplay; a French film, *A Cage of Nightingales*, for original story; and still another British film, *Black Narcissus*, for color cinematography and art direction. W.R. Wilkerson, who as publisher of the *Hollywood Reporter* was the official voice of the studios, warned that America had helped them with the war but didn't need to help them get "our Oscars." (This time foreign films won four Academy Awards, becoming a growing menace to the studios.)

1948 brought down the house! Months before the first Oscar balloting, Laurence Olivier's *Hamlet* opened to wildly enthusiastic crowds in New York and, later, in Hollywood. This time everyone was going to see the British film. The men at the top set their chins grimly and realized that gossip was already giving the best picture and best actor awards to Olivier. J. Arthur Rank's ballet film *The Red Shoes* opened a couple of weeks later and was also being talked as an Oscar caliber movie.

Before Christmas of 1948, angry executives from the "big five"—Warner Brothers, Paramount, MGM, Twentieth Century-Fox, and RKO—flew to New York and called a joint emergency session—the first time the five studios had met together since the labor crises of the thirties. The big five had Oscar on a short leash, and they knew it. Since 1939 the studios had subsidized the Oscar ceremony as an international publicity event. They'd given $87,000 in 1947, and had already agreed to pay $57,000 in 1948.

Never in their wildest dreams had the studios expected to pay the costs of an Oscar ceremony which honored a limey film.

Academy President Jean Hersholt, renowned as Doctor Christian in the *Dr. Kildare* movies, had known on December 16 that the studios were

Academy
or
Motion Picture Arts and Sciences
Organization Banquet
May 11, 1927.
Los Angeles Biltmore.

The second anniversary banquet of the Academy at the Hollywood Roosevelt Hotel indicates the party atmosphere in which the Oscars were conceived. Everybody was supposed to get together, have a few laughs, and hand out Oscars to actors selected by a handful of Hollywood's finest. King Vidor, the veteran director who never got an Oscar, says that, contrary to the Academy's own claims, Oscar winners were picked by five people "gathered together for a few drinks."

threatening to pull out. But he said later he figured the studios would "come around" as Oscar time neared. The industry simply swept the controversy under the rug until the night of the Academy Awards, when Hersholt told a national radio audience of the pullout. He added that the studios were out to wreck the Academy.

Caught off guard, the big five claimed the Oscars won by *Hamlet* had nothing to do with their withdrawal of the life-giving dough. "We just didn't want it to seem as if there were conflicts between us—the studios—and the awards," said a spokesman for the brass. It was just a bizarre coincidence that the pullout came in a year that honored a British film. "Give us a break, boys," the execs said to the press. And many of the Hollywood journalists bought it. Several even ran mild retractions explaining that "British films had nothing to do with it."

At a joint press conference, Nicholas Schenck of MGM, Barney Balaban of Paramount, Spyros Skouras of Fox, Major Albert Warner of Warners, and Ned Depinet of RKO issued a statement so sweet it melted in their mouths: "We intend to continue our *moral support* of the idea of making awards of merit for superior achievements in motion pictures. We shall continue our financial support of the original function of the Academy of Motion Picture Arts and Sciences. But we shall no longer pay the costs of this ceremony."

Somehow they also managed to say, "The step is not a commercial one. In fact it is in the interest of 'less commercialization.' Remember the companies as companies were never members of the Academy. That is as it should be." The last paragraph of their statement, however, betrayed their full intention: "The artistic standards of our industry are NOT dependent on this annual competition. There are, in fact, many awards by many groups for which the creative talent of our industry could strive."

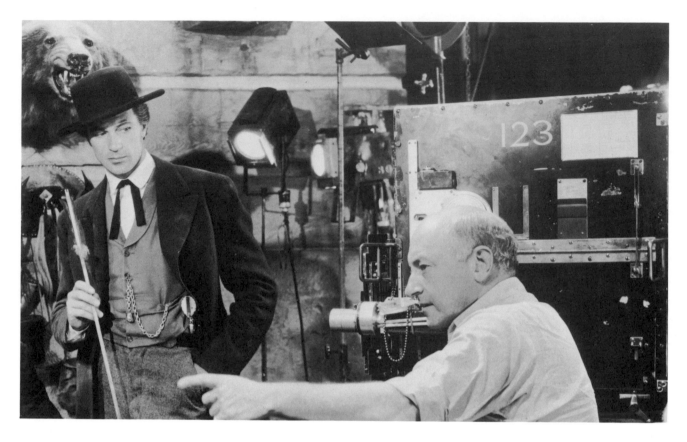

Now there! Academy. Take that and stuff it down *Hamlet*'s throat.

Back in Tinseltown, the *Hollywood Reporter*, which was part of the problem, trumpeted that the voting in the 1948 Oscars may not have been quite up to snuff and, therefore, highly traitorous.

The *Reporter* said flatly that the accounting firm counting the ballots should hand the ballots back to the Academy board for a public recount. "We have yet to run across a single voter who favored *Hamlet*," said the *Reporter*. "From ANY WAY you look at it," said the trade paper, "*Hamlet* was not the best picture of the year, and the Academy voting, which gave it the top honor, was not as a direct result of the voters (IF THEY VOTED THAT WAY) preferring it to our own-made top pictures but was rather a vote against the studios that pay them."

Hersholt's address at the awards turned Hollywood Boulevard into a political hotbed. The Academy prexy said a spokesman for the studios told him, "We don't want the Academy standards foisted on us; we want to make commercial pictures unhampered by considerations of artistic excellence."

At a press conference the morning after, Hersholt said Columbia, Universal-International, and Republic had withdrawn not just Oscar show funds but "all funds including money for operation and research."

Eddie Mannix, a former carnival bouncer who rose to the top of the MGM corporate ladder, answered Hersholt by saying, "In America it is still not a disgrace to be in a business that makes money. It isn't a crime. We're going to continue making the kind of pictures the public wants and will pay for."

Columbia's Harry Cohn was ready to count Oscar out: "It looks to us as if the Academy Awards is going to fold. This studio will therefore reserve

Gary Cooper and Cecil B. De Mille from *The Plainsman*. Cooper appeared in several De Mille epics at Paramount during the late thirties and early forties. Here, Cooper played "Wild" Bill Hickock, a far cry from his award winning performance as Marshall Will Kane in *High Noon* years later.

judgment as to any future plans for financial support. Maybe the Academy has far outlived its usefulness."

As the dust settled it was only too clear why the bosses ripped open the Academy's gut. New financial studies of Oscar-winning pictures from 1945–1947 showed that an Oscar for best picture adds an extra gross of two million smackers a year. Emmet Lavery, a noted screenwriter, penned the best postmortem in *The New Yorker*: "So we come now, in the twenty-first year of the Academy's existence, to the parting of the ways between the major Hollywood studios and the Academy. And a happy parting it is. The only cause for wonderment is that it did not happen sooner—preferably at the very beginning. This does not mean the end of the Academy. On the contrary, it means an expansion and development on an independent level. There can now be little question that the annual awards are the free choice of the 1,800 members of the Academy. At the ripe old age of twenty-one, Oscar has shown that he is free to vote as he chooses."

As usual, the studios were speaking out of both sides of their mouth. They took back their marbles, but they retained their votes. (And the Oscar did not go to another foreign film for fourteen years.)

Time magazine called him Little Orphan Oscar. And that he was—for a sticky couple of years. Radio commercials, increased dues, and a fund drive tided the Oscar ceremony over until 1952, a year in which the Academy recovered from twenty-five years of money problems in one fell swoop.

Television rode in like "The Lone Ranger." Television—the arch-enemy of the movies; the unmentionable; the devil in video clothes. The money men at RCA had watched the 1951 ceremony with greedy eyes. What they saw was a veritable Aladdin's lamp of movie stars appearing entirely free of charge—Marlene, Marilyn, Ethel Barrymore, Helen Hayes, Fred Astaire, Gene Kelly, Martin and Lewis. The guys from RCA knew that TV was going begging for superstars; Hollywood had forbidden them to even breathe a line on network TV. Oh, maybe a line or two on a talk show. But nothing more. And certainly not glamour.

What if RCA and its stepchild NBC picked up more stars than there were in the heavens on one show—and free at that. They went to the Academy and laid it on the line: a hundred thousand bucks for your Oscar show, and we'll do most of the work.

In 1952 the studios, who had set the Oscars adrift, watched the Academy Awards drift forever from their control. Millions stayed home from the movies to watch the Academy's show. (Later, Academy officers revealed that there would have been no Oscar ceremony that night if NBC hadn't come to the rescue.)

The television era was on; the Academy Awards were suddenly the property of the world. Ladies in Paris saw how Grace Kelly did her hair; movie buffs in Lincoln, Nebraska, got their first look at Cecil B. De Mille; Audrey Hepburn's bangs became an international rage. And the Oscar was suddenly worth countless millions of dollars to a winning picture or, more importantly, to a triumphant actor. And it was TV that finally freed the Academy from its bondage to the studios on one hand and the actors on the other. Starting with the hundred thousand dollars in 1952, the network and advertising money rolled in until it reached the millions: with the Oscars being broadcast to three hundred countries. Only the Superbowl has a larger audience, and ABC, the Academy's contractee, began charging advertisers an incredible two hundred thousand dollars a minute. Neither ABC nor the Academy will openly discuss the contract terms, but it's probable the network is paying more than two million dollars for the rights to the ceremony. Even though the Academy, which produces the show, pours more than $1.6 million back into the Oscar cast (Johnny Carson alone takes home $15,000 for one night's work), more than $400,000 is left to pay for the massive Academy library, film restoration projects, and festivals.

One way or another, three hundred million people saw Dustin Hoffman take home the prize as best actor of 1980. Since Hoffman's film *Kramer vs. Kramer* was named best picture and copped a passel of other awards, Oscar should be worth a cool $25 million to the film, and that's a conservative estimate. In the last five years the monetary power of the Academy Awards has reached awesome proportions. Economists put the value of a major Oscar at a million dollars in 1965; now a nomination alone is worth that—to a picture or to a star. When Olivia Newton-John appeared on the Oscar stage to sing the nominated song "Hopelessly Devoted to You" (from *Grease*), record stores across America and in England and France, particularly France, couldn't get enough copies of the soundtrack to meet demand.

Oscar began turning from gold to platinum in the early seventies. Billy Friedkin, director of the Oscar-winning *The French Connection* believes the award added "at least $5 million dollars to that picture's gross income. If a movie wins several Oscars—big ones—then the payoff is doubled." "There's no money in getting an Oscar per se," says Ernest Borgnine, Oscar winner for *Marty*, "but in time you may be offered a million dollars in parts." A prime example of this Oscar upmanship is Gene Hackman, who took one of the Oscars for *The French Connection*. Hackman's fee per picture jumped from $200,000 to $500,0000 after he won the best actor honor. And his fee had previously reached the six figure level after his Oscar nominated role in *Bonnie and Clyde*.

Hollywood's bankers watched the Oscar winning films of the early seventies reap massive money harvests in the months following the ceremony. And their busy little minds came up with a better mousetrap— specifically designed to maneuver the post-Oscar box office. It all started with *One Flew Over the Cuckoo's Nest*, the best picture of 1975. Three weeks before the Oscars, United Artists, which distributed the Jack Nicholson-Louise Fletcher film, took a staw poll in Hollywood and deduced that *One Flew Over the Cuckoo's Nest* would be an easy winner. UA released the film in a big blast toward the end of 1975—taking in major holiday ticket sales and then pulling the movie back in the mid-winter. Then the movie won all five of the major Academy Awards—the first film to do so since *It Happened One Night* in 1934. The morning after Oscar, the United Artists booked the film into 1,000 theaters in America, Canada, and Great Britain. Film writer Gregg Kilday, formerly of the *Los Angeles Times* and later with the *Herald-Examiner*, wrote that the five Oscars probably added an additional forty-three million dollars to the *One Flew over the Cuckoo's Nest* take. *Forty-three million dollars!* And this is not random coincidence; Universal also announced that the best picture award added thirty million in profits for their winner, *The Sting*. In still another example United Artists and MGM got their heads together before the 1976 ceremony and paired up two Oscar caliber movies—*Network* and *Rocky*. The duo divided most of the big Oscars in 1976, and the films opened as a double bill in 900 theaters—pulling in a total of twenty million in eight weeks. Naturally, this puts great pressure on the studios to get the films nominated and bag at least one Oscar. The ad line "Oscar winning film" has become a cure for what ails the box office of the eighties. (In 1980 when Paramount was stuck with the turkey *Star Trek, the Movie* and Walt Disney was carrying the disaster *The Black Hole*, the publicists at both factories stumbled over each other trying to get nominations for the films—ANY nominations.)

Actually, Twentieth Century-Fox wrote the book on Oscar exploitation. The men over at Fox learned that even the most dismal of films could get

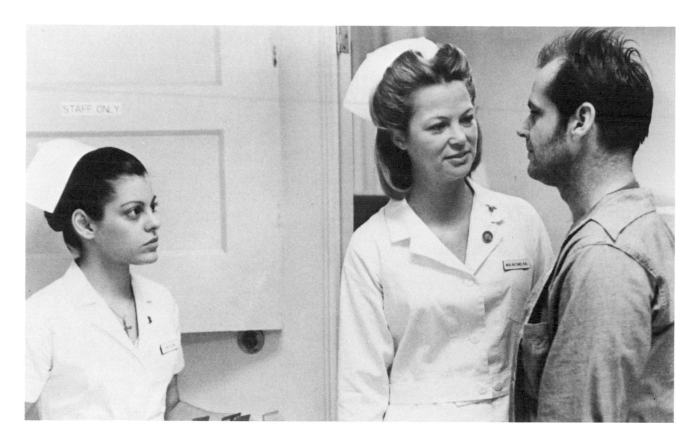

Jack Nicholson and Louise Fletcher in *One Flew Over the Cuckoo's Nest,* which won the top four Oscars and went on to gross an additional fifty million dollars—most of it due to the monetary value of an Oscar win.

a best picture nomination if it cost enough and if the studio kept repeating all over town, "This film is Oscar class; this film is Oscar class; this film. . . ." The tactic won picture nods for *Cleopatra, The Sand Pebbles, Doctor Doolittle,* and *Hello, Dolly!,* all pictures that probably shouldn't have been in the top ten, much less the top five.

"This means some pictures HAVE to get an Oscar to make it in the marketplace," says a publicist for Paramount. "That's a dangerous situation. When a film has to win in order to make back its cost, some of us will have to do everything short of killing to get them. It'll be a whole new ball game in the eighties."

3

SECRET BALLOT

"As of 1931, if I, a director for a minor league studio, wanted to win an Oscar, making good films was not good enough."
Frank Capra.

Joan Blondell was fighting mad. Her cheeks flushed up under her makeup, and her platinum hair waved in the wind like a flag. "They did it again! They did it again!" she yelled across the Warner Brothers lot, aiming her voice at anyone willing to listen.

She was in the middle of a musical number from *Stage Struck* being directed by tap-mad genius Busby Berkeley when the master called a coffee break, and Blondell ran to a newsstand near the front gate. It was February, 1935. "They delivered the *Citizen* yet?" she asked. "Just got here," said the paper seller, sailing a copy through the air to her outstretched arms. Blondell scanned the front page, searching for a report on the Academy Award nominations. "Those bastards. What the hell do you have to do to get nominated anyway?" Back on the set, she waved the front page before co-star Dick Powell's face. "They passed Bette up again. Not a mention—not for Bette or the movie." Dick reached for her hand and said, "Don't take it so hard. You know as well as I do that the Oscar business is all politics. Bette will understand."

And Bette Davis, Joan Blondell's pal, *did* understand. And more! She knew damn well why her incredible performance in *Of Human Bondage* didn't win an Oscar nomination. Hadn't Jack Warner ordered her not to appear in the Somerset Maugham classic—a decision he had rescinded only to shut Bette up? "Nobody in their right mind would want to play that vicious bitch," warned the boss of Warner Brothers. "You'll live to regret it."

As it turned out, the only thing she regretted about the movie was the Academy Award scandal that surrounded it. It sure wasn't the first time Oscar had overlooked the best Hollywood had to offer. King Vidor's triumph *The Crowd*—considered to be one of the best two or three pictures of the twenties—didn't even rate a best picture nomination in 1927. And in 1929 the Academy handed Norma Shearer an Oscar for a couple of limp-wristed roles, passing over Greta Garbo in *Anna Christie* and Gloria Swanson in *The Trespasser*.

A young Bette Davis and Leslie Howard in 1934's *Of Human Bondage*, a brutally frank film that wowed Hollywood and America with its brilliance and unleashed a storm of bitterness when it was passed up by Oscar voters. Bette's performance was surely the best of the year—one of the best of a decade. But political incest within the Academy froze her out of the nomination lists, a fact that almost destroyed Oscar.

This time, though, the Academy had gone too far. Nobody in Hollywood—unless he was deaf and dumb—could have overlooked Bette's performance in *Of Human Bondage*. It opened at New York's Radio City Music Hall on June 28, 1934. The reaction was violent; people cheered and clapped when the final credits were shown, and some eastern critics called Davis the best actress, so far, of the talkies. Nobody disagreed; in fact, it was common knowledge in Hollywood that the actress had gone through hell to even win the part and had given so much of herself, during filming, that superstars fought with each other to get tickets to the sneak previews. She was finally given permission when Jack Warner found out he could make a bundle on Bette by loaning her out at an inflated fee to RKO to play Mildred. "Go on, hang yourself!" Warner said to the actress before dismissing her.

Bette just jutted out her New England chin, took home her copy of the Somerset Maugham novel, and began trying, painstakingly, to master a cockney accent. She even hired a transplanted Englishwoman to help her. The lady moved into Bette's house (slept on the couch) and began her coaching.

"For eight weeks. Morning, noon, and night, I was at it," says Davis. "I even answered the phone with it. And naturally, I drove the family mad, but it was worth it when I found that I had mastered the accent well enough to win the praise of the British cast."

The performance was so stunning that some directors dropped by the RKO lot to see the daily rushes—if they could get permission. The success of the film should have only strengthened Bette's chance to win the Oscar.

When the Academy failed to even nominate her, almost everyone in Hollywood screamed "foul!" It was time, everyone decided, to take a good, hard look at the Oscar ballot box. Who in their right mind would nominate Claudette Colbert (in her fine, but lightweight, bit in *It Happened One Night*), Grace Moore (an opera singer who hit the high notes but little else in *One Night of Love*), and Norma Shearer (for shedding tears and holding a hankie in *The Barretts of Wimpole Street*) and NOT Bette Davis in *Of Human Bondage*? It was even harder to take because the Academy had the option of expanding the list from three to five if performances warranted.

There was no way around it. Bette Davis was passed over on purpose. It was only the latest—but the worst—sign of the political rottenness eating at the inner soul of the seven-year-old Academy of Motion Picture Arts and Sciences.

The conspiracy against Bette Davis, however, started at Warner Brothers. Jack and Harry Warner, both founders of the Academy, made it known that THEY were not supporting Bette Davis for the Oscar. The implication was clear; the Academy members working for Warners should not support her either. "My bosses certainly didn't help by sending instructions to all their personnel to vote for somebody else. So naturally, it worked!"

And over at RKO, which had managed to get less than twenty nominations (few of them major) in the first five years of Oscar, the bosses were only lukewarm over Davis. She was not, after all, under contract to RKO. And an Oscar to her would only succeed in making the Warner brothers wealthier at their expense.

The Oscar slighted Bette Davis and *Of Human Bondage* for other reasons as well. In 1934 Oscar was held by his privates, so to speak, in the iron grip of a few big studios: Paramount, United Artists, and Metro-Goldwyn-Mayer—particularly Metro-Goldwyn-Mayer. Louis B. Mayer himself conceived of the organization, hosted its first dinner meeting, and had his own lawyer draw up the bylaws. Eleven of the founders were from MGM, and that studio had taken the hog's share of nominations and Oscars since

Joan Blondell, an actress who averaged thirty films a year in the Warner Brothers' factory, braved the wrath of studio boss Jack Warner and led the drive to gain a nomination for Davis's Mildred in *Of Human Bondage*. The Academy, sensing its own vulnerability, allowed voters to "write in" Davis, the film, and Leslie Howard, but the landslide for Frank Capra's *It Happened One Night* tossed Oscar to Claudette Colbert and Clark Gable. The surprise of Colbert's victory over Bette Davis was revealed when Claudette had to be pulled off the train and rushed through the streets to collect her award.

1927 (155 nominations and 33 Oscars in the first decade—twice as many as Warner Brothers, three times as many as RKO, and four times as many as Columbia).

Louis B. Mayer's personal Oscar power was even more insidious. During the first several years, he apparently had an almost royal veto power over some of the ballot decisions. (And ballot is too kind a word for the first ten years of Oscar decisions.) It was Mayer, and Mayer alone, who kept King Vidor's monumental film, *The Crowd*, from being nominated in 1928. Looking back from 1980, this act seems not only stupid but quite near-sighted. *The Crowd*, the first film to really deal with the bleakness of lower middle-class life, was a classic when it was released. Mayer made it clear to the hand-picked nominating committee that he wished them to "bypass MGM to avoid appearance of a conflict of interest." It was all right, he said, to nominate King Vidor for best director. The other nominees were Frank Borzage, a studio-popular director; and a forgotten man, Herbert Brenon, for a forgotten film, *Sorrell and Son*. The decision that was made in the finals remains clouded in mystery. Who decided on Borzage over Vidor? The Academy historians say the Oscars were decided by an impartial panel.

"Well, that's a crock," said Joan Crawford, when she was reminiscing in the sixties, "The committee only formalized decisions that were already made by a few key producers. You've got to remember, the Academy, then at least, was only an extension of the 'executive suite.'"

King Vidor also tells it differently: "At the start the voting was done by five people only—a situation which fortunately didn't last very long. The first year Sid Grauman, Mary Pickford, Douglas Fairbanks, Sr., and Louis B. Mayer voted for everybody. I figured I had a good chance to win. My film *The Crowd* had gotten spectacular reviews, and Mayer himself had produced it. After an all-night voting session Sid Grauman called me at 6 a.m. and told me he'd held out for my work in *The Crowd* until daybreak."

"Well?" said Vidor. There was a pause on the other end of the line: "Your problem, Vidor, was Mayer. He wouldn't vote for it because it wasn't a big money-maker for MGM." Vidor hung up the phone in disgust. "Even then money mattered—though it didn't earn an extra million dollars like it does now."

"I'm a great admirer of the Academy," says Vidor, who never did get a regular Oscar—though he's now thought of as one of the top twenty directors in U.S. films. "But it was nearly ruined by tampering from the big studio men who founded it."

Hollywood directors screamed like Aunt Paddie's Pig over Vidor's loss, so the Academy dropped the cozy little committees that decided the winners during the first two years. But not before the bosses made sure that Mary Pickford got an Oscar for *Coquette* and MGM took home a best picture award for its choppy, moderately successful *Broadway Melody*. Mary Pickford's Oscar was, to be fair, a "career Oscar" for her twenty years of monumental contributions as the movies' first superstar. She earned it, but it was to set a precedent for the Oscars that continues today. They give awards, over and over, not for the best performance of the year but for years of fine duty under fire.

The Bette Davis bypass happened under different rules. The entire membership, such as it was, had been making the nominations since 1930. But hundreds of writers, scores of directors, and thousands of actors had deserted the Academy in unhappiness and hatred over the use of the organization by studio executives to keep the unions—and therefore fair wages—out of Hollywood (see Chapter Two). Perhaps history will never know how few people decided the Oscars in the thirties; one thing is certain, the processes were dominated by the producers and studio bosses.

Frank Capra took over as president of the fast fading Academy in 1936, and he says the membership was down to fifty. Another director, Walter Wanger, has said several times that the membership was forty or below. (Wanger succeeded Capra as Academy president in the early forties.)

The voters were a veritable Hollywood handful, that's certain. Capra says he had to beg the members of the Screen Actors Guild, the Directors Guild of America, and the Writers Guild of America. "At that time, any support of the Academy, even voting, was taboo."

Studio politics, pure and simple, cost Davis the nomination and, probably, the Oscar. It had happened before and it would happen again. (But it could never happen now because the voting membership is so much larger.)

Still, the "Bette Davis Affair" scared the hell out of the Academy. Bette's friends and admirers, including Joan Blondell and Dick Powell, stirred Hollywood gossip (always the city's greatest force) to create general outrage in the acting community. Mayer and the rest of the bosses took the bait. On February 15, 1935, the Oscar committees announced that write-ins would be permitted in the voting for the 1934 Oscars. But this was only a grudging gesture. Claudette Colbert won, followed by Norma Shearer and Grace Moore. "I suppose there was no chance for any part of the process to be fair because everybody had quit the Academy," said Joan Blondell. "But when they left Bette out, we all began taking a closer look and decided: 'Hey, something's rotten in Beverly Hills.'"

The scandal was the end of an era for Oscar. Six years of tea party voting was finally over. Marie Dressler, an early winner, described the syndrome as "cream and sugar with my Oscar, please." The year Mary Pickford won, virtually all the voters had been guests in her palace, Pickfair, at least once. In Norma Shearer's case, her husband, MGM production

"I have to shamefacedly admit that I was heartbroken not to win the Oscar for *Of Human Bondage,* the actress told interviewer Dick Cavett. "Due to the acclaim from the critics and my friends, I just naturally assumed I would win. I learned quick never to take the Academy Award process for granted. And when I won the next year for *Dangerous* I knew the award was really for *Of Human Bondage.*"

Frank Capra coaches Clark Gable and Claudette Colbert on the set of *It Happened One Night*, the film that brought him the Oscar, which was his personal "Holy Grail," as he called it. "I was Oscar crazy," Capra said. "Did everything in the world to get one." But Capra learned quickly that "making good films was not good enough." Capra had to join the Academy and work his way up to the board of directors before he won the big one. A familiar story.

chief Irving Thalberg, delivered the executive vote; most of the other voters had been guests at Irving and Norma's wedding.

"This is not to say that these early awards didn't hit right on target," says writer Frances Marion, an early winner. "I think it had more heart to it then."

The big winner in 1934 was Frank Capra. His film *It Happened One Night* took Oscars for: best picture; best direction; best actor, Clark Gable; best actress, Claudette Colbert; and best screenplay, Robert Riskin. But even Capra knew the voting process had to be overhauled or it would bring Oscar's walls down around the Academy. Capra immediately opened up the ballot box—extending voting power to all the guilds: actors, directors, extras, etc. It was then possible for voters to number about 20,000. "But we still had to beg the guilds to let their people get the ballots through the mail. Many, many people felt the voting was a tacit support of the Academy and that support of the Academy was anti-labor."

Capra's plan helped. But not Capra, nor Wanger, nor even Bette Davis (Academy president briefly in the forties) could successfully cure the Oscars of their near fatal domination by the big studios. The ballot box was the tender issue in the beginning and it remained that way until the mid-seventies when Gregory Peck, the president, finally got a slippery handle on it.

Academy voters have littered fifty years of film history with the carcasses of creative giants who have gone Oscarless in the name of box office success and big studio politics. Bad voting was the issue in 1935; it was the issue in 1945. And it was still the issue in 1970.

Oscar's history is characterized as much by the movies and performances it slighted as by the ones it honored.

It was Oscar voters who passed up Greta Garbo and handed sob-sister

Luise Rainer two of the little gold men. It was Oscar voters who named the mawkish musical *Oliver!* best picture of the year while failing to nominate *2001: A Space Odyssey* or *Easy Rider* (two films that were listed by *Time* magazine and the *New York Times* as best of the decade).

Academy members gave Elizabeth Taylor an Oscar for *Butterfield 8*, one of her worst movies, but did not nominate her for *A Place In the Sun*, one of her best. They named *The Greatest Show on Earth* as best picture over *High Noon, Moulin Rouge*, and *The Quiet Man* (while failing to nominate *Singin' in the Rain, Come Back, Little Sheba, The Bad and the Beautiful*, and *Viva Zapata!* in the same year).

In 1939 they nominated Mickey Rooney for *Babes in Arms* and not Henry Fonda in *Young Mr. Lincoln*. In 1943 they nominated Mickey Rooney for *The Human Comedy* and not Henry Fonda in *The Ox-Bow Incident*. In 1955 they nominated Spencer Tracy in *Bad Day at Black Rock* and not Henry Fonda in *Mister Roberts*. The example of Henry Fonda is particularly important because it demolishes the Academy's greatest defense against its incessant critics. The men and women who have apologized for the Oscar in speeches, articles—even books—always say that the Oscar adheres to one golden rule. Oscars are not always given, so say the apologists, to the actor or actress who gives "the best performance of the year." But, so they say, the Oscars do even out the odds by honoring actors or actresses who have consistently given a career full of fine performances. But what about Greta Garbo or Irene Dunne or Cary Grant? Or Henry Fonda.

Fonda is perhaps the prime example. First, because he's only been nominated once (for *Grapes of Wrath*) and second, he's still turning in one good performance after another in a career that began forty-five years ago. His Oscar calibre roles are too many to list, but have included *Jezebel, Jesse James, Chad Hanna, The Male Animal, Daisy Kenyon, Twelve Angry Men, War and Peace, Advise and Consent*, and *Once upon a Time in the West*. The Oscar bosses say that Fonda's numbers just didn't come up right—his years were always during years of bountiful male performances. That's not true, of course. In 1957, when *Twelve Angry Men* was nominated for best picture, the voters opted for Marlon Brando in *Sayonara*, Alec Guinness in *The Bridge on the River Kwai*, Anthony Franciosa in *A Hatful of Rain*, Charles Laughton in *Witness for the Prosecution*, and Anthony Quinn in *Wild Is the Wind*. Only Guinness' performance was as good or better than Fonda's.

Other Academy big-talkers are quick to say that "Hank knows the score; it doesn't really affect him; he knows about the politics."

Maybe. But Hollywood columnist James Bacon has another impression. When Fonda was backstage at the 1970 Oscars, Bacon noticed him pacing around nervously. "You worried because Jane might not win?" asked Bacon. "No," Fonda replied, half in jest. "How would you like to have a daughter who's about to get an Oscar before you? And you've been a film actor for thirty-five years." Henry Fonda has made light of that statement, even issued a semi-denial. But Bacon sticks to his guns.

The Academy has passed up Fonda so many times that it's become an inside joke. In a delicious bit of irony Billy Wilder cast Fonda as the president of the Academy offering a long overdue Oscar to an aging movie star in 1979's *Fedora*. Unfortunately, Fonda wasn't on screen long enough to bag a nomination for best supporting actor—but the thought was there.

The domination of the Academy by the studios seemed just another example of the quaint and madcap way Hollywood did things. "Oh, you know how it is out there," said Elsa Maxwell, discussing the Oscars with the Duchess of Windsor. "They just play dress-up once a year. It's not to be taken seriously."

Then came 1941 when the Oscars passed up *Citizen Kane*, by everybody's estimate one of the ten best films ever made. "It's just a good thing

Henry Fonda and Lee J. Cobb in a scene from Fonda's self-produced *Twelve Angry Men*, which was nominated for best picture in 1957. Fonda, one of Hollywood's first great freelancers, failed to earn a nomination for his performance in the film—he had no studio and therefore no big buck hype behind him. Far lesser talents (Spencer Tracy and Bing Crosby, for example) took home the golden man while Fonda created a mass of film work equaled in longevity and excellence only by Laurence Olivier.

John Ford's harsh "Depression-style lighting" emits a Rembrandtesque quality in this scene from *The Grapes of Wrath* with Fonda and Jane Darwell (in the truck). Fonda's distraught and driven Tom Joad brought him his first and only Oscar nomination in a career that has included *The Ox-Bow Incident, Young Mr. Lincoln, Jezebel, Drums Along the Mohawk, Jesse James, Chad Hanna, Mister Roberts, How the West Was Won, Advise and Consent, The Longest Day*, and *Once Upon a Time in the West*. With a wry sense of irony, director Billy Wilder cast Fonda as the Academy president in *Fedora* and had him awarding an Oscar to Marthe Keller.

that *Birth of a Nation* didn't have to face these voters," said writer Dalton Trumbo. "They'd have given it an honorable mention for cinematography and tossed Lillian Gish a bouquet for best supporting actress."

Then television, the infidel, forever ended any quaintness the Oscars may have possessed. People turned on "I Love Lucy," and quit going to the movies. It happened overnight. In 1948 the films had one of their best years in history. In 1950 they had one of their worst. The Hollywood bosses were grabbing at straws; pulling things out of the hat such as Three-D and Smell-O-Vision to get them back to the ticket windows. Overnight, the Oscar became a deadly serious matter. The fat men in the front offices had discovered an amazing thing in 1947. A special box office study showed that *The Best Years of Our Lives*, and *Gentlemen's Agreement* both earned about two million dollars extra after they won the best picture Oscar. Louis B. Mayer and others thought it was a whim of the times, at first. But a Dow-Jones study published in *Fortune* magazine proved that both films had virtually finished their normal box office runs by Oscar time. The Oscars, said the Dow-Jones men, caused the films to "make two million extra— each!" Thus ended, forever, Oscar's virgin objectivity. From that day, Oscar had a cash value. And Oscar is nice for a lot of other reasons, too. But agents, public relations men, executives, and the national theater chains— particularly the chains—see it as money in the bank. This era is far from over. What else can explain the defeat of *Network* by the sappy *Rocky* in 1976. (And *Rocky* was surely the weakest picture of the five, the others being *All the President's Men, Bound for Glory,* and *Taxi Driver. Marathon Man, The Shootist,* and Ingmar Bergman's *Face to Face* weren't even nominated.)

The use of Oscar as a blank check was already an institution by the time the first true critics of the awards appeared on the national scene. Sad to say, most of the movie press accepted the Oscar decisions as being of unassailable virtue until the fifties.

Then, the first true critic wasn't a Hollywood reporter but a writer of mysteries—Raymond Chandler, author of *The Big Sleep; Farewell, My Lovely;* and many others. "It isn't that the awards never go to fine achievements as that those fine achievements are not rewarded as such. They are rewarded as fine achievements at the box office," Chandler wrote in *The Nation.* "They are not decided by the use of whatever artistic and critical wisdom Hollywood may happen to possess. Instead, they are bally-hooed, pushed, yelled, screamed, and in every way propagandized into the consciousness of the voters so incessantly in the weeks before the final balloting that everything except the golden aura of the box office is forgotten."

Chandler, writing in the late forties, came to many of the same conclusions that other critics would reach in the seventies. Namely, that the voters normally do not heavily attend the movies they vote on, and the percentage of the Academy that actually votes is never higher than sixty or sometimes seventy percent and is often less than fifty percent.

Studio bosses will deny this even now. "Why, studios can't control votes," Darryl Zanuck used to say. "It's a SECRET ballot for chrissakes." True, how true. But to quote Joan Crawford, "You'd have to be some ninny to vote against the studio that has your contract or that produces your pictures. Your future depends on theirs—so to speak. And if an Oscar means a better future, then so be it."

The Hollywood brass has talked out of the other side of its mouth when outraged by an occasional show of Oscar impartiality. Most notably, execs yelled when the Academy chose a British production as best picture of the year in 1948. And it was a picture that wasn't even being distributed by a Hollywood company. The film was Laurence Olivier's monumental *Hamlet,*

Child star Jackie Coogan returns his signed contract to MGM studio manager Joe Engel. Star babies were little more than money-makers in early Hollywood—darned cute little bundles of revenue reared in platinum nurseries. The Academy treated them the same way—designing a series of tiny "toy Oscars" to honor their work in films. "It became obvious that they shouldn't compete for the grown-up awards," said Louis B. Mayer. This pattern wasn't broken until Patty Duke won a real, adult Oscar for *The Miracle Worker.*

"Play it, Sam"—Bogart, Bergman, and Dooley Wilson in the wartime Oscar winner *Casablanca*. The stylish saga bagged the best picture award plus better-late-than-never recognition for director Michael Curtiz. But it would be giving the Academy voters too much credit to say they knew what they had on their hands—a monumental classic. More likely, it was the war that earned the votes. And 1943 was a fairly weak year. *Casablanca*'s main competition was the Ernst Lubitsch comedy, *The More the Merrier*.

for which Olivier was also named best actor. (It won two other awards.) And, don't this beat all, a second limey pic, *The Red Shoes*, was also up for best picture in place of perfectly good red-white-and-blue efforts like *I Remember Mama* or *The Luck of the Irish*, for God's sake (see Chapter Two).

This seemed so fishy that the bosses bad-mouthed the Oscar voting process which they had always defended like the Statue of Liberty. W.R. Wilkerson, publisher of the *Hollywood Reporter* and the media voice for the studios that fed his paper with ads, said right out that the ballot box must have been stuffed. "It's a mystery to us as to who actually did cast a vote for *Hamlet*, said Wilkerson in his front page column, "Trade Views." (It was no secret that Wilkerson spoke for the studio establishment.) Wilkerson figured out that, according to his convoluted arithmetic, *Hamlet* would have to have gotten 317 votes to win the Oscar. "Where are the 317 that voted for *Hamlet*? Can you find them? We can't!"

A day later Wilkerson wrote: "We wonder what would have happened in the balloting for the best picture of the year had *Hamlet* been made in one of our own Hollywood studios. Our guess is that it would never have been voted best picture if it were Hollywood made." (Hinting that the studios would hardly have let it get that far.)

He concluded: "Have we a bunch of goofs among our Academy voters, who, like many of those New York critics, kid themselves into believing that Britain is capable of making better pictures than Hollywood? Now really!"

Wilkerson decided to let the matter drop with the warning: "If they can't honor American pictures then perhaps they've outlived their usefulness." The Academy voters took the hint. Not until 1962 did the best picture award go to a foreign-made film, *Lawrence of Arabia*.

The soft tones of a California sunset treat the Oscar kindly on its thirty-eighth anniversary when Liz Taylor and Paul Scofield took home the top acting prizes. It was to be the last year of the dinosaurs, and unsettling winds were blowing through the audiences—both out in America and inside the Santa Monica Civic Auditorium where the ceremonies were still held. A couple of years later the Academy bylaws were changed, stipulating that a third of the board of governors be either under thirty-five years of age or have been members for five years or less. This infusion of youth began to show up quickly. Jane Fonda's win for *Klute* could never have happened under the old era.

The first Academy Theatre on Melrose Avenue in Hollywood. After the Awards had moved, the "Theatre" was used as the Academy library. The library is now located at the Academy's new offices on Wilshire Boulevard in Beverly Hills.

The studios decided early that the Academy Awards ceremony was a glorified publicity stunt, the ultimate public relations tool in a city ruled by flaks. Publicists, in fact, have their own Academy branch (ranging from 150 in the fifties to almost 190 now). The men who run the Oscar campaigns are a part of Oscar's inner-sanctum. They are privy to the secrets of the Oscar voting, have representation on the Academy's board, and are on the receiving end of the largesse from Oscar campaigns competing against them. Happily, the public relations branch of the Academy is one of the few that appears to be shrinking. The Oscar brass has never been able to adequately justify the existence of the P.R. branch—or for that matter the branches devoted to executives and administrators. They give no Oscar for the best ad in a Technicolor medium or the finest cold cuts and champagne supper for voters. Likewise, there's no Oscar for best use of the executive washroom or most creative hype memo from a studio president. If there is a hint of shameful conflict of interest within the Academy, then it's probably to be found in these three branches—administrators, executives, and public relations executives. Every other branch—ranging from acting to art directors—gives awards to the supposed best of their branches. The executives, administrators, and flaks are actually holdovers from the twenties and thirties when the Academy was still a pseudo company union. And there are 490 of them—a full one-seventh of the Academy's voting strength of about 3,500. "And these members VOTE," said former *Los Angeles Times* columnist Joyce Haber, now a celebrated author of caustic books about Hollywood (*The Users*, et al.). "A lot of those other branches get very apathetic and scattered. The executives and the flaks all have something to gain—or to lose—in the sweepstakes."

As for the acting and artistic branches (see Appendix for statistics), they're a different breed of political cat. They are biased toward big box office pictures, usually honor age over youth (no matter how deserving), and some of the branches, particularly editing and cinematography, are locked into voting patterns that are twenty-five years old. Since each artistic branch nominates its fellows (the actors nominate the five best actors, the composers nominate for the music award, and so on), all of the Oscar mistakes and preposterous awards start here.

It puts an awesome amount of power in a very few hands. To quote Charles Champlin, entertainment editor and chief film critic for the *Los Angeles Times*, "Nominations alone can mean additional playing dates for a film, possibly more favorable rental terms," plus more business and longer runs. In the early spring of 1978, for instance, a ballet film, *The Turning Point*, was laying embarrassing eggs throughout suburban America. Then the Oscar people gave it a whole bushelful of nominations, including best picture, best actress (both Anne Bancroft and Shirley MacLaine), plus a supporting pick for sexy ballet star Mikhail Baryshnikov. It was like the cavalry to the rescue, and those little match box theaters in America's shopping centers drew moderate crowds through the final Oscar ceremony.

Year after boring year, film critics have wasted so much newsprint crying over the final results that they have missed the forest and seen only the Oscars.

It's the nomination process that's criminal—outdated, prejudiced, careless, and backward. Analysts of the National Association of Theater Owners now say that five or more nominations for a movie can often do as much for profits as a final victory. A best picture nomination with a couple of acting nods thrown in will get a movie priceless exposure on the Oscar show—with its 300 million viewers. In 1980, for instance, film clips from Bette Midler's *The Rose* (which wasn't even nominated for best picture), pushed the six-month-old film back into the top ten box office list and sent

the original cast album to the top of the *Billboard* chart.

So the nominations themselves can well mean the difference between profit and loss for a film that's failing at the box office.

The long road to the Oscar starts the first week in January when the members receive a list of eligible films—which is, more or less, every new feature film that played fifteen days in Los Angeles. All the Academy members vote for best picture nominees, but all the other five finalists are determined by the branches (writers pick writing nominees, etc.).

But before that, most branches pick a quarterfinal list of ten nominees. The one hundred photography directors in the Academy's cinematography branch are in full control of the lists of ten and the later lists of five. A hundred is only a handful in the hotbed of jealousy, hypocrisy, and spite that is Hollywood. But most Oscar watchers say the preliminary voter turnout ranges from forty to sixty percent. Therefore a place on the list of five cinematography nominees is undoubtedly determined by four or five votes either way.

The hundred-member Cinematography branch is perhaps the prime example of the Oscar's internal rottenness.

Year after year, decade after decade, the men behind the camera have worshiped at the altar of the box office and studio bosses. They have repeatedly honored nonsense (such as *Cleopatra* in 1963) and have frozen out innovation (such as the work on *Tom Jones* the same year). Because cinematography is probably the most essential of the movie arts, its branch's old-fashioned voting patterns and outright favoritism begs for a much closer look.

Charles Champlin, who has been publicly monitoring the nomination process for twenty years, took a close look at the ten cinematography lists

Bette Midler, here in the closing number from *The Rose*, called by some "the best bad movie of the decade." Midler, a concert and record star for more than a decade, performed with such athletic and raw emotion that an Oscar nomination was assured from the night the film, based loosely on the life of Janis Joplin, opened. Sally Field's more traditional performance in *Norma Rae*, however, won the Oscar.

Rex Harrison could have "talked to the animals" in *Doctor Doolittle* by turning in his performance on the telephone. The super-expensive musical was a dismal product from its first chimp to last yak. And there's no doubt that Twentieth Century-Fox knew it. Still, Fox played the Oscar game as well as Harrison played his role, gaining it an important handful of nominations: for its ho-hum photography, for its mediocre set decoration, for its grating sound, even for best picture. The victory spoke for the finesse of Fox P.R. men who coaxed, wined, and dined a shoddy product into Hollywood's golden circle.

in 1968 and came away annoyed. He found that Twentieth Century-Fox, pushing the disastrous *Doctor Doolittle* and Paramount, pushing the so-so *Barefoot in the Park*, may have been responsible for freezing out some dazzling examples of photography.

Apparently, Fox let it slip that *Doctor Doolittle* was to be the choice of the studio photographers in the Academy. So the inane film about animals made it into the ten while the trend-setting photography for another Fox film, *Two for the Road*, was offered up as a sacrificial lamb. Across town, Paramount's flaks wined and dined Oscar's cinematographer voters, bagging a top ten spot for their film *Barefoot in the Park*, freezing out *Far from the Madding Crowd*, *Accident* and *Cool Hand Luke*.

"The omissions, some of them, are worrisome. So is the cumulative suspicion that cost is a plus consideration," wrote Champlin. "Look at the case of *Camelot*, which took six nominations, including editing and cinematography. And this is a film," said the *Los Angeles Times* critic, "whose principal disappointments were visual."

But Champlin's public warnings fell on deaf photographic ears. A year later, the cinematographers ignored the innovative photography of *2001: A Space Odyssey*, *Rosemary's Baby*, *Rachel, Rachel*, and *Faces* in order to nominate the pedestrian work on *Oliver!*, *Funny Girl*, *Ice Station Zebra*, and the lead-weight disaster *Star!* The one nominee with inventive work, *Romeo and Juliet*, fortunately took the Oscar.

Champlin again unfurled the newsprint. "Among the movies not, I repeat not, nominated for cinematography were *The Charge of the Light Brigade*, *Petulia*, *The Thomas Crown Affair*, *The Fox*, and *Hell in the Pacific*. But *Star!*, lavish and unimaginative throughout, was nominated.

"The Academy membership is probably less and less a fully accurate

Jane Fonda's matchless portrayal of call girl Bree Daniel was equaled in intensity by the photography which used harsh light and dark with hints of a bloated color scale to set the tone of the realistic film. The photography in *Klute* was a breakthrough—the work of young cinematographer Gordon Willis. But he wasn't nominated by the Academy's cinematography branch—which is under the iron political glove of the old guard. To keep Willis off the nominees list the photographers were forced to nominate one of its own officials, Robert Surtees, twice in one year—for *The Last Picture Show* and *The Summer of '42*.

reflection of the fast changing industry and even less of the moviegoing public," Champlin wrote. "What emerges still smacks less often of a pinpointing of excellence than of local pride, sentiment, correction, consolation, retribution, study of the grosses, and an orientation toward what WAS rather than what is."

Public embarrassment, however, has not fazed the elderly voice of the Oscar cinematographers. (And they mirror voters in such branches as editing and music as well.) There are dozens of examples. One is a real case of the photo establishment against one young maverick photographer. His name is Gordon Willis, a camera wizard who burst on the movie scene in an incendiary display in 1971. The film was *Klute*, the moody study of a New York hooker played by Jane Fonda. Willis used light and dark to paint the screen like a modern Rembrandt. Willis' camera panned across Fonda, in half shadow, as she unzipped her dress, and his images exposed the soul of her character. The stills—frozen from the film—are achingly beautiful.

The Oscar photographers had a tough time excluding Willis from their nominations that year. In fact, they had to nominate one man twice in a move that leaves little doubt about their bias. The double nominee was Robert Surtees, sixty-four, nominated for *The Last Picture Show* and *The Summer of '42*. Other nominees included the boring *Nicholas and Alexandra*, *The French Connection*, a stunner, and so-so *Fiddler on the Roof*, which took the Oscar.

Then came *The Godfather*. Paramount began preview showing of Francis Ford Coppola's masterpiece far ahead of the Oscar votes. The jaded critics, artists, and movie bigwigs walked out of the previews stunned—by the performances, the emotion and, most of all, by the raw, jagged style in which the movie was filmed. Willis used dazzling light and deepest shadow

The cinematography of Coppola's *The Godfather, Parts I and II* was as much a departure from American cinema's old American kitchen style as impressionist art was from academic French painting. In scenes like these with James Caan and Robert De Niro, Gordon Willis let his camera career through the dramatic landscape like an emotional X-ray. Indeed, the photography was at the heart of the film's success and should surely have shared the saga's Oscar glory. That Willis was refused even a nomination for either film is one of the modern shames of the Oscar race. Bigotry and conflict of interest in the cinematography branch have locked Willis—and many other young photographers—out in the cold. There's no relief in sight.

to penetrate the gothic world of crime, religion, great love, and basest evil. The trip his camera made across Brando's face exposed ridges and craters of personality unequaled in film history. Francois Truffaut said cinematography would "never be quite the same." Not since Gregg Toland's work on *Citizen Kane* in 1941 had film photography moved into such experimental depths.

Critics predicted a cinematography nomination and, probably, the Oscar.

They hadn't reckoned with the Oscar's creaky cameramen. They froze Willis out again, nominating an incredible list: *Butterflies Are Free, 1776, The Poseidon Adventure, Cabaret,* and *Travels with My Aunt.* A common saying in Hollywood about Oscartime is, "Don't take it personal." But sometimes it is personal. From 1970–1978, Willis never made the nominees lists in spite of his work in *The Godfather Part II, The Paper Chase, The Drowning Pool, All the President's Men, Interiors, Comes a Horseman,* and *Annie Hall.* In order to bypass Willis for *Annie Hall,* the voters had to nominate Fred J. Koenekamp for *Islands in the Stream* and William A. Fraker for *Looking for Mr. Goodbar.* But Willis is a young and relatively new cinematographer, and none of the artists nominated in 1977 (the year of *Annie Hall*) were younger than forty-eight. One was seventy-two, one sixty-six, and another fifty-three.

"Taste is undoubtedly a factor here," says Champlin. "Willis' work, like the work of young Caleb Deschanel (*The Black Stallion, Being There,* and *More American Graffiti*), tends to be poetic, dark, and moody, far removed from the clean, well-lighted style that was the norm in an earlier age when some of the branch's voters did their best work. Deschanel, in all events, was also snubbed by the cinematographers this year."

The cliquish cameramen have excluded many excellent nominees by their insistence on voting for themselves. Only eleven of the fifty-seven

cinematographers nominated since 1966 were not members of the 100-member Academy branch. Of those eleven, eight were foreign.

"The controversies in some of the nomination processes suggest to me that Oscar's health would be improved by making several more of the nominations Academy-wide," Champlin continued. "The argument, of course, is that it takes an editor to know editing. Some of us would endorse this view more wholeheartedly if the excellent Dede Allen in New York (*Bonnie and Clyde, Dog Day Afternoon, Rachel, Rachel, Alice's Restaurant, Little Big Man,* and *Night Moves*) had even been nominated. But she hasn't been."

Charles Champlin's renewed pleas for more open voting were made just before the Oscar ceremony in 1980. And it is only the latest chapter from what has been a twenty-year, painstaking crusade for him. His analyses of voting processes have amounted to more than a thousand newspaper inches since 1968 alone. His force has already been felt in better procedures for foreign film and music voting. One former Academy president believes that "Academy members listen to Champlin because his reports on the Oscar races tell 'all sides' of the issue. You know those radical ones—Andrew Sarris of the *Village Voice* and Aljean Harmetz of the *New York Times* are only interested in ripping us apart."

Champlin's strongest words were written in February of 1980: "Putting the nominations on an Academy-wide basis would get rid of the in-breeding and in-fighting. It would make the Academy Awards a popularity contest, but they are anyway. And the 3,600 voters are, after all, men and women who make their living from motion pictures and know a jump cut from a slow dissolve and sunlight from shadow."

"This is a transfusion," says Champlin, "that might save Oscar from hardening of the arteries—a frequent complaint in gents of his generation."

Woody Allen and Diane Keaton photographed by Gordon Willis in a staging scene from *Annie Hall*. Allen managed to woo Willis away from Coppola for his recent string of hits—*Annie Hall, Interiors,* and *Manhattan,* with the latter proving that the photographer was equally adept in black and white. Other Willis accomplishments ignored by the Oscars include *All the President's Men* and *Comes a Horseman.* The wooden-headed arrogance that has kept Willis off the nominees lists is important basically because it publicly bares the termite holes of crookedness that run through the leadership of all the Academy branches—where only a handful of people determine who will and will not be nominated. There is also strong evidence that hundreds of voters in their respective fields don't even bother to see the films they are judging.

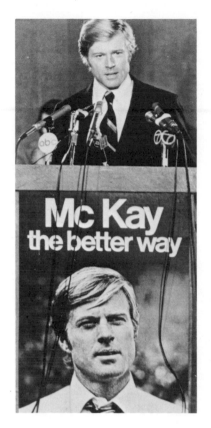

Robert Redford's acting tour de force in *The Candidate*, one of the actor's growing list of quiet but adept performances. Had Redford been slightly less handsome and somewhat less of a superstar his portrait of the bitter political contender might have brought him the nomination and maybe the Oscar. But Academy voters have tended to buy the town's own P.R. line that brains and beauty don't mix, so Redford's work in *Downhill Racer, The Way We Were, Jeremiah Johnson, All the President's Men,* and *The Electric Horseman* has been largely ignored. Only when he played his own image, the easy-going but handsome scoundrel in *The Sting,* did the Academy toss him a nomination. Similar fates went to Burt Reynolds, Clint Eastwood, Rock Hudson, Ryan O'Neal, and now, it appears, to Richard Gere.

The critic is being kind. Academy-wide voting would, in plainer terms, take the nominations out of the hands of the studio bosses, the flaks, and, sad but true, out of the hands of artists somewhat past their prime.

The money men who head the conglomerates such as Gulf & Western and MCA learned long ago to coerce, cajole, and even buy the votes of the cliques within the branches.

It's not as easy to buy votes now, and the cliques have cracked a little— *Annie Hall* would never have taken the 1977 Oscar otherwise. But voting by box office is far from dead . . . witness the defeat of *All the President's Men* and *Network* by the sappy *Rocky.* (We can consider ourselves lucky, I guess, that super-fists Sylvester Stallone didn't take the acting prize from the incomparable Peter Finch.)

As few as ten years ago, Oscar voting practices were pretty much "the worthless, grotesque circus" that Dustin Hoffman described. The huge studios, particularly Twentieth Century-Fox could still force dreadful but expensive films down the throats of Oscar voters much as French farmers make pâté by forcing massive amounts of food down the throats of captive geese.

Oscar bigwigs like president Fay Kanin just shrug. "Hey, why bring up the past? That's behind us. Isn't it?" Well, no. It isn't. With Oscar, nothing is over. The old voting patterns come back as frequently as Bette Davis. And the Academy constantly holds up the glamour and the rightness of its decisions. Luise Rainer WAS the best actress in 1936, the Academy tells us over and over again. *Patton* WAS the best picture of 1970, they tell us again . . . and again. We may know, down in our artistic psyches, that Garbo was better than Rainer and *M*A*S*H* was certainly finer than its militaristic competitor. But then the Oscar show comes on with its drivel about the old days, and the world once again has reason to believe that *How Green Was My Valley* was—is—better than *Citizen Kane* and Yul Brynner was a better actor than Montgomery Clift.

Ten years ago it was so bad even the gossip columnists were yelling. Joyce Haber, then the lady with the nastiest pen, said the worst thing about Oscar voters was that "they don't even see the films; they rely on ads in the trade papers." But almost as bad, said Joyce, was the voter turnout. "You'd have to describe it as 'pitiful.' I know one producer who lives abroad, and his doctor, a specialist, but not in films, fills in his nomination and voting ballots every year. I know a producer who lives in Beverly Hills and has his college-graduate son do the job for him. And I just had dinner with a Broadway star, who is also a sometime movie actress and a member of the Academy. She admitted to me that she had not seen ANY movies. She'd been on tour, don't you know. She kept asking me how to vote," said Haber in mock scandal. "I refused to add to the problem. Suddenly, she looked at me and said, 'I'm going to vote for Paul Newman and *Butch Cassidy* because I think he's SO-O-O handsome." Haber, once *Time* magazine's Hollywood editor and later the columnist of the *Los Angeles Times,* says she didn't find any of this cute. "These people are serious. I have to ask, 'Did *Butch Cassidy* get a best picture nomination because of Paul Newman's beautiful baby-blue eyes?'"

The same era brought Andrew Sarris, the eastern critic, to the coast, and he found even less to cheer about than Haber. "It is a matter of conjecture, to be sure, but I find myself annually depressed by the strong suspicion that few of the 3,000 members of the Academy see as many as a dozen films a year." His suspicions appeared in the *Village Voice,* so the Oscar brass just shoved their hands in their Sy Devore suit coats and drawled, "Well, you know that type of paper." (Ironically, the workup for Universal's Oscar campaign for *Airport* indicated that only forty-six percent

Jon Voight and Dustin Hoffman as the lonely and eroding heroes of John Schlesinger's *Midnight Cowboy*, which was named best picture by the Academy in 1969. Since the movie rested entirely on the shoulders of the two actors, it seemed inevitable that one of them would take the best acting prize. But the spectre of ill and ageless superstar John Wayne in *True Grit* threw the Oscar voters into an old dilemma: 1969 might be the last chance to give Wayne Oscar's tarnished glory. And so they did. Oscar's promise came true: "If you live long enough and can still talk," said Hedda Hopper, "then you'll get an Oscar."

Hello, Dolly! was perhaps nominated as a salute to Hollywood's well endowed taste buds since Twentieth Century-Fox shunned traditional Oscar campaigning and spent megabucks on fancy buffet dinners. "The technique of unlimited liquor and prime rib au jus had worked so well for Fox in 1967 when *Doctor Doolittle* was nominated for best picture," wrote Aljean Harmetz in the *New York Times*. ("It was all so silly," remembered one film editor. "All the editors standing around and knowing they'd been bought.")

could be expected to see more than two of the nominated films. The studio direct mailed *Airport* propaganda to the stay-at-homes, gaining the flyby a nomination over *Ryan's Daughter, Little Big Man, Women in Love,* and *The Great White Hope.*

"It seems likely that a huge number of ballots are cast for pictures and performances purely on hearsay," said Sarris. Then he quoted Academy president Walter Mirisch: "As an Academy we also seek excellence in judging the work of our peers." Sarris answered, "Peers, schmeers. Have you guys and dolls seen many movies this year? I doubt it." The hearsay and voting by prejudice is still a part of the Academy. In 1979 tap dancer Ann Miller told an interviewer, "My friends all say they don't know how they're going to vote this year. Why just look at the sloppy appearance of those actresses, Jill Clayburgh, Jane Fonda, Ellen Burstyn, etc. There's no glamour left. I don't even think I'll vote."

In 1970 the Academy voted on its stomach. Free food, free booze, and enough gifts to gag Nero lured Oscar voters into silk-lined traps. Gorged on food, dazed by advertising, laden down with free record albums and desk sets, the electors lined up in mobs to vote for the turgid *Anne of the Thousand Days,* the disastrous *Hello, Dolly!,* and a foreign film, *Z,* which pigged in far more than its share of nominations. Critics started yelling, "What the hell happened?" The normally timid "Entertainment World" asked "How did *Anne of the Thousand Days* win ten nominations and *Midnight Cowboy* only seven? It's incomprehensible." And Aljean Harmetz of the *New York Times* said, frankly, "The fact that *Anne of the Thousand Days* received ten nominations and *Hello, Dolly!* tied *Midnight Cowboy*—including a best picture nomination for both—had more to do with beef stroganoff and imported champagne and three-inch prime ribs than with any quality in the films."

Caterers imported from Paris prepared a buffet table for those who attended the free showings Universal Pictures held for Oscar voters in the winter of 1969–1970. (The food alone cost thirty-five dollars per person, according to Universal sources.) And thirty-five screenings were held— many of them exclusively for the Academy's nominating branches. The cinematographers—whose branch is still the easiest bought—were ushered onto the Universal lot for a cocktail hour and buffet supper before the 8:30 p.m. showings. Suntanned ushers—wearing silk tights and velvet doublets—handed the voters high priced propaganda about *Anne of the Thousand Days* and guided them to the buffet room. The tables were literally sagging under the weight of the food: cocktails, seven hot appetizers, cold roast beef, cold ham, chicken breasts Hawaiian, beef stroganoff, imported rice, fresh fruit salad (with out-of-season fruits costing $3.95 a pound), cheeses, and French pastries. The next day the voters who showed up received a special delivery letter from Universal, thanking them for coming and offering still more propaganda about the Richard Burton, Genevieve Bujold movie (both of whom were nominated). "We cultivated the hell out of the artistic branches," said a public relations spokesman for Universal. "And, boy, did it work." And work it did! *Anne of the Thousand Days,* a creaky movie that might as well have been made in the thirties, got an entirely undeserved bouquet of nominations. The artisans who were wined and dined by the studio all included the film in their lists of five nominees. The film was not missed by a single branch.

Twentieth Century-Fox had to try harder. The greedy studio brass had a $25 million lemon on their hands, the ungodly *Hello, Dolly!* "We decided that lavish advertising would do no good for this one; the whole town was already gossiping about how bad it was," said a Fox publicity man. "We decided to blow the budget on prime ribs from Kansas City and imported champagne. Then we had the showings. The branch voters then saw the movie through champagne-colored glasses."

The cinematographers can be excused on this one; *Hello, Dolly!* had several seconds worth of fine camerawork during the movie's opening titles. What it did NOT have was good editing. It had miserable editing, in fact! Its scenes jerked from one to another like a rusty trolley car, and musical numbers bumped into each other on the screen. But it's simply amazing what good drink and a fine table will do. The editors saw to it personally that *Hello, Dolly!* was nominated. "It was all so silly," said one editor, "all of us editors standing around the party tables—knowing we'd been bought." There were, of course, examples of very fine editing that year—*Downhill Racer, The Wild Bunch, The Gypsy Moths,* and *Easy Rider* to name a few. But what could the poor editors do? After they had given away places to *Hello, Dolly!* and *Anne of the Thousand Days,* they had to at least nominate the better known films *Midnight Cowboy, They Shoot Horses, Don't They?,* and *Z,* an Algerian film that had the most expensive campaign of all. After that, there was no more room.

The big losers that winter were *Easy Rider* and Sam Peckinpah's *The Wild Bunch.* Nobody today looks twice at *Hello, Dolly!* or *Anne of the Thousand Days. Easy Rider* and *The Wild Bunch* are not only revived, they are part of the regular curriculum at many film schools. Peter Fonda knew enough to keep quiet in 1970. Peckinpah's people knew immediately that the nominations were a poor call. "I don't understand why two drinks and a bad hors d'oeuvre should make a difference in your critical judgment," said Joel Reisner, Peckinpah's principal assistant.

The Wild Bunch might have had a chance, but its studio, Warner Brothers, refused to plug the film in any way. "In December of 1969 Warner Brothers told me that the grosses of *The Wild Bunch* didn't justify extra ad costs," Reisner said. "The studio probably didn't believe Sam Peckinpah would get nominated no matter what they did. The Oscars are merely a popularity contest, and Sam has fired an awful lot of people over the years. Warners also knew *The Wild Bunch* was an unfriendly, unpopular film." (As Aljean Harmetz pointed out, the film was so far outside the establishment that only five members of the 150-member Academy editor's branch showed up for the screening.)

The bored, disinterested Oscar voters are primed and waiting for fresh winds of hype. Last year's hype won't do. Or last week's for that matter. The 2,400 voters (and the voter turnout is never higher than that) exist in a rarified atmosphere. Paperweights, posters, toys, and books flood through the mail—to Kathryn Grayson's house on the Riviera Country Club, to John Travolta's penthouse above Sunset Boulevard, to Ginger Rogers' ranch in the foothills of Oregon.

The studios, agents, and flaks spent about $7.5 million during the three months of Oscar campaigning in 1980. That's $2,500 per voter, if most of the Academy members—by some miracle—happened to vote. The grand pageants are carefully staged. Take Bette Midler's bid for a best actress nomination. The ballyhoo started in November—six months before the final vote. Fox, which made her film, *The Rose,* let the word get around that Midler was "sensational" in her portrayal of a Janis Joplin-like rock singer's rise and fall. Then the previews began—with the first screening set for a Tuesday.

Tuesday morning—Beverly Hills and Hollywood had been graven in Bette's image. Black and red posters (with Midler screaming her song in front of a vivid red rose) blanketed the city. On Sunset Boulevard, Bette had risen above the strip like a cardboard phoenix with sixteen-foot arms spread to enfold the voters on their way to work—Alan Ladd, Jr., heading

Barbra Streisand's commanding presence in *Hello, Dolly!* helped the film gain a basket of nominations and three Oscars. But it was the film's big budget and shameless Oscar hype that impressed the voters. Fox had long before become a master at trapping Academy Awards for ploddingly mediocre movies. At the box office, Fox learned, it didn't matter so much WHICH Oscars you won so long as you can use the golden phrase "Oscar-winning movie" in the advertising. Besides, *Hello, Dolly!'s* safe and bland theme made it more palatable to the Academy's "better safe than sorry" digestion. Landmark movies such as *Easy Rider,* with its questioning of established order; *Taxi Driver,* with its slap at the loneliness of urban life; *The Wild Bunch,* with its portrait of the violence inside all of us; and *Sunday Bloody Sunday,* with its look at modern sex hangups are all examples of film genres that DON'T win. It's so much easier to honor *Hello, Dolly!'s* costumes and hairstyles. Who can argue with that?

Bette Midler in a quiet moment from Mark Rydell's *The Rose*, which repackaged Midler from rock superstar to Oscar-calibre actress. Her home run the first time out echoed the similar triumphs of Julie Andrews in *Mary Poppins* and Diana Ross in *Lady Sings the Blues*. Unfortunately, Hollywood's reaction to such quick Oscar jackpots is often near-sighted and paranoid. "You should see the worthless scripts I've been offered since *The Rose*," Midler told Phil Donahue. And Ross said, "Scores of offers appeared that would have had me playing Billie Holiday over and over again." In the case of Julie Andrews, Fox built such musical dinosaur films for her that she was caught in a big-budget prison.

for a meeting at Warner Brothers, Jane Fonda driving in to her Sunset Boulevard bank, Natalie Wood going to an exercise class.

Car radios suddenly swelled with lullabies in the Bette Midler voice—her soundtrack album had been released that morning, not so coincidentally. (Members of the music branch received soundtrack albums in the mail.)

Tuesday night came! The parade of Rolls-Royces lined up at Twentieth Century-Fox was flagged through the V.I.P. gate into a parking lot with ample spaces—an unheard-of luxury in the city of cars. But necessary. Nothing must jangle the nerves of the Oscar voters on their way to see the film debut of "The Divine Miss M," as they call her in rock circles.

A bleached-blonde secretary somehow crammed into Jordache jeans checks off the names as they enter the Fox screening theater, which is just off Peyton Place Square—still intact from the television series of the sixties. No inch of film will roll until the last voter is ushered to his red velvet seat.

Finally the theater darkens, and Bette's voice begins a rock 'n' roll cry. For the next two hours not a sound is heard as one of the most dismal films of the seventies unfolds on the screen. Not one hand claps as the film ends and the titles run off. But no matter—the hype has been planted so firmly in the minds of the voters that Bette Midler made the list of nominees in flying colors.

The whole process is done so smoothly, so quickly that nobody really notices; Bette Midler as a great actress has seeped into Hollywood's creative consciousness.

Often, it's not money but moxie that outfoxes all other contenders. That's what got the Algerian film Z—which in 1970 became the second

Jane Fonda's personal odyssey toward the Oscar started here with *They Shoot Horses, Don't They?* in 1969, the first role for which she abandoned the kittenish glamour that had made her a star. "When it got around that I was doing *They Shoot Horses, Don't They?*, and that I wanted to cut my hair for it, you know what people said?" asked Fonda. "They said 'Jane, dahling, you're out of your mind. Don't cut your hair!' I thought, oh wow, so that's what I've become—a lotta goddam blonde hair." But Fonda was bested by Maggie Smith in 1969—a victory caused by Smith's virtuosity and Fonda's negative, anti-war publicity.

foreign language film to be nominated for best picture in Oscar history. (The first was France's *Grand Illusion* in 1933.) And *Z* was nominated for five Oscars—each one of them due to the wizardry of free-lance P.R. man Max Bercutt, who was hired by the distributor to get *Z* as many nominations as the traffic would bear. The five Oscar bids probably added $5 million to the grosses of the movie in this country alone.

Bercutt told Aljean Harmetz that he had to fight the two basic biases to get the film nominated. "Academy members nominate first out of loyalty to their studios or connections. Second, they nominate out of loyalty to the 'Hollywood product.'"

Bercutt had seen the system from the inside, also, and that was a plus. He was publicity director for Warner Brothers during the sixties—one of its golden epochs.

The first targets of the campaign for *Z* were the ever-present core of Oscar voters in the ranks of the retired—at least 500 actors, artists, and executives who've served their time and have now been turned out to celluloid pastures. "These people haven't worked in five to ten years. But these old-timers are very important. They're the keepers of the bees of Hollywood's past. This was the toughest target. How could I get them to vote for a film with subtitles? I decided that the answer was to show them the film and to try to instill in their minds that it is the greatest picture in ten years."

The P.R. man took a new print home with him. "Those voters don't go out much, so I took the print to their houses. I screened it for twenty people or for one person. I told them that a nomination for *Z* would make the Academy look important worldwide."

The voters also had sound-track recordings delivered to their front doors. (The music nominations were already released and *Z* wasn't named.) "It was great advertising with the great big 'Z' on the cover. I hoped that enough members would play the album, like it, and say, 'Poor film, why didn't it get a nomination?' Then they'd vote for it in one of the other categories."

Hollywood's gossip mill caught on quickly that *Z* was getting special treatment. Other studios and public relations men began telephone campaigns asking the voters to "vote Hollywood—vote against *Z*."

But they were too late. *Z* got the nomination—shutting out the Hollywood products *They Shoot Horses, Don't They?* and Peter Fonda's and Dennis Hopper's *Easy Rider*.

It goes without saying that Oscar hype wouldn't be worth it if the economic stakes were not so high. Still, the harm is not major. Some quite dreadful films get nominated. (Some even win—*The Greatest Show on Earth, Oliver!*) Some quite wonderful films aren't even mentioned. (*Papillon, Singin' in the Rain.*)

But occasionally the quest for an Oscar crushes some good guys under. (The silent conspiracy by MGM and Warner Brothers against Judy Garland's *A Star Is Born* ended the chances of a major film comeback.)

And once or twice a decade a studio's greedy-minded Oscar campaigning turns dark and nasty. This happened in 1973 when Warner Brothers was trying to get an Oscar for Linda Blair, the fourteen-year-old star of *The Exorcist*.

The Exorcist had a bizarre and difficult birth to begin with. Billy Friedkin was only thirty-one when he began directing William Peter Blatty's story of demonic possession. It took two years out of his life and aged him, he said, five years. First, Friedkin tested 500 young girls to cast the lead—finally picking an incredibly gifted girl, Linda Blair, who was then twelve. Almost from the first day of filming, a demon or demons stalked the

Linda Blair's double threat performance as the sweet young girl and her demon-possessed flip side in *The Exorcist* easily gained the fourteen-year-old a nomination for best supporting actress. Flaks at Warner Brothers quickly began figuring the box office draw of a Blair *Exorcist* victory. To insure it, the studio carefully erased the identity of a potent and secret ingredient in Linda Blair's performance—the "voice of the devil" furnished by former Oscar-winner Mercedes McCambridge. The veteran actress was denied credit on the film and the record album. Writer Charles Higham found out, however, and delivered an explosive story to *New York* magazine, a story which probably lost the Oscar for Linda Blair and seriously hurt the picture's chances to take other awards for the film itself and for the direction by William Friedkin.

production. Things disappeared from the set; an almost impossible fire roared through a set that had taken five months to build; a character actor playing a motion picture director who gets murdered by the demonic child dropped dead a week after his movie death scene. "There were even some strange images that showed up on film," said Friedkin. "These were things that were unplanned—double exposures on Linda's face."

But the film came in only a million or two over budget—hardly anything in the inflated overruns of the seventies. Friedkin, who'd won the directing Oscar for *The French Connection*, delivered the film to Warner Brothers—and all hell broke loose. The limited engagement openings in New York and Los Angeles broke every known box office record. The film brought in a hundred million dollars in the first six months. A hundred million dollars! And this was before *Jaws* or *Star Wars*. In eight months both *The Sound of Music* and *Gone With the Wind* were toppled from first and second place in the all-time box office. Every studio in town was into Devil worship. And agents were signing up sinister looking kids by the handful.

That big a hit does strange things to studio executives. First they look over their shoulders—wondering if it's real. They then try and guard the goose that laid the golden egg. Warners had two geese: Billy Friedkin and Linda Blair, a bit of a star to be protected, nurtured, and gently shoved into one vehicle after another. In Linda's case she was rushed from *Airport '75* to *Exorcist II: The Heretic*, to *Hard Ride to Rantan*, and, in 1980, to *Roller Boogie*.

To protect and nurture Miss Blair, *The Exorcist*'s producers and Warner Brothers apparently decided to get her an Oscar at all cost. I mean, my Gawd, here's a twelve-year-old girl who spoke in the voice of the Devil, played the full erotic range from nymphet to ancient whore, and whose voice, said a critic, had "the timbre of Orson Welles, the depth of the

Ryan O'Neal and daughter Tatum in *Paper Moon*, the Peter Bogdanovich comedy about a Bible salesman during the Great Depression. Tatum's acceptance of the best supporting actress award was the final legitimization of the Academy's two-faced relations with child actors. In the beginning there was some outcry over the nomination of ten-year-old Jackie Cooper for *The Champ*. The Academy's solution was to create a school of little "toy Oscars" which were given to Shirley Temple, Deanna Durbin, Mickey Rooney, and Margaret O'Brien (but, ironically, not to Jackie Cooper). Patty Duke's victory in the adult Oscar race ended the silliness, and Tatum O'Neal made it official.

Vatican choir, and the range of the Royal Shakespeare Company." Isn't that amazing? said the Warner Brothers' press corps: isn't that amazing? Why not even Patty Duke . . . .

The Academy voters, also shaking their heads and clucking in amazement, quickly nominated Linda Blair for best actress in a supporting role. "Her voice leaves scratches on your soul," said *Paris Match*. "Incomparable," said the *Times* of London.

Warners just basked in the afterglow of Linda Blair. Not even Tatum O'Neal, with her incredible debut in *Paper Moon*, could give her a race. The Oscar, everybody decided, was hers.

But Linda Blair's voice would come back to haunt them all—Hollywood, Billy Friedkin, and Warner Brothers. Because it wasn't Linda Blair's voice at all. It was the voice of Mercedes McCambridge, a former Oscar winner with vocal chords like Gideon's trumpet. And Mercedes McCambridge, some of the big guys decided, would just have to be sacrificed in the quest for Oscar gold. After all, Billy Friedkin was her pal. She'd understand. Case closed.

It might have ended that way. And Linda Blair might have taken home her Oscar—however falsely. Worse things have happened in the name of Oscar.

Mercedes McCambridge had no official credit on the release print. She had none on the posters, the advertisements, or on the jacket of the record album—for which her voice was undoubtedly the main drawing card.

But one of Hollywood's veteran journalists got the drift of a particularly nasty rumor about the denial of McCambridge's contribution to *The Exorcist*. So Charles Higham, writer for the *New York Times, Los Angeles* magazine, and the *Directors Guild Magazine*, picked up the phone and gave her a ring. He found a story of horrific, but typical, Hollywood greed. McCambridge

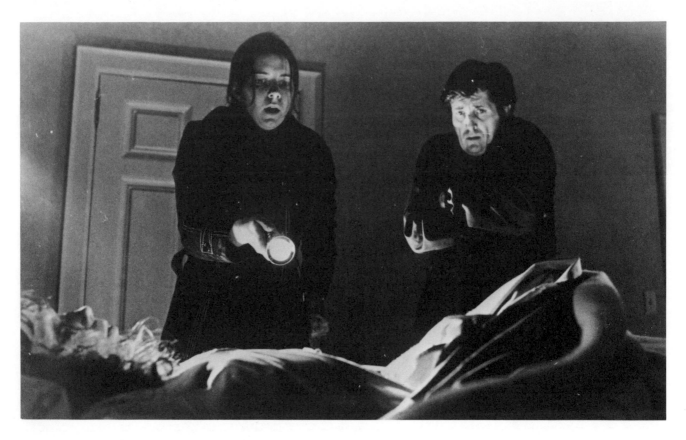

poured out the story in anger and hurt—her words tumbling one over the other as they had on *The Exorcist* soundtrack. "I gave the most difficult performance of my life. Warners didn't give me a single credit on the picture or in the advertising." (A frightening thing in a town where an actor is only as good as his last credit.)

"Even the man who supplied the jewels got a credit," said Miss McCambridge. "I cried. Billy Friedkin promised me a special credit—'And Mercedes McCambridge' it was supposed to say. Doing that soundtrack was a terrible experience. I didn't just do the voice; I did all the demon's sounds. That wheezing, for instance. My chronic bronchitis helped with that. I did it on one microphone; then on another, elevating it a bit; then on a third and fourth, two tones higher each time. The wailing just before the demon is driven out, that's the keening sound I once heard at a wake in Ireland. I used moaning cries I had used when playing Lady Macbeth for Orson Welles. For the groaning sounds, I pulled a scarf around my neck, tight, and almost strangled."

McCambridge, who became a radio actress when she was still in college, won an Oscar for her first film, *All the King's Men*, in 1949. Orson Welles called her "the world's greatest radio actress," and she was nominated again in 1956 for her work in *Giant*. When the word got out about her dilemma there was immediate outrage, so much so that some Academy officers began investigating the legality of giving an Oscar to actors whose contribution is solely audio. "We don't know if that could even happen, but it's obvious, we're going to think about it," an Academy spokesman told the *Los Angeles Times*.

The actress, in interviews, described the job as one of the toughest, mentally, she ever faced: "I had to imagine the incredible, bottomless agony

Why did *The Exorcist* lose to a lesser work, *The Sting*? Critics asked the question then, and it seems more pressing now—after dozens of films have appeared as part of the genre created by the William Friedkin film. Now that the dust has settled, it appears that the movie was badly crippled by Warner Brothers' attempts to suppress the contributions of Mercedes McCambridge (opposite) and the film's gore finished it off. "I think that many voters were worried that the subject matter of the film might reflect poorly on American films as a whole," says NBC's Rona Barret. "People just didn't want the movie to be representative of Hollywood." Oscar voters are also late in picking up on fresh trends or genres—a decades-old condition: this is the Academy, of course, that failed to even nominate *King Kong, Singin' In the Rain*, and *Things to Come*.

of a lost soul. I drew on memory for that. I've been an alcoholic, saved by A.A., and I've seen people in state hospitals, vegetables in straitjackets, the hopeless, abysmal, bottomless groaning and screaming. I used imitations of those hellish cries. Who better than I would know how the Devil feels? I'm out of hell; he's there forever.

"And when I spoke the scene in which the little girl spits out green vomit, when I made the sounds of violent expectoration, I swallowed eighteen raw eggs along with a pulpy apple. Sometimes I was so exhausted and my circulation so sluggish, I couldn't drive home."

Higham acknowledges that his stories probably "cost Linda Blair the Oscar." But in Oscar's double-dealing history that is something to be proud of.

If he needed any reassurance, he got it while attending a press party honoring Linda Blair's birthday. It was at Chasen's, an exclusive Beverly Hills restaurant. And Higham had just settled down when a flak from Warner Brothers pushed his way up to him—waving the proofs of Higham's story on Mercedes and her experience with *The Exorcist*. "What's your idea in writing a piece like this?" said the man from the executive suite. Higham, an acute observer of Hollywood greed in his books on Hepburn, Cecil B. De Mille, and others, looked up calmly and said, "What was your idea in smuggling the proofs out of the paper before their removal was authorized?"

Linda Blair did not, as it happened, win the Oscar. It went to Tatum O'Neal. And *her* whole performance was up there on the screen.

The shabby Oscar plotting involved in *The Exorcist* is hardly surprising. More surprising was the failure of the mass media to really pick up on the scandal. Day in and day out, year after year, more than seven hundred

reporters—from as near as Long Beach to as far away as Calcutta—spend part of their year covering the Academy of Motion Picture Arts and Sciences. (Eight hundred members of the press were accredited to cover an Oscar ceremony in the seventies.) Less than five of those reporters do any objective reporting on the Oscars, and two of those are from the *Los Angeles Times*—Lee Grant and Charles Champlin.

A study of more than 7,000 articles on the Academy Awards—all published in the last five years—shows that only fifty articles portrayed both sides of the Oscar story. Twenty-five of those were by Champlin with the others divided between less than ten reporters. (Namely, Andrew Sarris, Aljean Harmetz, Rex Reed, and an insider, Peter Bogdanovich.) The rest of the press swallows the Oscar decisions as if they were handed down by Moses on stone tablets.

And this is why a red herring of a film like *Oliver!* can be named best picture of the year without worldwide laughter.

Few realize that Shirley Temple was a "Vargas Girl." This publicity photo was taken at Fox during the mid-thirties. Shirley has long since retired from show business, but the amazing Vargas continues to illustrate for *Playboy* magazine.

An obnoxious little muppet, Mark Lester hugs his bowl of porridge in the "Food, Wonderful Food" production number from the 1968 *Oliver!*, a truly awful film that was named best picture. "That it was even nominated gives sufficient cause for a world-wide chuckle," said new-era critic Andrew Sarris of the *Village Voice.* "

4 IN THE NAME OF OSCAR

"Hearst, with his whim of iron, became obsessed with winning an Oscar for Marion Davies—no matter the cost. . . . The quest loomed like a holy grail." F. Scott Fitzgerald in *Esquire*, 1940.

Marion Davies was already one of Hollywood's ghosts by 1942—a film star of fast fading beauty and evaporating fame.

On Oscar night, 1942, she was far out of the Hollywood swim, whiling away the war in a dank hunting lodge with her megamillionaire lover William Randolph Hearst at her side. Her dressing bungalow of sixteen rooms was now only so many cartons in a Los Angeles warehouse, and untouched prints of her films were sealed in an air-conditioned bin.

The career of Marion Davies lasted from 1917 to 1936 (long by Hollywood standards), and was remembered as a bizarre Hollywood footnote.

But on February 26, 1942, Marion's shadow fell over the Academy Awards like a cultural fog bank, and her silent voice drowned out the silly sentences of the presenters. In a deliberate manner, category by category, Orson Welles' masterpiece, *Citizen Kane*, lost to far inferior films.

Gary Cooper's "yep" and "nope" portrayal of Sergeant York beat out Welles' incendiary Kane. Gregg Toland's masterful photography lost to Arthur Miller's so-so work on *How Green Was My Valley*, and Robert Wise's editing was bested by William Holmes' for *Sergeant York*.

It was an Oscar freezeout with the Tinseltown establishment throwing its weight behind *How Green Was My Valley* and, says Hedda Hopper, "almost any other film EXCEPT *Citizen Kane*." So *How Green Was My Valley* was named best picture of the year with no surprised gasps from Hollywood. "The REAL surprise," hissed Hedda, "was that this 'little' picture got any nominations at all." Then she threw one arm around Coop, the other around Joan Fontaine, and posed with the happy winners.

Today those faded pictures serve as blatant reminders of Oscar's lowest artistic point. Staunch Academy defenders would repeat through the years that *Citizen Kane* would not be thought of as the greatest film in American movie history until a number of years had passed. Back in 1942, they would plead, there was only a mild twitter of acclaim for Welles' study of power and egomania.

Marion Davies in *Peg O' My Heart*, the movie her sugar daddy William Randolph Hearst thought would win her an Oscar. Marion even claims that the original idea for the Academy of Motion Picture Arts and Sciences came from W.R., who, said Marion, "had his heart set on winning the award for me."

That is, of course, apologetic hogwash—the reviews at the time the picture opened were as strong and unanimous as they would ever be. And even in Hollywood, at the cozy little parties given by Basil Rathbone and Walter Wanger, some iconoclasts whispered the word "genius" when talking about Welles. The movies' collective artistic mind felt bested for the first time since D. W. Griffith. To quote Dorothy Parker, "The town was upended, and Welles could have whatever he wanted—except an Oscar and a job."

Nobody denies—then or now—that Welles' KO from the Oscar was only a political defeat not an artistic one and that the knockout was sealed the minute Hollywood realized that the doomed, alcoholic mistress in *Citizen Kane* was meant to be Marion Davies. (So eerily correct was Dorothy Comingore's performance that Marion's walk and hand mannerisms were duplicated.)

And nobody denies—then or now—that Welles' withering depiction of Marion would never have occurred if Hearst had not become morbidly obsessed with having the actress crowned as the dramatic queen of Hollywood with her Oscar becoming the sceptre royal.

"To him, it would have meant the seal of approval for his whole relationship with Marion Davies," said Zelda Cini, a major Hollywood correspondent for *Time-Life*. "The Oscar, he felt, would make up for the marriage Hearst could not give her. And Lord knows it wasn't the first or the last time that somebody would try and buy an Oscar."

The real irony is that Hearst's quest for a Davies Oscar and the *Citizen Kane* defeats, coming together as they did in 1942, would resemble nothing so much as one of Hollywood's own gothic scripts. Underneath their Adrian gowns and silk tux coats, the Academy voters who gathered at the Biltmore all had a warm spot in their hearts for Marion Davies—the hostess of Hearst's massive castle at San Simeon, a lady who knew most of them by nicknames and who had sent their children christening gifts. By anybody's standards Marion had been the official hostess for the movie capital from 1925–1939.

It must have been soul wrenching for Oscar voters to decide whether to vote for a film they knew to be a monumental work of art or honor social debts to an old friend, a Hollywood damsel in distress.

"It was easy for everyone to assume, since Hollywood is a community conditioned to think the worst of anyone rather than the best, that they were at last getting the truth about Marion's erratic career," said Fred Laurence Guiles, in his 1972 book, *Marion Davies*. "Word of this reached Marion quickly. Bad news always travels the fastest. But Marion pretended that it didn't bother her, and she could not guess how far the film would go in obliterating her name as a film queen."

Guiles, in his exhaustive study of Hearst and Davies during the *Citizen Kane* period, does not buy Welles' later apologies that Susan Alexander in *Kane* was never meant to be Marion. "There was no doubt in anyone's mind, once the film was released, that it WAS Hearst. And before many months passed, people in Hollywood would be referring to Susan Alexander as 'the Marion Davies part.'"

The day Hedda saw the film, she borrowed a phone in the lobby and phoned Hearst directly at San Simeon. Louis B. Mayer of MGM, the studio that made the best of Marion's movies, wept as he came out of a private screening. The next day Mayer tried to buy the negative for $800,000 from RKO. "*Kane* is an important film, and we're proud of it," answered George J. Schaeffer of RKO. "No sellout."

There was good reason for the tears. *Citizen Kane*'s scriptwriter Herman Mankiewicz, who had been the guest of Marion dozens of times, had

Hearst at San Simeon with his beloved dachshund, Helen. The publishing magnate used the considerable magnificence of San Simeon to lobby for Marion during Oscar season . . . but no amount of champagne and imported food could persuade the film community to take Marion Davies seriously. When that failed, Hearst threatened Louis B. Mayer with the wrath of his newspaper empire—telling L.B. to deliver the MGM votes for Marion or else. But MGM's second in command, Irving Thalberg, always delivered the studio votes to his wife Norma Shearer.

Marion busy emoting in a thirties film. "The Oscars were designed to create incentive, but they became a cruel joke. It was only natural that they create jealousy," said Marion. "You would go to the show and think you were going to win and somebody else did." If Marion was complacent about her chances for an Oscar, Hearst only became angrier as each year passed: he pushed her into lavish musicals, bought the services of Clark Gable, Bing Crosby, and Gary Cooper to star with her, and, finally, pulled her off the MGM lot and switched her to Warner Brothers when nothing worked.

virtually created the woman character in Davies' image. The film star's sad and growing affair with alcohol, her loneliness among the crowds at the Hearst mansions, and her gnawing wish to become Mrs. Hearst were all paraded before Welles' cameras. But Mankiewicz used these "details only a friend would know" to create a portrait of a failure, a lady totally unredeemed by talent.

"In this they went too far, and Mankiewicz, of all people, knew better; he'd seen all Marion's triumphs, and he KNEW," said one of Hearst's managing editors. "But the millions who have seen the movie accept it as the gospel truth—so goes history."

The movie myth so completely engulfed the truth that Marion Davies, if she is remembered at all, it's as the inspiration for Susan Alexander.

But six decades ago—about the time Hearst began creating her in the image of the Virgin Mary—Marion Davies was a big star, on her own and with no help from any of her sugar daddies. Ziegfeld had seen her in the second chorus line of a minor Broadway musical and signed her on for his *Follies*. There, while coming down a stage staircase as a March daffodil, she was spotted by Hearst. She was eighteen; he was fifty-four. (And restive from his marriage with an earlier chorine, Millicent Hearst.)

"I don't know if he decided then and there to make her the second Mary Pickford," said screenwriter Frances Marion. "But he had definitely decided on that course by the time he, and she, came out to Hollywood." Hearst summoned Miss Marion to his office after finding out that she was the one who wrote Mary Pickford's cutesy filmplays.

"He looked at me, and I could tell he was going to ask me to write Marion's movies," she said. "My heart sank. I liked this warm-hearted Irish girl who was prettier than peonies in a horticulture catalogue. But her pictures were weighted down with such elaborate sets and bejeweled costumes that they dwarfed the actors." The writer hedged her way through a second cocktail and finally blurted out: "Mr. Hearst, I really don't want to work on Marion's pictures."

Hearst's eyelids dropped a little: "Why not? Don't you like her?"

"I like her very much," said the writer. "And that's exactly why I don't want to do anything that would hurt her career." She waited for Hearst; he finally said: "I don't understand what you're saying. I'm willing to spend a million dollars on each picture."

The paper magnate had given Frances Marion the opening she was looking for: "Lavishness doesn't guarantee a good picture, Mr. Hearst. Marion is a natural born comedienne, and you are smothering her with pretentious stories and such exaggerated backgrounds that you can't see the diamond for the setting." Frances Marion then took in a relieved gasp of air. She'd said it; gotten it out—told Hearst what all Hollywood had been wanting to tell him.

And Hearst, the writer said, gave her a "look that curled me up on the edges."

She had hit it on the head. Hearst, who decided he could as easily be a Svengali of the films as he had of publishing, remained on his pig-headed course—virtually smothering Marion Davies' fragile gifts under an avalanche of hokum. She was never able to crawl out.

When the Oscar came along ten years later, Hearst was the first to see the little statue as a vial of holy oil just meant to anoint his lover's saintly gifts. So he pulled her out of the simple comedies (for which she might have legitimately won an Oscar) and shoved her into a dismal parade of bad musicals (*Going Hollywood*), weary soap operas (*Peg-O-My Heart*), and sorry backstage epics (*The Floradora Girl*).

Hearst had contracted all the symptoms of a Tinseltown blight that

Time magazine called "Oscarmania—an irrational search for awards at the expense of all reason."

In this, the newspaper mogul was an original. But he blazed a course of silly lavishness that would be repeated in later decades by other idealistic swains trying to pick off an Oscar for their ladies as if it were a Kewpie doll with pink feathers on its head.

In the forties, movie genius David O. Selznick (producer of *Gone With the Wind*) would lose all reason grappling for a second Oscar for his wife, Jennifer Jones. Several decades later Peter Bogdanovich apparently suffered cultural amnesia as he created the dubious *Daisy Miller* for his blonde nymphet Cybill Shepherd. For entirely other reasons, Samuel Goldwyn spent ten million dollars on a forgettable star, Anna Sten, and Joseph Kennedy helped Gloria Swanson spend most of her fortune on an Oscar-aimed movie, *Queen Kelly.*

This "Oscar greed," in all fairness, has always been discouraged by the Academy. However, since Academy voters quite often honor even dreadful films which cost too much (*Cleopatra, The Alamo, Doctor Doolittle,* and *Hello, Dolly!*), spending often takes precedence over common sense and good taste.

This form of greed first reared its head in 1934—quite early in Oscar's history, in an artistic cold war between Marion Davies and Norma Shearer, and therefore between Hearst and MGM's boy genius Irving Thalberg, Miss Shearer's husband and the man who had guided Shearer to her first Oscar (in 1929–30 as best actress in *The Divorcee*).

Thalberg, who siphoned off all the best MGM properties for Shearer, seemed to view the first Oscar as basically "an early sound launching pad" for Norma. And who should have known better than he that the Academy Awards race was held in the pudgy little hands of a few studio bosses in 1930. So Shearer really needed a second Oscar to bring her career to its harvest point.

Thalberg, then only thirty-five and two years away from his death, drew up an acting plan for Norma Shearer that was as cold-blooded as a fighter plane—and as ambitious as the Maginot Line. First, Shearer would get out her lace handkerchiefs to play Elizabeth Barrett Browning in *The Barretts of Wimpole Street*. Then, at the age of thirty-six, she would take on Shakespeare's love tragedy *Romeo and Juliet* (as the sixteen-year-old Juliet). Finally, in 1938 Norma would shrug off her youthful demeanor to play Marie Antoinette from minuet to guillotine. So ambitious was the Thalberg plan that scouts were sent to France to buy the French queen's OWN furniture and wigs; meanwhile MGM artistic wizard Cedric Gibbons began building Verona on the backlot.

This was like waving a red flag in front of Hearst. And he responded like a raving bull. After all, hadn't Hearst draped $80,000 worth of pink roses around the screen when Marion's *Cecilia of the Pink Roses* opened (sending hundreds of moviegoers rushing home with hay fever)? And hadn't he hired Victor Herbert, at almost $100,000, to compose the "Marion Davies March" for the opening of *When Knighthood Was in Flower* (at a premiere so lavish that Dorothy Parker said, "Well, at least we now know what the Second Coming will be like.").

The newspaper publisher pushed his way into Louis B. Mayer's office without an appointment and began pounding on the sacred desk. "I brought my film company to you with an agreement that Marion would get a choice of properties. We had our heart set on *The Barretts of Wimpole Street* and *Marie Antoinette.*

But Mayer was having trouble keeping Thalberg happy. And, since the studio's prestige and much of its success depended on the whiz kid, Mayer

Hearst's Oscar rejection wrath focused its full force on Irving Thalberg and his wife, Oscar-winner Norma Shearer—here at their elaborate wedding (where ironically Marion, to the right of Norma, was matron of honor). This cozy little wedding party (from left, Edith Mayer, Irene Mayer, Louis B. Mayer, Sylvia Thalberg, Thalberg, Norma, Marion, Douglas Shearer, and Bernice Ferns) only served to demonstrate Norma's dominance of the MGM circle.

Hearst's pathetic search for Marion's Oscar was to have devastating consequences in Hollywood when Orson Welles in *Citizen Kane* used Marion as the inspiration for the doomed, alcoholic mistress in the 1941 movie. Welle's brilliant film provided a far more damaging portrait of Hearst himself—the model for Kane. About this Hearst said he "cared not a damn." But the slurs against Marion broke his heart and, secondarily, scared the hell out of Hollywood moguls—who quickly saw that *Citizen Kane* was denied the Oscar it certainly deserved.

let Norma keep her gilded bouquet of roles.

Hearst trumpeted like a wounded elephant. He called up Jack Warner and said, "We're bringing our business to Burbank." Warner, of course, was delighted. And why shouldn't he have been? Marion Davies meant Hearst; and Hearst meant the combined power of the old man's newspapers; and the papers meant Louella Parsons, a lady who could make or break an Oscar nomination with a remark over her morning croissant.

That night a construction crew on double time pulled down Marion's two-story bungalow (with its Renoirs on the wall) and drove it out the MGM gate. Louella said that L.B. cried as he watched it drift out of Culver City. (But if Mayer had cried as many times as Louella recorded, there would have been a salinity problem in Culver City.)

The Barretts of Wimpole Street came out; Norma got her nomination, and George Cukor was hired to direct *Romeo and Juliet*.

Across the hills at Warners, Marion's sugar daddy bought her the services of Dick Powell (for *Hearts Divided*), of Clark Gable (for *Cain and Mabel*), and of Robert Montgomery (for *Ever Since Eve*). By the time *Cain and Mabel* opened, the Oscar election was in its most vulnerable position with Academy membership down to fifty and the race decided by only a handful. Still, Hearst couldn't wangle even a nomination.

Thalberg had earned his wife the nomination for *The Barretts of Wimpole Street*, but Claudette Colbert won for *It Happened One Night*. The town's actors, however, nearly brought down the Academy when Bette Davis was not nominated for *Of Human Bondage*. Thalberg was unconcerned: *The Barretts* was only a curtain raiser for *Romeo*.

"Juliet will win Norma an Academy Award in her maturity as an actress just as *The Divorcee* did for her in her young womanhood," Thalberg told

Tyrone Power and Norma Shearer in a scene from *Marie Antoinette*. This film created a breach between Hearst and Metro-Goldwyn-Mayer. Hearst told the Thalbergs at a San Simeon costume party that he "expected Marion to play Marie Antoinette in one of the biggest productions of all time." Twenty years later, Marion said Norma told her, "If you want it, you can have it." But Louis B. Mayer told Hearst he didn't "dare build such a lavish production around so meagre a talent." The entire legend that demeaned Marion Davies's talent was born that night.

Basil Rathbone, John Barrymore, and Leslie Howard in one of the fight scenes from *Romeo and Juliet*. Thalberg preposterously cast thirty-six-year-old Norma as the fourteen-year-old Juliet as part of his mania to get a second Oscar for his wife. But Shearer, sighing and mooning about in gauze and shot through a silk screen to hide her age, appeared as a lightweight when compared to the brilliance of Rathbone and Barrymore, who were both passed over for Oscar nominations. Shearer, however, got her nomination. The voters recoiled at the thought of giving her the best actress award, choosing Luise Rainer for *The Great Ziegfeld* instead.

his friends. "It's true that Norma is past thirty and Juliet a teenager, but her artistry will easily overcome the discrepancy." To balance the scale, he hired an artist even older than Norma, forty-two-year-old Leslie Howard to play Romeo. (Howard was later to play Ashley Wilkes in *Gone With the Wind* but to remain Oscarless.)

The movie had such an endless budget that the balcony scene was filmed indoors using all of MGM's huge sound stage fifteen. Director Cukor needed thirty arc lamps to light the set and took seven days to film the one scene.

Late one day, Cukor noticed a man standing in the shadows, and sent an assistant director to investigate. "It's Mr. Thalberg, sir," said the kid. "Tell him to come on over," said Cukor. "But he said to ignore him." And for hours Irving Thalberg watched his wife toil through the most famous love scene in history.

A year later Thalberg was dead, and *Romeo and Juliet* was well on its way to losing more than a million dollars.

Neither it nor Norma won an Oscar. (*Marie Antoinette*, filmed after Thalberg died, would fare no better, with Shearer receiving a sympathy nomination for her twittering, inept portrayal of the French queen.)

It was this legacy that brought Hollywood to the Oscar table in 1942 where Marion Davies and Orson Welles would both become victims.

Joan Fontaine, who won her Oscar at that ceremony for *Suspicion*, said that you could smell the envy and fear at the ceremony with "people just waiting for you to stumble."

When Orson Welles' name was mentioned (as it was for his personal nominations as best actor, best director, and producer) there were loud hisses and boos. Everybody looked the other way when the words *Citizen*

Kane were spoken. "People fiddled with their furs, adjusted a hat pin—anything to get them past the shame," said an actress who was there. "This was a freeze out that was decided long before the voting."

Critic Pauline Kael, in her brilliant series, "Raising Kane," spent months researching the background for this public crucifixion of *Citizen Kane*. And she believes the Hollywood establishment denied the film distribution access not because of any overt threats from Hearst, but because they feared what he "might" do. "Had it not been for the delays and the nervous atmosphere that made the picture 'seem' so unpopular and so become unpopular, it might have swept the Academy Awards. But the picture had an aroma of box-office failure about it when the Awards were given—an aroma that frightens off awards in Hollywood."

This aroma has become such a legacy that this scent of fear often stains the Oscar derby—a possible explanation for the embargoes against such films as *Easy Rider* and *2001: A Space Odyssey*.

But more than aroma clobbered *Citizen Kane*. Hollywood was hit with the full brunt of a Hearst power machine that had been abuilding for a half century. The first sign came when the premiere—set for February 14 at the Radio City Music Hall—was suddenly canceled. George Schaeffer, RKO's top production chief, called the Rockefeller offices in New York City (they owned the Music Hall) and asked, "What gives?" The first answers were vague. Finally, after Schaeffer went all the way to Nelson Rockefeller, he was told: "Louella warned me off it. She asked me, 'How would you like the *American Weekly* magazine section to run a double-page spread on John D. Rockefeller?'"

It took pressure from a lawsuit to finally get Warners Theaters—which had agreed to distribute—to offer booking dates for *Citizen Kane*. Then Schaeffer had trouble getting papers to take ads for the movie. Some theaters paid for the film but then sat on it, according to Kael's research. And Mayer's campaign in Los Angeles not only got Welles evicted from his offices at RKO but cost Schaeffer his job as well. RKO employees who had cooperated with Welles were given assignments on "B" pictures.

Only magazine and newspaper critics (on non-Hearst magazines and papers, of course) retained any courage.

To quote Miss Kael, "Contrary to rumor it got smashing reviews."

Like this one in *Time*, March 17, 1941: "To most of the several hundred people who have seen the film at private showings, *Citizen Kane* is the most sensational product of the U.S. movie industry. It is a work of art created by grown people for grown people."

And this one by John O'Hara in *Newsweek*, also on March 17, 1941: (I) "have just seen a picture that must be the best picture I've ever seen. And I've just seen the best actor in the history of acting. Name of picture: *Citizen Kane*. Name of actor: Orson Welles."

And this one by Gilbert Seldes for *Esquire*: "Welles has shown Hollywood how to make movies. . . . He has made the movies young again, by filling them with life." And this one by Archer Winsten in the *New York Post*: "It goes without saying this is the picture that wins the majority of 1941's prizes in a walk. For it is inconceivable that another will come along to challenge it."

And this, by Cecilia Ager in *PM*: "It's as if the motion picture was a sleeping monster; a mighty force stupidly awaiting a fierce young man to come and kick it to life; to rouse it; shake it and awaken it to its potentialities. Seeing it, it's as if you never really saw a motion picture before."

This Greek chorus of praise was the final ingredient needed to convert the Oscar ceremony, 1942, into a full-blown tragedy of classic proportions.

Orson Welles in *Citizen Kane*. Welles was a victim of rotten Oscar politics. *Citizen Kane* was the best film of 1941, and everybody in town knew it. But the men in charge of the studios also knew the power of Hearst's wrath, so they cautioned their employees to vote for any other film but *Citizen Kane*; for any other actor but Orson Welles. The conspiracy went beyond the Academy Awards when the major film distribution networks were bullied into refusing the film, relegating it to art houses in America's big cities. Welles's film is now considered by many to be the best American film ever made. In 1972 the University of Southern California Performing Arts Council asked fifty film executives to name the most significant American movies; *Citizen Kane* placed first. A 1975 poll of 1,500 key members of the film community placed *Citizen Kane* sixth, and the movie was high on the 1977 poll of the American Film Institute.

John Barrymore, his eyes red and his face distorted by alcoholism, points a finger at the camera in a 1940s publicity stunt. The same gutter politics that turned Marion Davies's comic talent into a crude joke barred Barrymore from the nominee ranks. In the first five years of the thirties, critic Spencer Berger pointed out, "Barrymore conjured up his magic, creating a gallery of characterizations that surpassed in variety and effectiveness the range of every other actor of his time."

"The members of the Academy destroyed Orson Welles that night," wrote Kael in *The Citizen Kane Book.* "*Kane* was Welles' finest moment. Their failure to back him was the turning point. He had made *Citizen Kane* at twenty-five, and he seemed to have the world before him. The Academy members had made their token gesture to *Citizen Kane* with the screenplay award. They failed what they believed in; they gave in to the scandal and to the business pressures. They couldn't know how much guilt they should feel: guilt that by their failure to support *Kane*—they started the downward spiral of Orson Welles—who was to become perhaps the greatest loser in Hollywood history."

But Kael is counting out Marion Davies—the only other loser from an Oscar scandal comparable to Welles. One of the silent films' most gifted artists, her image remains unrescued—may always remain unrescued.

1941 is one of those years that puts a chink in Oscar's fragile armor of objectivity. It is a permanent chink. If only the Oscar weren't held up by the mass media as a high watermark of quality. But it is. If only a single nomination couldn't make the difference between a big career and a moderate one. But it can.

Far worse than Oscar's infrequent lapses of objectivity and trust are those producers and directors who, occasionally, set out to make not a good movie—but an Oscar winning movie and achieve not a fine performance but an Oscar-winning performance.

Oscarmania has also caused several bits of high farce in Hollywood's rather humorless history. Under its influence David O. Selznick made the now hilarious *A Farewell to Arms* in 1957. And it was surely "Oscaritis" that caused normally tasteful Samuel Goldwyn to create Anna Sten, a costly star who proved to be bankrupt both financially and artistically.

It was painful, contemporaries said, to see how much David O. Selznick wanted to create an Oscar-winning role for his future wife, Jennifer Jones. Under the pressure of competition from his early success with *Gone With the Wind* and her Oscar-winning first effort, *Song of Bernadette*, Selznick's artistic judgment faltered. He smothered her talent in overblown productions that bombed with the critics. Some of the most powerful men in Hollywood have mounted similarly massive and doomed efforts to win statuettes for their favorite starlets—Samuel Goldwyn with Anna Sten, William Randolph Hearst with Marion Davies, Irving Thalberg with Norma Shearer.

The "Anna Sten Affair" came first. In 1932. Oscar was still young, and Goldwyn was prickly with jealousy over the nominations being chalked up by Dietrich and, later, by Garbo.

With two foreigners packing the theaters of America, a third, newer one could only do better, to Sam's thinking. (He couldn't know that Hollywood would soon be calling his import "Goldwyn's Last Sten" as Oscar voters chuckled over their ballots.)

Sam saw the German actress when he was on a tour of Europe in 1932. The film was *The Brothers Karamazov* and the producer was entranced. "Listen to her," he told an adjutant. "She sounds like Garbo—only better."

"But Mr. Goldwyn," said the aide, "she's speaking in German." Goldwyn bristled, "She speaks better than Garbo."

"But Mr. Goldwyn, Garbo's Swedish, not German."

Goldwyn would hear none of it. He met Anna Sten, toasted her with champagne and then, with Sam bobbing his head and speaking English and Sten bobbing her head and speaking German, the star was signed up at $3,000-a-week plus expenses. Anna stuffed the fat Goldwyn marks into her almost empty wallet, headed for Paris shops, and left her new boss to overcome the fallout from his own largesse.

A month later, American film editors found their mail suddenly cluttered with a barrage of German cheesecake. Sten! Sten as an Arabian temptress; as a coy milkmaid with Clara Bow lips; as an apple-cheeked Hussar popping from her vest. "Sexier than Dietrich; more mysterious than Garbo," said the releases from the purple pen of Goldwyn publicist Lynn Farnol.

Sten was in Hollywood by then, fatter and speaking much less English than he remembered. No English, in fact. Sam told Gary Cooper that she seemed able to do only two things—bob her head and gain weight.

Goldwyn made her sign up at the Beverly Hills Tennis Club to cure the latter and sent her to a passel of voice coaches to cure the former. As for Sam, he took an Alka-Seltzer and screamed for his story editors. "She has to start at the top," he told writer Willard Mack. "In a classic by ANOTHER foreigner. You know, Zola or something. Yeah, Zola'll do fine."

And Zola it was. *Nana* to be specific—the story of a whore adrift in nineteenth-century Paris. The scripters started sweating while Goldwyn's bills piled up. "Teach her to sing," he ordered an MGM vocal coach. "But Sam," he cried, "this is a woman with a small but disagreeable voice." "Change it then," answered Sam. "Teach her to dance," he ordered a veteran ballet master. "But she has no coordination," he pleaded. "I'll come see myself," said Goldwyn.

Which he did. Goldwyn's biographer Arthur Marx said Goldwyn, after about five minutes of watching the lessons, "jumped off his chair and hopped around the rehearsal hall on his left foot to show that anyone, even a middle-aged man, could learn to do the cancan."

The evidence was dismal, but Sam set a starting date for *Nana* anyway. "This is the girl that's going to win the next Academy Award," he said. "Just you watch."

George Fitzmaurice took the helm, slowly coaching Sten line-by-line through a script that was simply waterlogged by attempts to make it fit Goldwyn's standards of "Academy-seriousness." The producer tried to ignore the rumors coming from the set, but finally ordered a rough cut to gauge the progress of "Project Sten." "When he saw a picture that was definitely without the Goldwyn touch, Sam ordered the whole thing scrapped and announced that he was starting over from page one with a new director," said Marx in *Goldwyn*. "I don't care how much money it costs," he yelled at his distraught accountants. "It is my money I'm spending. We will shoot until I'm happy."

Sam brought in the town's only woman director, Dorothy Arzner, and tried to tell Anna it would be more pleasant from that point on. Sten thought he was talking about her dress and asked, "What's wrong with it?"

Arzner pulled Sten through the picture with a maximum of artistry and a minimum of confusion. But even Arzner could not correct what the Goldwyn scriptwriters had done to Zola. They had changed *Nana* from a prostitute into a nice girl in trouble and jettisoned Zola's gruesome death from smallpox. In the Goldwyn version *Nana* commits suicide freeing two brothers who love her to fight for France.

And Sam had an alternate plan in case the critics caught on. A week before *Nana* opened in New York, twenty-five percent of the downtown billboards were plastered with Sten—a full story high with the subtle hint that here was next year's Academy Award winner.

"By the time *Nana* opened at the Music Hall on February 2, 1934, Anna Sten was better known to some Americans than Charles Lindbergh and the Burma Shave sign," said Marx.

It was futile; *Nana* lost money—only Sam knew how much. To dampen the rumors of "failure," Goldwyn quickly put Sten with Gary Cooper in a sure winner, *Barbary Coast*, with William Wyler directing. Nobody ever talked about what happened on that set. But Anna came tumbling out of the role after only four days. (She was succeeded, successfully, by Miriam Hopkins.)

"Well," said Goldwyn, unruffled, "we'll try Tolstoy." Then he hauled out and dusted off the Russian's difficult novel, *Resurrection*, a minor success. The critics liked it; the public didn't. No Oscar.

Sam again drafted Cooper and scrapped together a little pastiche called

You can be forgiven if the screen credits of Anna Sten have escaped your memory; her major films—*Nana, Resurrection,* and *The Wedding Night*—hardly set the thirties on fire. Sten, shown here during her "Garbo period," was imported from Russia by Samuel Goldwyn. When she docked in New York and was driven into Manhattan, Goldwyn had billboards already plastering the city. Later, when *Nana* was released, her face, in this kerchief pose, stood seventy-five feet above Times Square. Goldwyn said quite frankly that she "is better than Garbo, sexier than Dietrich, and a finer actress than Norma Shearer." But the Oscar voters were unimpressed.

Selznick, failing to win an Oscar for Jennifer Jones in the bloated *Duel in the Sun*, went from the idiotic to the incredulous with *Indiscretion of an American Wife*, directed by Vittorio De Sica and centered entirely in the new Rome railroad station. De Sica got the screen credit, but Selznick butted in so dreadfully and so often that De Sica finally threw up his hands, saying, "I really don't care what happens to this movie. That man (Selznick) has become a walking disaster."

The Wedding Night, with King Vidor at the controls. "He can direct anybody," Lillian Gish had said, not counting on Sten.

Halfway through filming Goldwyn showed up on the set to watch a love scene. "I tell you that if this scene isn't the greatest love scene ever put on film, the whole goddamned picture will go right down the sewer." Which is exactly what it did.

The third time was a knockout. Goldwyn threw in the towel and said goodbye to Sten. (She later reemerged in minor roles during the forties.)

Years later Rosalind Russell, after losing the Oscar on the almost certain *Mourning Becomes Electra*, said: "It seems to be a case of the Gods saying to those self-conscious 'Oscar pictures'—well, just you watch, you aren't going to win."

David O. Selznick knew all this when he began tilting Academy Award windmills in the name of his love (later his wife) Jennifer Jones. She'd already won the Oscar on her first time out for *The Song of Bernadette*. That only put more pressure on Selznick; not only did he have to top himself (after the Oscar rich *Gone With the Wind*), he had to find the role of roles, the film of films for Jennifer.

The producer shuffled through a couple of minor projects for Jennifer before settling on *Duel in the Sun*, an overblown western that critics would call *Lust in the Dust*. The $5 million film had King Vidor to direct, Gregory Peck, Lionel Barrymore, and Lillian Gish to star, and, as a special consultant for Jennifer, Dietrich's former mentor, Josef Von Sternberg.

"From the artistic little western, *Duel in the Sun* grew to epic size," said Associated Press writer Bob Thomas, Selznick's biographer. "David was especially meticulous in matters concerning Jennifer. Her costumes were

Jennifer, here with Gregory Peck and looking like a cross between a Mongol princess and a cigar store Indian, was so hopelessly adrift in outlandish costumes and distressing music that her own, wonderfully natural style of acting was buried in an avalanche of kitsch. Josef Von Sternberg, the German wizard who created Marlene Dietrich, was hired by Selznick to create a glamorous presence for Mrs. Selznick—which he did with broad swatches of body paint, wildly shoveled hair, and lips the color of a Tahitian sunset. "It was," said Hedda Hopper, "simply ghastly."

redesigned again and again. Her makeup and hairstyles were tested again and again."

Then came the "affair of the orgasm music." Dimitri Tiomkin found out about that only after Selznick hired him, sending him a Western Union memo, declaring that the film's score must have eleven separate themes: Spanish theme, ranch theme . . . love theme. Desire, too. And, oh yes, the orgasm theme. Tiomkin told Thomas it might have been funny if David weren't so serious. "Love themes I can write. Desire, too. But orgasm? How do you score an orgasm?"

Well, you'll just have to try," said Selznick as an afterthought. The composer came up with a heavy air that he thought might fit his employer's idea of orgasm music. David seemed to like it. At a sneak preview, however, the producer began stirring in his theater seat. He rushed back to Tiomkin: "Whistle the orgasm theme for me!"

The composer with a shelf full of Oscars wet his lips and whistled a weak approximation of the score. "No, that isn't it," said Selznick. "That's just not an orgasm." Back to the music sheets. Weeks later, Tiomkin unveiled the new theme. He combined cellos, trombones, and the pulsating of a handsaw.

David still wasn't happy, but the score stood after Tiomkin blew up, yelling "Meestair Selznick, you . . . your way, I . . . mine. To me, THAT is . . . music. Case closed."

The low point of Selznick's movie meddling came as King Vidor was finally filming the death scene. Jennifer Jones and Gregory Peck were sprawled in the hot sun expiring for the camera. Vidor loomed over them in intense concentration.

Suddenly, new splashes of blood slopped onto the actors. Then a hand appeared dubbing more Indian face makeup on Jennifer's contorted face.

It was Selznick. Vidor closed his script, rose from his chair, and looked Selznick in the eye. "David," he said, "you can take this picture and shove it."

Many another producer would have been shaken from his obsession by this incident with its embarrassing publicity. Not Selznick. When the Oscar nominations were announced, Selznick's carefully mounted ad campaign worked: Jennifer was nominated for best actress. (This is what makes Oscarmania so venal—even for lapses of taste, this strategy works; it ropes in the voters long enough to get a nomination.)

Bob Thomas, in *Selznick,* wrote: "David became obsessed with Jennifer and with her career. She was unlike any woman he had known before— enigmatic, enchanting, quintessentially feminine. He saw in her the limitless potential of a consummate actress. There was nothing she was incapable of; no role she could not play. And David took charge of every aspect of her career."

So Selznick began writing the "Jennifer memos," a series of insanely long instructions to directors, makeup artists, lighting technicians, and producers, advising them ad minutiae on the intricacies of handling Miss Jones (by then Mrs. Selznick). One memo to the cameramen on *A Farewell to Arms* ran for twenty pages (single spaced). Selznick, point by point, told the cinematographer how to properly photograph Jennifer.

A Farewell to Arms was Selznick's last grab for the gold ring on the Academy's Oscar merry-go-round. He hired John Huston to direct, Rock Hudson to co-star, and every extra in Italy for support. Huston, on location in Italy, was soon buried under paper. "I am very much on my guard, and unless I hold you to the line on this as a love story, with the war as the background, the military emphasis is going to throw the picture way off balance," Selznick wired.

Huston was still dizzy from this one, when a second cable arrived. "If this picture is going to fail, it must fail on my mistakes, not yours," in a $700 telegram that also hinted strongly that Huston should resign (which he did).

In came Charles Vidor (no relation to King). Vidor had a week's grace before the memos started. Then this, one of Selznick's most comical: "I must say that Jennifer, Charles, knew what she was doing when she asked for a 'business appointment' to discuss with me her deep disturbance concerning changes we have made in her first scene with Henry (Rock Hudson) in the Milan hospital. We have with the rewrite lost entirely the desperate hunger of these two people for each other—in what Hemingway has called his *Romeo and Juliet.* As I think you will discover, Jennifer is a very creative artist, who brings to every scene the benefits of intense study. Incidentally, please let me mention that I think you would be well-advised to always let her play the scene for you first, of course, then feel free to redirect her as you see fit."

The memo exposes for public scrutiny some of the hysteria he felt during this last attempt to bag an Oscar for his wife. Rock Hudson told Thomas that he quietly watched Selznick, lost in concentration, walk into a wall. Another time, when Hudson was in deep embrace with Jennifer, he looked up at the camera to see Selznick whispering in Vidor's ear. "David," said the actor. "Oh, sorry," said Selznick. Several days later he told an associate producer, "This picture has got to have love, love, love. And there isn't enough of it yet."

Finally Selznick and Jennifer Jones headed home with their picture under their arms.

A Selznick advisor took one look at it, then advised his boss to release

A prematurely aged Selznick with Gregory Peck on location for *Duel in the Sun.* Even with Lillian Gish and partial direction by King Vidor (he quit in disgust over Selznick's meddling), the film won only two nominations—one to Gish for flatly obvious reasons, and a bow to Jennifer Jones, which Selznick had to wring from voters through a multithousand dollar advertising campaign. It was the end of the line for Selznick, Oscar-wise; his films received only one more nomination— a best supporting actress bid for Ethel Barrymore in 1947's *The Parradine Case.* If Selznick had been able to relax—and to escape from his fear that he'd never again equal *Gone With the Wind*—his Academy Award record would probably have stretched far into the fifties. Even so, his Oscar record was equaled only by Irving Thalberg, Darryl Zanuck, and Jack Warner. Thirteen Selznick films earned thirty-six nominations and nine Oscars. Two of his most personally produced films were named best picture—*Gone With the Wind* and *Rebecca.*

it gradually in California to get audience reaction. But the bigwigs at Fox wanted it out quick, whispering sycophantic nothings into David's ear.

That was just what he wanted to hear; being anxious to have *A Farewell to Arms* qualify for both the Oscars and the New York Film Critics Awards. The producer was literally seduced by the yes-men at Fox. And he let the film go out without viewing the final cut, sailing to Jamaica with his wife.

The reviews were crushing, with critics calling the picture old-fashioned, over-produced, poorly acted, and ineffective. Even Hemingway, who had been offered a share of the profits, cabled that he thought little of the profits from a film in which "the forty-one-year-old Mrs. Selznick portrayed the twenty-four-year-old Catherine Barkley."

Bob Thomas said, "Selznick was devastated by the failure of *A Farewell to Arms*, and what hurt him most was the feeling that he had failed Jennifer. He had intended the picture to be the crowning achievement of her career. David, his confidence shattered, never made another film."

A Farewell to Arms received only a single nomination—Vittorio De Sica for best supporting actor (a man with whom Selznick had feuded in this and an earlier movie).

And the Oscar Svengali tradition didn't die there.

What, after all, is megaproducer Bob Evans when it comes to Ali MacGraw, the frozen-faced girl who got an Oscar nomination for "never saying I'm sorry" to Ryan O'Neal in *Love Story*?

Evans, an incredibly handsome man who made a million in the women's sportswear business and then worked his way up the Hollywood production ladder, showed almost unerring judgment as a Paramount helmsman (with *The Godfather*, *Rosemary's Baby*, and *Love Story* to his credit). When it came to human sleepwalker Ali MacGraw, however, Evans finally lost all sense of taste in 1979 when he tried to create a tennis version of

Producer David O. Selznick and director King Vidor on location with *Duel in the Sun*. Selznick had a policy of watching every move his wife, Jennifer Jones, made, exasperating several directors.

Steve McQueen, another celluloid knight after the Holy Oscar for his lady—this time out, Ali MacGraw, who did less real acting to earn her nomination (for *Love Story*) than any "actress" (used loosely) in the Academy's history. But here McQueen handcrafted a trucker epic, *The Getaway*, as a glove-tight vehicle for Ali. A disaster resulted. McQueen himself received only one nomination—for *The Sand Pebbles*. Where were the voters looking when Steve made *Love With the Proper Stranger, Baby, the Rain Must Fall, Bullitt*, and *Papillon*?

Rocky with Miss MacGraw and the equally vapid Dean-Paul Martin (son of big Dean) in *Players.*

Where *Rocky* had won the Oscar, Ali MacGraw, as a female cross between Sylvester Stallone and Burgess Meredith, drew only laughter. They snickered at a foreign press preview, they chuckled in Westwood, and they laughed out loud in Atlanta. The frightful dramatic climax of the film featured the masklike Ali pushing the bleach-haired Martin through a tennis training workout. "You have pigeon toes," said Ali, squinting over her Gucci scarf. Dino rolled his eyes (buried in blue contacts) and mumbled: "Segura was pigeon-toed; Laver was pigeon-toed; Gonzales was pigeon-toed. And me—now me." Then they called it match, game, and set.

"How can two people who look so good, act so bad?" groaned Gene Shalit on the "Today" show.

According to Marie Brenner's stylish 1978 book, *Going Hollywood*, Evans' grand dramatic design for Ali was formed long before *Players*. "Ali had plans for *The Great Gatsby*," said Brenner. "Gatsby's Daisy was her literary self-image. She nagged Paramount for two years, convinced Evans it had to be *Gatsby*.

But first came *The Getaway*. And Steve McQueen. The whole world knows the rest. According to Brenner, Ali forgot Evans but remembered *Gatsby*. "Evans had an ultimatum for her. If she stayed with him, she'd be in the movie. If not." So Mia Farrow played Daisy to Robert Redford's Gatsby, saving MacGraw from one of cinema's five biggest flops.

There are echoes of both Selznick and Hearst in Evans' "Ali fixation." And while Evans is not the kind to admit right out that he's been tilting for an Oscar, his campaigns for *Love Story* and *The Godfather* long ago unmasked his Academy Award fever.

Peter Bogdanovich's celluloid tinker toys for Cybill Shepherd fit more

Cybill Shepherd and Timothy Bottoms in Peter Bogdanovich's *The Last Picture Show*, a black-and-white masterpiece of control and tempo. Awards went to Ben Johnson and Cloris Leachman.

easily into the classic mold set by Hearst. Shepherd, an also-ran for Miss Teenage America, might have made it better on her own than with Bogdanovich's heavy directorial hand. She had blazed to glory in *The Last Picture Show*. Her mentor, however, had far bigger plans for her: a hand-tailored version of Henry James' *Daisy Miller*. He then surrounded her with the immense talents of Cloris Leachman and Eileen Brennan. Cybill came off like a living Barbie doll in a Hollywood wax museum.

Ho-hum, one down. Then Bogdanovich bought most of Cole Porter's song catalogue and cast Shepherd in a dinosaur of a musical called *At Long Last Love*. A singing Burt Reynolds, literally crammed into tight thirties' black tie, reported as Miss Shepherd's co-star. "It's a good thing Cole wasn't alive to see this," Ethel Merman said through clenched teeth.

As if this weren't enough, Peter pulled Cybill into one of America's best recording studios to record a personal album of naughty songs by Porter, such as "In the Morning, No." A disc jockey, trying to play one of the songs on a New York station, laughed so hard the needle jumped through an entire band.

Is it any wonder that Cybill retired to Memphis—with no Oscar on her bookcase.

"To some," said Hedda Hopper, "the Oscar is like a one-armed bandit. They just have to pull that lever—no matter the cost."

Cybill in all her Gothic regalia—frozen-faced and granite-chinned. But this wasn't the last of Cybillmania; Bogdanovich paired her up with Burt Reynolds, bought the complete Cole Porter song catalogue, and fashioned a thirties musical for two stars who couldn't sing, didn't dance, and chose not to act. Said *Variety* of the film, *At Long Last Love*, "It just lies there—and it dies there."

IN OSCAR'S CLOSET

"The REAL show is backstage and out there in the audience. It's written on the faces of the losers, in the hearts of the winners, and told in whispers behind perfumed hands." Dorothy Kilgallen, 1963.

The young usher blushed through his deep tan and tried to smile, "Uh, ma'am, the show's already started. You can't go in now."

The raven-haired lady in buckskins and beads stared right through him and sized up the door keeping her from the orchestra seating for the 1972 Oscar show. She grabbed her turquoise necklace and shifted nervously from one moccasin to another.

The costumed intruder turned to her companion, who was dressed to the Beverly Hills' nines. "Let's try the other door."

They glided noiselessly over the two-inch carpet at the Los Angeles Music Center and stormed a second wall of doors. The six-foot traffic cop on guard hooked his thumbs in the top of his skin-tight pants and looked down at the Indian. He opened his mouth to bark, but the Indian's companion beat him to the punch.

"Brando!" she said. "We're here for Marlon Brando." "Oh, wow!" said the cop. "Wow!" He almost saluted and led the pair to a side door. They ducked down a slight hall, opened a second, smaller door. This time they just flashed their tickets and whispered, "Brando." "You'll have to wait until the next break," said another usher, who dropped his programs and burst into a run—headed for Oscar's inner-sanctum behind the golden curtain.

The usher grabbed the arm of a sweating assistant director and gasped, "Brando's being represented by an Indian." "So what?" said the A.D., thinking to himself that Brando's first wife was, after all, a former Indian movie star—Anna Kashfi. But the usher, second-guessing him, said, "No, I mean an American Indian—you know, in moccasins, beads, leather." The assistant director's arrogant grin contorted into an expression of almost sheer terror.

He began elbowing his way through America's most famous backstage scene. Past Raquel, past Jane, past Charlton. Finally he found him—Howard W. Koch, Oscar producer for the Academy of Motion Picture Arts and Sciences, and, for a night, the most powerful man in Hollywood. "Uh, Mr.

She called herself Sacheen Littlefeather—Indian princess for a night at the 1974 Academy Awards. When she stepped up to refuse the Oscar for Marlon Brando there was an angry buzz from the audience and a mild fury backstage.

Koch," stuttered the A.D., "there's an Indian here representing Marlon Brando. And she's got this big, long speech to read." Howard Koch threw his fists up to his face in frustration. This, he thought, is too much, as his mind whirred over the Academy's rough sailing through recent political controversy (a history made unavoidable with Jane Fonda a winner and Vanessa Redgrave a multiple nominee).

"I quickly called a pow-wow offstage," said Koch. "We considered everything. We even considered arresting her on the grounds that seats are nontransferable." (A move that might have been disastrous since stars and nominees have sent proxies since the awards began.)

Koch tugged the satin lapels on his coat and decided to risk the ordeal under fire—he had to confront her. "Might as well learn the worst now," he told a confederate as he slipped out into the darkened auditorium.

Onstage, Julie Andrews was presenting the best director award to Bob Fosse for *Cabaret*. Koch's first words were drowned out by screams from Liza Minnelli and Joel Grey in nearby seats. The Oscar chief's face was as blank as Buster Keaton's as he stood face to face with his adversary.

She was well figured, lovely, composed. Five thousand dollars worth of New Mexican turquoise was on her neck; her white buckskin had been rock hammered in Canada, and she had made her leather thong headdress herself. "I am Howard Koch," said the flustered official. "And *I* am Sacheen Littlefeather," said the dark-haired beauty.

"You can't read *that*," he said, pointing to the sheaf of papers in Miss Littlefeather's hand. "We're running late. You just can't read it."

Sacheen lowered her eyelids, "If Marlon should win, I *am* going to read it." (See appendix.) "If you try to read that, I'll cut you off the air," he repeated, as the Oscar show quickly moved through the major awards and toward the climax.

"Okay! Okay!" said the Indian maiden. "I won't read it." Koch headed backstage while Sacheen Littlefeather and the beautiful girl with her, Brando's secretary, Alice Marchak, were seated next to Brando's pal Jimmy Caan.

Caan leaned over and grabbed Alice's hand, "He's gonna win, Alice, he's gonna win!" The lights dimmed at that second. Roger Moore and Liv Ullmann walked to stage center and read the nominees, as clips from the performances rolled onto the screen: "Marlon Brando, for *The Godfather*, Michael Caine for *Sleuth*, Laurence Olivier for *Sleuth*, Peter O'Toole for *The Ruling Class*, and Paul Winfield for *Sounder*."

There was the usual breathless pause as Hollywood and 300 million people around the world waited to crown Hollywood's "King for a Day."

"The winner is . . . Marl—" There was a mighty roar because this was a comeback. And Hollywood, above all other things, loves a comeback. Sacheen Littlefeather moved from the protective darkness into the Oscar spotlight, and the audience began to buzz with rumor and speculation. She held up her hand as Roger Moore tried to give her the Oscar and then blushed as he realized she would not take it. Then she declined for Marlon Brando in her own halting words, explaining that Brando was protesting the treatment of Indians by America, generally, and by the movies, specifically. The silence was stunning as Sacheen Littlefeather drifted offstage and was mobbed by press.

Koch sighed, partly in relief. It was, he thought, not as bad as it could have been. Visions of Marlon's hand typed, five page speech danced in his head. Anyway, the show was over and he was off the hook.

But not the Academy. And not Brando. For a year later the Battle of "Little Big Oscar" raged in Hollywood and America. Brando was pilloried by conservative critics; turned into a hero by liberal critics; and alternately loved, hated, and suspected by the powers that be in Hollywood.

Rona Barrett screamed "Coward!" over network television. Conservatives wrote mailbags of protest to the Academy. And a Beverly Hills shirt parlor began selling "Marlon-Sacheen" T-shirts the next week, with Brando's jowls peering from the chest and Sacheen, band and beads included, glaring from wearer's shoulder blades.

Finally, even Sacheen herself became a public commodity complete with her own P.R. man. She wasn't really Sacheen Littlefeather, it turned out. She was a sometime bit actress named Maria Cruz, formerly of Salinas, California, and formerly Miss Vampire U.S.A. But she was part Apache and other tribes, she was an Indian activist, and the most comely veteran of the tribe that took Alcatraz in a highly publicized 1969–1970 protest.

It was on that windy prison rock that an Indian leader had told Marie Cruz, "I dub you Sacheen Littlefeather." How Brando met the Urban Indian Maiden has never been clarified—mainly because Brando's public reaction to his Oscar win was the most terse since Gary Cooper said "Aw, shucks" in 1941. "Outta-my-way," said the "Godfather" to reporters at the airport. "Outta-my-way."

The furor in Hollywood died the minute producers realized they couldn't make a film about it. Sacheen drifted into Oscars-past. And Brando reported to the set of *The Missouri Breaks*, for which he would collect $1.3 million and a percentage of the profits.

It was another matter in the skyscraper headquarters of the Academy of Motion Picture Arts and Sciences in Beverly Hills. There, Academy prexy Daniel Taradash called an emergency board meeting to discuss what insiders called a cure for Oscar's misuse as a public soapbox. "I don't know what we can do," Taradash told the *Los Angeles Times*. "We don't know if anything will work, but we have to look at the use of the Oscar lectern as a platform."

One thing was sure: there was no going back. Brando's political coup had worked. Hate mail against Brando was not large enough to hurt either him, the Oscars, or *The Godfather*. So Oscar big chiefs like Charlton Heston and Gregory Peck simply girded their loins and waited for successive waves of politics to wash through the seventies and into the eighties.

"You might as well cancel the Oscars if you're going to muffle winners," said Koch to a friend. "We'll have to bank on the good faith of most winners."

Until Sacheen shuffled up to the stage in 1972, most of Oscar's backstage trouble had resulted from confusion—such as the hysteria which erupted when Liz Taylor and Katharine Hepburn were given the same dressing room—or from spiteful tiffs among movie stars:

—Such as the long-running feud between Oscar-winning sisters Olivia De Havilland and Joan Fontaine which bubbled to the surface at the 1946 ceremony. Olivia had just accepted her award as best actress for *To Each His Own*, when Joan walked over to congratulate her. She held out her hand and saw Olivia turn away from her, clutching her Oscar to her bosom. Unluckily a *Photoplay* magazine photographer just happened to have his camera aimed right at the siblings and turned it into a legendary moment.

—Also typical was the tiff between Bette Davis and Joan Crawford which percolated to a hard boil at the 1963 Oscar ceremony. Bette was nominated for *What Ever Happened to Baby Jane?* Joan was not. To make it worse, Bette had gone on the "Tonight" show two days earlier, saying that one producer told her, "Hollywood won't give you a dime for those two old broads." Crawford wired Davis two hours later, "Please do not refer to me in that way again." Curtain time for Oscar saw the two actresses (both former winners and nominees several times) spitting mud. Crawford sailed into the Santa Monica Auditorium that afternoon and set up a wet bar in the largest dressing room. She was there, she said, to accept the best actress award for Anne Bancroft. "There's no doubt she'll win." Bette paced up and down backstage as the announcement neared, at one point gripping nervously the arm of her longtime friend, Olivia De Havilland. Finally. "And the winner is, Anne Bancroft for *The Miracle Worker*." Bette felt a cold hand on her shoulder. "Excuse me," said Crawford, her voice dripping ice. Then she sailed out to thunderous applause. "It was a moment I'll never forget," said Bette Davis.

Oscar has even seen wave after wave of absentee winners, culminating in 1966 when the *Hollywood Reporter* noted that fifty-seven of the nominees were missing. (One notorious absentee, Claudette Colbert, was coaxed from a Santa Fe train and rushed across town in a police car to receive her award for *It Happened One Night* in the thirties.)

And Oscar had even been refused before—most notably by George C. Scott, who blasted the whole process in 1970 when he won for *Patton*.

But Oscar's new role as a soapbox opened a Pandora's box of troubles that are certain to continue as long as the ceremonies last.

Interestingly enough, Brando's grand gesture began almost innocently. Brando had already rejected the New York Film Critics Award, the Golden Globe, and the Reuters News Agency World Film Favorite Prize when he was nominated for the Oscar. He sent the same telegram to all three organizations: "There is a singular lack of honor in this country today—what with the government's change of its citizens into objects of use, its imperialistic and warlike intrusion into foreign countries and the killing of not only their inhabitants but also indirectly of our own people, its treatment of the Indians and the Blacks; the assault on the press, the rape of the ideals which were the foundation of this country. I respectfully ask you to understand that to accept an honor, however well intentioned, is to subtract from the meagre amount left. Therefore to simplify things, I hereby decline any nomination and deny anyone representing me."

The wire got scant press and much of that was distorted. Joyce Haber, a former *Los Angeles Times* columnist and author of *The Users*, wrote, "Brando, who won the Reuters Poll for World Film Favorite presumably sent a wire to that agency using such foul language that it could not be read on the air." Such callous disregard for the truth quickly convinced Brando that he would either have to turn down the Oscar in person or send someone he could trust.

The Academy virtually bombed Brando's secretary, Alice Marchak, with letters and phone calls asking if Brando would come. Over at Paramount Pictures, which made *The Godfather*, the brass became increasingly jumpy as the rumor mill predicted the star as a hands-down winner. Paramount threw up its hands and publicly announced that Robert Evans, its handsome production chief, would collect Brando's Oscar.

Somewhere in the South Seas Brando decided otherwise. He jetted into Los Angeles the day before the ceremony and asked Alice to meet him at his house: "I want you to go to the Awards—with Sacheen," he said, sending his secretary running to the phone. "I remembered we didn't have tickets. So I called Mr. Koch's office at Paramount and asked him to send two tickets to Brando's house." Since Hollywood is still the smallest back fence town in America, the news spread like wildfire. Brando's coming to the Academy Awards . . . In Person. The wire services sent it out as a bulletin, and newscasters in the East led off their broadcasts with the announcement.

Rumor had it that Brando (here in a key scene from *The Godfather*) was far away on a Tahitian island the night he won the Oscar, but he was actually in the living room of his Beverly Hills pied-à-terre, drinking with friends and packing a suitcase for a trip to America's Indian reservations. Up until the last few minutes Paramount studio boss and sometime matinee idol Robert Evans was set to pick up the Oscar. Network cameras were already trained and focused on Evans's handsome profile when a flustered usher ran down the darkened aisle with Brando's secretary Alice Marchak and Sacheen Littlefeather. The rest, of course, is history. The actor's connection with the Oscar race began twenty-three years earlier with his first nomination for *A Streetcar Named Desire*. He was nominated again in 1952 for *Viva Zapata!* and again in 1953 for *Julius Caesar* before winning his first Oscar in *On the Waterfront* in 1954. The final nomination of Brando's early period was in 1957 for *Sayonara*. In the fifteen years between *Sayonara* and *The Godfather* Brando had become far more interested in political causes than acting. His rejection of the Oscar was a natural outgrowth. There are signs, however, that he regrets the decision. Prodded by Dick Cavett a year later Brando sputtered: "Would I do it again? Well, uh, I don't think so."

Bob Wise presenting Alfred Hitchcock with the Irving Thalberg Award, April 10, 1967.

Many Oscar watchers were primed for a theatrical event; some even thought the Academy had staged it to build ratings for the show—their biggest (about $1.7 million) source of revenue. After the show, however, some critics, notably Charles Champlin, entertainment editor of the *Los Angeles Times*, and Rona Barrett, despaired of the future.

"What Marlon Brando did this year could signal the death of Oscar as we know him," said Rona on "Good Morning, America." "I suggest that perhaps we should take a look at whether it still works to give the Academy Award to just one person. Perhaps the nominations should BE the awards . . . so that one winner is *never again* tempted to feel so omnipotent that he can misuse his recognition as Marlon Brando has done."

Champlin, whose moderate voice has brought winds of change to the Academy, stated, "Brando was arguing in absentia that attention must be paid, and he took the occasion of a very promotional evening. The question is whether the gesture, in all its arrogant sincerity, succeeds in dramatizing or in trivializing the problem."

Then the columnist threw an off-handed compliment to Brando: "Say what you will about him, he's an electrifying nonpresence as well as an electrifying presence."

But "What will happen next year? Or the year after? Or in 1979?" asked Rona Barrett.

A year later, the Academy found out.

The Oscarcast on April 2, 1974, was so star-glutted that buses were sent to Los Angeles International Airport to collect the herds winging in from England and France. There was Twiggy and Francois Truffaut, Liza Minnelli and Linda Blair, Susan Hayward and Alfred Hitchcock. And, as an added Roman candle, Katharine Hepburn, an Oscar first. She won the press over with her candor: "I'm so glad," she said, "that people didn't

Elizabeth Taylor abandoned her su- perstar image and probed the dark of her own soul in *Who's Afraid of Virginia Woolf?* and won a second Oscar in 1966. This time she re- mained in Europe for Oscar night and, after her victory was an- nounced, spoke frankly: "I'm happy about it, but the victory is dimmed by the fact that Richard lost—he was the one who deserved it." Fellow Briton Paul Scofield defeated Burton in 1966 for his work in *A Man for All Seasons,* a film that has lacked the staying power of *Who's Afraid of Vir- ginia Woolf?* By staying home Taylor was able to voice a powerful protest about the injustices of Oscar politics. In earlier years Taylor's own social fortunes had been chronicled poig- nantly as she appeared on the arms of Michael Wilding, Mike Todd, Ed- die Fisher, and, eventually, Richard Burton. Her first Oscar, incidentally, was for a ho-hum performance in a terrible movie, *Butterfield 8,* in 1960.

call out, 'It's about time.'" While Hollywood was bowing low to Kate, an offstage drama began unfolding in the Navy blue halfworld behind the curtain. Before it was finished the staid Academy officers were gulping Valium like Life-Savers and reporters were running to the phones.

The man who caused all the trouble, Robert Opel, had no trouble getting backstage. His tuxedo was super-expensive, his black shoes were shined like a mirror, and he had the look of a dashing producer or at least a young director on the make. But most important, Opel had a bright yellow badge tacked onto his velvet lapel. That meant he was "V.I.P. Press" and not to be bothered in that Oscar fifth circle of Hell—the fighting, clawing press room. Somehow Opel used a big smile, matinee idol looks, and perhaps another badge to edge past a black ribbon that separated the news room from the murky darkness of the backstage. Nobody gave Opel a second glance, so he ducked behind a cellophane and papier-mâché stage set. Good, he thought, it's dark enough; just barely, but dark enough.

David Niven was just coming onstage. And the orchestra played "Around the World in Eighty Days," the theme from Niven's best known film. The Englishman acknowledged the applause, bowed in his Saville Row tuxedo, then began his fond introduction of the evening's second super-luminary, Elizabeth Taylor.

Opel had already slipped out of his coat and draped it over a prop. He slipped out of his shoes and unbuttoned his shirt.

A policeman walked by and Opel held his breath, waiting only a sec- ond before unzipping his pants and letting them fall to the floor. Then his briefs.

Niven was almost through when Opel, jogging in the arrogant strides of a cross country track man, burst into public view. There was a gasp; then a roar. David Niven let his guard's officer bearing drop long enough

"Now you see him . . ." The phantom streaker of the Oscars, Robert Opel, appears in the national television frames behind David Niven, who dismissed him with a few wry comments. Raquel Welch, however, was more impressed.

to almost stutter. But he immediately caught sight of the display on the big television monitor. "Isn't it fascinating that probably the only laugh this man will ever get in his life is by stripping off his clothes and showing his shortcomings."

Opel was gone by then. He had accomplished his "streak" so quickly and so smoothly that hundreds in the audience weren't sure what they had seen.

A flying wedge of security guards thundered into the backstage area with dazed looks on their faces. The streaker had simply vanished into murky darkness. They thought that Opel had sought sanctuary in a superstar's dressing room; maybe in Liz Taylor's.

But Opel had used the confusion to run, even faster, into the wings, around the back of the stage, and to the secure darkness of his set, which was shattered apart as the athletic Opel crashed through it.

"Hmm," said Raquel Welch, "must have been the Schlitz Malt Liquor bull. I'd like to meet him."

He was back in his pants and was fumbling with a shirt and cummerbund when a security guard found him and began hustling him into the rest of his clothes. To Opel it looked like a trip to the slammer. Then he was saved—by an Academy P.R. man. After all, you can't lock up the hit of the evening. Can you?

"What else can happen now?" asked a pristine young secretary from the Academy. "How could it have happened? Really, how could it?" And it was quite a good question. If Bob Opel could get backstage, shuck his clothes, run the 100-yard dash, and then climb back into his tux, then anyone could do it. The Oscar brass, it turned out, weren't at all interested in the streak. They were horrified at being caught with their press badges down. "We've got fifty of the world's most famous people backstage. I always felt they were completely safe—until now," said an Oscar chief. Academy flak Marty Cooper scurried to his master list of registered press. "We looked through all 500 credential certifications," he told producer Koch. "There's no Opel; not even anyone fitting that description."

Opel was suddenly the darling of the press; flash cameras caught his image for the world to see. "I have no official connection with the Academy," stuttered Opel, who seemed far more timid with his clothes on than he had in his tanned birthday suit. "Well, how the hell did you get in here?" asked a reporter from CBS. "Press badge," said Opel, shrugging a little. "Where is it?" asked the reporter. "Dunno," said Opel. And that might have been the end of "the case of the missing badge." "I crumpled it up, it must be somewhere backstage," said Opel. "What color was it?" "Yellow, sure, it was yellow," Opel answered, looking down on a sea of yellow press passes.

But a tall deputy sheriff was listening in. And he told another story. "I saw the guy when he first came backstage," said the cop. "He had a white badge. I'm sure it was white." The faces of the Oscar brass turned a collective shade of white. A white badge, they knew, was the most guarded commodity on Oscar night—going only to presenters, stars, and Academy officials. Still, that would explain the security breach—which in Washington would have been the equivalent of Watergate burglars in Roslyn Carter's bedroom.

Thus began the rumor that Opel's naked romp was staged by Oscar director Jack Haley, Jr. "No truth to that," said Opel. "I've got nothing to hide. But I'll tell you one thing, I'm not gonna say where I got the badge."

Then Opel smiled and ambled off into Oscar history. And if Jack Haley, Jr., had staged the spectre of a naked Oscar, he wasn't about to admit it. He only smiled a Cheshire cat smile as the 1974 Oscar show bumped other news off the front pages of papers around the world. "I got off light," he said to a Hollywood columnist. "This was just a bit of window dressing."

Right he was. In 1975, Howard Koch was back, and his backstage exploded into a battlefield for superstars.

Bert Schneider, a man who won the documentary Oscar, brought down the house when he thanked Hollywood for the Oscar and then took out a telegram sent that day from Hanoi. Thanks, America, said the wire. Thanks for liberating South Vietnam. As Schneider read the halting words, the celebrity audience was a bit slow on the uptake. Since Schneider had just accepted the Oscar for his controversial anti-Vietnam War film, *Hearts and Minds*, many people thought the producer was delivering his own sentiments.

There was no such confusion backstage. Bob Hope's face turned ruddy, Frank Sinatra's chin jutted out in hostility, and both men headed for Howard Koch. "This is too serious to let slide," Sinatra said. And Koch later remembered that Hope was furious. (One thing that gets overlooked often in the "Hearts and Minds Affair" is that Sinatra and Hope were merely speaking for thousands out in the audience.)

Hope began scrawling a message on a program with Sinatra adding a phrase here and there. They showed it to Koch, and he nodded his head. (Academy president Walter Mirisch was out in the audience and could not be consulted.)

"If you don't want to do it I WILL," said Hope. Sinatra just shook his head. "I'll do it," he said.

Actress Shirley MacLaine, also backstage, took immediate offense. She spit out a few words to Sinatra, a longtime buddy.

But the singer walked onstage and read the simple statement: "We are not responsible for any political references made on this program tonight. And we are sorry that they were made."

Shirley collared Sinatra the minute he came offstage. "Why did you do that?" she asked. "You said you were speaking on behalf of the Academy. Well, *I* am a member of the Academy."

"Well, did you agree with that telegram?" asked Sinatra.

"It seemed like a very positive, friendly telegram to me," she answered.

Sinatra, one of the most popular winners in the history of the awards, realized as perhaps nobody else did that night, that blatantly political outbursts like Schneider's would only lead the Oscar show into deeper and deeper political waters. (Network stations reported that the thousands of calls that came in were running at least three to one against Schneider's action.)

"The attempts to keep the world of rain and thunder out of the Academy work better some years than other," said Charles Champlin, in the *Los Angeles Times*. "This year the fact that Hollywood is sharply divided politically, as it always has been, slipped through the smooth, self-congratulatory surfaces."

There was a permanent hole, however, in Oscar's public relations dike. By April 3, 1978, on Oscar's fiftieth birthday celebration, the hole had become a crashing waterfall. The guys putting together the birthday show had their first bout of nerves when they realized that Vanessa Redgrave was the odds-on favorite to win the supporting award for *Julia*. Worse than that, Vanessa was flying into town to collect the award in person. Nerves were certainly in order. Miss Redgrave, a four time nominee (for *Mary, Queen of Scots, Morgan, Isadora,* and *Julia*), is one of the world's finest actresses. But she has never made for burpless Oscar banquets. To the Academy, she was Vanessa of the Hanoi headband, Vanessa the socialist candidate for Parliament, and Vanessa the free spirit. She brought down the house in the sixties when she showed up in a billowing sari with lantana blossoms intertwined with her flying red tresses. In 1978 she was better known for her recent film *The Palestinian*, a movie considered inflammatory and anti-Zionist. (Ironically, Miss Redgrave's nomination and eventual win was a triumph of mature thinking among the Academy's heavy Jewish voters.)

"It wasn't too hard to tell," said Gregg Kilday, a film writer for the *Los Angeles Times*, "that it was going to be a bumpy evening." Indeed. The Nazi storm troopers and growling members of the Jewish Defense League were hardly grouped outside to root for singer Debby Boone, whose appearance would, itself, become an international issue before the evening was over.

Finally, Vanessa arrived. She was in black—with her red hair catching the rays of a California sunset. She was neither unnerved nor upset by the chanting and hostility outside. In fact, the minute she saw what was going on, she began rewriting her acceptance speech in her head.

Then there were sirens! Forty policemen from ten divisions were rushed to the streets near the Los Angeles Music Center which, as the Oscar curtain went up, was turned into a battlefield for the JDL and the Neo-Nazis. Suddenly, in the dusk, two men rushed up to the steps of the theater, hoisted an elaborate effigy with flaming hair, and then set it afire. The sign dangling from the doll's feet said: "Vanessa Is a Murderer."

Into this maelstrom marched still a third little band—the Arabs, members of the Palestine Arab Fund. And their signs said, "Zionism Is Racism." The Los Angeles police S.W.A.T. troopers linked arms and began steering the 400 away from the theater and into isolated groups. But the disappearance of the press proved to be the final wet blanket, and the militants on all sides, seeing their chances of fame disappearing, hightailed it for home.

Oscar's only card-carrying socialist, Vanessa Redgrave. Her victory for *Julia* in 1978 was a tribute to the new liberality and objectivity of Academy voters—who had to walk through violent anti-Redgrave protestors outside the Los Angeles Music Center. The militants, members of the Jewish Defense League, were bitter over the actress's narration for a Palestine Liberation Organization documentary. Earlier traces of the Academy's open mind came with their recognition of the 1970 film *Woodstock* and the nominations given to the short film *Interviews With My Lai Veterans*.

The 1979 Academy Awards. Fans of actresses Jane Fonda and Bette Midler boosted their choices as the nominees filed into the Music Center.

If only, Howard Koch might have mused, it had ended there.

The problem would not disappear with a whimper. Vanessa won. And after her thanks, added: "You should be very proud that in the last few weeks you stood firm and you refused to be intimidated by the threats of a small bunch of Zionists whose behavior is an insult to the stature of Jews all over the world and to their great and heroic . . ." And on, and on, and on.

Even if it had ended there, the Academy would still have had much to be thankful for. No such luck. Playwright Paddy Chayefsky couldn't resist mounting the soapbox to say, "I'm sick and tired of people using the occasion of the Academy Awards for the propagation of their own political propaganda. . . . I'd like to suggest to Miss Redgrave that her winning an Academy Award is not a pivotal moment in history. A simple Thank You would have been sufficient."

Paddy was so overcome with the love of his own voice and words that he completely forgot to read the names of the winners whose Oscar he was presenting. "These winners might have wished Mr. Chayefsky to have read their names," said a columnist. "Maybe it wasn't a big thing to him (Paddy), but it surely was to them."

Then came Debby Boone in virgin white, singing "You Light up My Life," as cloyingly sweet a song as the Oscarcast had seen in many a year. Daddy Pat Boone and his wife Shirley sat out in the audience, holding hands, saying wow and fighting the tears. To make it even more touching, Debby was surrounded—like Dorothy and the munchkins, with darling ten-year-old girls who interpreted the song in sign language. And within minutes there wasn't a dry eye in the house.

Bob Hope stepped out and announced in an awesome whisper that the girls were from the John Tracy Clinic, named for the deaf son of Oscar

© A.M.P.A.S.

Best actor Jon Voight, best actress Jane Fonda, and best director Michael Cimino greet four hundred of the world's reporters with their Oscars in hand. This picture notwithstanding, it was not all cookies and milk backstage. Neither the *Coming Home* alumni nor *The Deer Hunter* veterans could contain their animosity, and Cimino, at one point, pulled away from Fonda. Still later best supporting actor Christopher Walken of *The Deer Hunter* said, "I'm glad I beat him," referring to Bruce Dern of *Coming Home*, his major competition. Oscar had come light-years since 1944 when the winner, *The Best Years of Our Lives*, was cheered by a unanimous audience—many of them, like Clark Gable, still in World War II uniforms.

winner Spencer Tracy. Who could top that? Right?

The Academy quickly found out as the first calls began jamming the switchboards of the network. The sign language, as it turned out, was basically inept. And the deaf members of the audience picked it up. Oscar officers had to shamefacedly admit that the girls were not deaf and that they had come from the Sam Levy public school in nearby Torrance. "After all," said a P.R. spokesman for the Academy, "nobody actually *said* the children were really deaf. And a doctor at the Tracy Clinic *did* recruit them."

"But we're offended," said the president of a newly founded Alliance for Deaf Artists. "Because we have many, many deaf children who could have done the same thing if only they'd been given the opportunity. What happened on the Oscar show was really the last straw in that it represented the industry's traditional misrepresentation of the deaf."

The Academy blushed collectively and began looking hopefully ahead to 1979.

But 1978 was the year the movies finally came to grips with the Vietnam War; it was a case of better late than never. The fact that Jane Fonda had to fight for six years to scrape together the cash to film *Coming Home* speaks for itself. Hollywood was afraid of Vietnam films and more afraid of the ultraconservative audiences who might boycott them. But *Coming Home* with Fonda and Jon Voight, and Michael Cimino's *The Deer Hunter* with Meryl Streep and Robert De Niro broke the Vietnam embargo. They were fine movies, and the public lined up to see them. Both had fat parcels of nominations, and *The Deer Hunter* was the two-to-one favorite to win the big one—best picture of 1978. These odds were well earned. Academy voters were wined, dined, and wooed by Universal Pictures in the most cold-blooded and calculated campaign since the one for *Gone With the Wind*.

The fact that neither film needed help was of no consequence to the fearful Hollywood executives. They had learned to their distress and heartburn that a good campaign for a lousy picture could easily get it a nomination over the really great film. Columbia Pictures for instance had achieved an Oscar nomination for the dreadful *Oliver!* at the expense of one of the finest films ever made, Stanley Kubrick's *2001: A Space Odyssey.* Even worse was the fact that *Oliver!* was named best picture of the year.

But the $250,000-plus campaign for *The Deer Hunter* blazed new trails of hype in a town gorged on public relations. From the day the film was finished until the night it won the Oscar, the studio made no move that was not geared toward the Academy's 2,700 voters. Universal even turned to Tinseltown's king of hype, Alan Carr, producer of that celluloid bit of bubble gum, *Grease.* Carr's orders were to sell the movie, and to sell it by first winning the Oscar. First, Carr had to see the movie. He says he came away from his private screening "crying like a baby. Why, I was crying so hard I had to go to the men's room and put cold water on my face. I was having dinner with Governor Brown that night, and I was so emotionally undone I had to apologize personally to Jerry Brown." Carr told the Gov, "I've been affected so deeply I just can't speak tonight."

Carr left a trail of salt water all the way to the offices of those entertainment bibles, *Daily Variety* and the *Hollywood Reporter.* But he was certainly dry-eyed when he designed lavish supplements to those papers loaded with color stills from the film and heavily burdened down with positive reviews of *The Deer Hunter.* Special editions of the ads were immediately mailed to the homes of Academy members. Billboards soaring above Hollywood's Sunset Boulevard blazed in the winter sun—with a minimum of message. "I sensed right away that this is an 'event' movie. It's not *Grease* where it's ninety minutes in and out and turn over the box office grosses," Carr told a Los Angeles columnist. So Carr waited until the hype in New York and Hollywood neared hysteria and then opened the film for eight showings in L.A.'s university suburb, Westwood, and in Manhattan. "I knew it would be the Christmas cocktail party subject in New York," said Carr. "Everybody would be asking if you were one of the 500 people who saw one of the eight shows? They said to me, 'You can't give a film to New York and then just take it right away.' I answered, 'That's how you treat New York.'"

The opening of *The Deer Hunter* in Westwood is now legend. People mobbed the box office and everybody who was ANYBODY bombarded Universal with requests for "house tickets." Betty Bacall asked; so did Charlton Heston and Rudolph Nureyev. "Imagine everybody's reaction when we told them, There aren't any. We're saving this film for the Academy."

It worked! The members of the Academy of Motion Picture Arts and Sciences took the bait like underfed trout in the Colorado River. Universal royally used all its Oscar screening time to virtually guarantee that there was a time to fit the schedule of even the busiest Oscar voter. The studio even put a full time staff member at the door, carefully counting the number of voters showing their Academy cards to get in. The final tally was 2,400 of the 2,700 eligible voters. (This voter turnout is almost unheard of; most studios estimate that only twenty-five to forty percent of the Oscar voters see any given film.)

Carr believes the campaign was helped greatly by opening the film out of town. "L.A. is jaded and spoiled by the movies. At previews in Westwood they cheer for Telly Savalas chasing an airplane."

Then Carr scheduled a golden circle showing with an audience of two—directors Steven Spielberg (*Jaws* and *Close Encounters*) and Vincente Minnelli

Jon Voight, here with Jane Fonda in the wheelchair love scene from *Coming Home,* was eventually considered picture perfect casting as the bitter paraplegic hero of the anti-war film. In reality, he only got the part after Jack Nicholson and Sylvester Stallone turned it down. It wasn't that Voight's name didn't come up; Fonda had early mentioned him as ideal due to his close ties to veterans protesting the war. "They said they would rather pay another million dollars to get a star," says the film's producer Jerome Hellman. "Hal Ashby (the director) and I fought for him, and U.A. finally relented. But they told us it was entirely our responsibility. It was a chance we gladly took."

Meryl Streep and Robert De Niro in *The Deer Hunter,* which drew more overt protests from the public than any other Oscar-winning film. The Vietnam Veterans Against the War formed themselves into a censuring Greek chorus outside the Academy Awards show—cheering for Jane Fonda and hissing at *Deer Hunter* director Michael Cimino. But inside, Cimino said his film was "not even really about the war. The war is really incidental to the story—it's just a part of the characters' lives. The war was just a means of testing their courage and will power. But it could just as easily have been the Civil War." In another bit of Oscar irony, Jon Voight, who has long courted the press, was a popular best actor winner—thanking the international movie reporters as "my uncles and aunts." Yet there was a disturbing feeling among the press that justice had not been done. "It was silent but it was there," said Lee Grant, a film writer for the *Los Angeles Times,* "that vague knowledge that De Niro had given the best performance of the year."

(*An American in Paris* and *Gigi*). The young lion (Spielberg) and the old master (Minnelli) represented the two opposite polls of the powerful Directors Guild of America. When Carr bundled his select audience into the screening room, the D.G.A. Awards were only a week or two away. And Carr was obviously relying on his audience to be impressed and to spread the word. (For most of the past twenty years the director winning the D.G.A. has also directed the film ultimately winning the Oscar.) Right on target! *The Deer Hunter*'s Cimino was quickly named director of the year—an honor he would have undoubtedly won in any case.

Analyzing the strategy, the *Los Angeles Times* noted, "The making of the campaign for *The Deer Hunter* is a case study of what happens when a major studio incorporates a run for the Oscar into its overall marketing strategy for a commercially shaky film. And eight months ago *The Deer Hunter* was both a box office long shot and an Oscar dark horse.

"Carr's campaign seemed to have pinpointed timing and strategies of exposure. He was backed by the highest levels at Universal, who obviously counted on the Oscar to help them with a very tough marketing job."

But Carr hastened to add: "Of course, none of this would have worked if we hadn't had a brilliant film." (Many Oscar watchers worry that the strategy will spread to films that aren't quite so worthy, creating an entirely new way to buy the Oscar.)

So that's how *The Deer Hunter* came into the Oscar arena with a two-to-one shot. The film's only real competition, Jane Fonda's *Coming Home*, a soap opera about one woman's odyssey into the soul of a handicapped veteran of the war in Vietnam, was an odds-on favorite to take the two best acting awards (with Bruce Dern a dark horse for best supporting actor).

Unfortunately, Vietnam also dominated the streets and sidewalks outside the Music Center as members of Vietnam Veterans against the War, the Association of Vietnamese Patriots, and the "We Won't Go Away Committee" came to cheer Fonda and boo Cimino. *The Deer Hunter*, they claimed, was pro-war and anti-vet. Their placards—"No Oscar for Racism," "*The Deer Hunter* Is a Dirty Lie," and "Profit Is Their Holy Word"—were waved above the limos as Robin Williams, Christopher Reeve, and Donna Summer alighted and headed through Hollywood's golden arches. The protests were echoed inside in a chilly feud between the *Coming Home* Oscar winners and *The Deer Hunter* champs.

Lee Grant, one of the major film writers for the *Los Angeles Times*, was backstage from the first shout to the last yawn. And his description allows for a rare view from behind Oscar's curtain of hype: "Like everybody else, working or not, you root silently (and some reporters even openly) for the pictures you want to win. I was happy for *The Deer Hunter*, but I thought Robert De Niro gave the performance of a lifetime in the same film. But Jon Voight won. The reporters backstage whooped and hollered for Voight, who is popular with the press—if you remember, he called the Hollywood Foreign Press reporters, 'my aunts and uncles' when they gave him the Golden Globe. Backstage, however, Voight was soapy and even maudlin, 'I accept this for every guy in a wheelchair,' he said."

According to Lee Grant, Fonda's competitiveness apparently ran away with her tact. "She shimmied out on the press stage with her Oscar to her bosom; called the demonstrators outside 'My friends. . . . I know those people out there. They know a lot about Vietnam, and *The Deer Hunter* delivers the Pentagon's view of Vietnam.'"

Then Fonda said to the world, "Our picture (*Coming Home*) was better." But earlier Fonda had told Lee Grant, and others, that she hadn't even seen *The Deer Hunter*.

Television's Rona Barrett who, along with Charles Champlin of the *Los Angeles Times*, is one of the few voices of conscience by constantly policing the silliness and inequities of the balloting. Barrett, known to her peers as a top investigative journalist, not a gossip columnist, says she can count "on one hand the actors who have truly 'risked themselves' enough to deserve the Oscar." Backstage on Oscar night, Rona asks the questions many reporters are afraid of, such as her demand of *Midnight Express* scriptwriters: "Why did you cheapen the original and true story—and depart from the truth?"

"Michael Cimino, who also won the Oscar as best director, was on the same press stage with Fonda and Voight," said Grant. "He all but ignored them. A quiet man, whose upcoming *Heaven's Gate* is supposed to be brilliant, he said, 'I'm puzzled by those demonstrators. *The Deer Hunter* was not intended as a political film. It was an anti-war film. This (the Academy) is a good place to remember that we are moviemakers and are not trying to recreate newsreels.'"

The sparks of bad feeling between the *Coming Home* gang and Cimino's guys erupted again when *The Deer Hunter*'s Christopher Walken walked off with the Oscar for best supporting actor. Of Bruce Dern, his competitor, Walken said, "I'm glad I beat him."

Grant believes that Fonda was a popular winner among the press "because she's always good for a quote. However, professionally, most reporters felt the best performance of the year was Geraldine Page's in Woody Allen's *Interiors*, followed by Jill Clayburgh's in *An Unmarried Woman*.

Grant also offers a unique view of Rona Barrett, whose public voice is probably the second most influential among the film community establishment. (The most powerful voice is Charles Champlin's of the *Los Angeles Times*, whose calm, steady pleas for more objective voting have virtually revolutionized the Academy and its voting practices.) Rona, says Grant, functions as a sort of journalistic duenna and is a woman all the winners will have to face down sooner or later.

"Seated away from other TV reporters is the diminutive Rona," says Grant. "She loves these situations, to be mixing with other journalists and waiting for the stars to recognize her. Occasionally during the minor award winners, she'll slip away into the press reception room for a cup of coffee and a chat with other reporters. She can, of course, be a tough questioner. She hated *Midnight Express*, and when its screenwriter, Oliver Stone, walked into the interview room, Rona railed against him for writing an exploitive film." (Stone had, for one reason or another, wrought havoc on Billy Hayes' incredible true story of years in a Mideast prison for dope smuggling.)

A year later, in 1980, with Grant backstage watching, Rona Barrett leaped right into the middle of the Academy-wide dissension over Dustin Hoffman's *Kramer vs. Kramer*. "The film was not a particularly popular winner with the press corps as a whole," says Grant. "The reasons are not clear. But I think most of them knew that *Apocalypse Now* (Francis Coppola's saga of the Vietnam War) was a better picture.

"Dustin and Rona got into a verbal wrestling match," said Grant. "Hoffman, after making his speech about competition among actors (see Chapter One) defended *Kramer vs. Kramer* from Rona's charge that it was a soap opera and anti-feminist in nature. At one point, Dustin came down off the podium and put his head in her lap. He looked up at her and said, 'Well, the soap opera won.'" This is especially coy and cute of Hoffman who, a decade earlier, had publicly called the Academy Awards a "grotesque circus," ridiculous and outdated. Ah, the wages of youth; Hoffman was only thirty then.

Later, supporting actress winner Meryl Streep took over the *Kramer vs. Kramer* banner, saying, "I'm a feminist, and I don't think the picture is anti-feminist at all."

Grant says, "Meryl Streep was a very popular winner backstage. Earlier, after winning the Oscar, she just charmed everybody. 'How does it feel?' someone asked her. 'Incomparable,' she answered. 'I'm trying to hear your questions above my heartbeat.'"

The clothing of the winners and those who present them their awards

can also create controversy. "We had to have a crash crew backstage to make sure presenters didn't sneak onstage with irregular attire," says Edith Head, who guided the show's costumes for more than two decades. "I had three seamstresses, a prop man with a can of spray to dim the diamonds, and a large box of 'cleavage covers.' These last were the most important. We found we just couldn't trust our superstars who are about to go onstage. After their gowns were approved, some stars would have the cleavage enlarged just before going onstage. At the last minute, however, we would pull out of the emergency kit a yard of tulle or a big flower to match the costume. A couple of times we had to just sew a star's midriff up."

The superstars spent months preparing their gowns, says Head. "I remember Joan Crawford, who was a super-perfectionist, had me design the identical dress for her in both light and dark material so that in the event the star presented before her had changed, Joan could also make the shift. And it happened. Joan rushed back into her dressing room, changed to the lighter gown, and was the hit of the evening."

Princess Grace of Monaco (when she was still only Grace Kelly) created a world fashion when she was a presenter in 1954. Grace was on the set at Paramount until only thirty minutes before the ceremony. She ran through the lot to the hairdressers and had them pin up her hair. But it fell as her limo rounded a sharp corner in downtown Los Angeles. "Somebody had given Grace a lovely bunch of pink roses," said Miss Head, "so she calmly pinned up her hair, stuck a rose over her ear and, presto—a new fashion was born."

In 1957 Joanne Woodward accepted her award for *The Three Faces of Eve* in a dress she had made herself on an apartment sewing machine. "I knew I didn't have a chance to win. So I didn't want to invest a lot of money in a dress." In 1956 one of the show's emcees, Jerry Lewis, reported backstage wearing a custom-made blue shirt, complete with midnight blue studs and ruffles. NBC had already decided that blue shirts were taboo because of the glare factor. "I had only two hours to make a shirt, vest, and high collar," said Sy Devore, who is often called "tailor to the stars." "Five of us working just managed to get it finished by curtain time." Devore came dashing in the back door and deposited his creation in Lewis' dressing room.

But the funniest backstage disaster came in 1972 when the show had to open without its host, Charlton Heston, which is the equivalent of a Vatican Mass minus the Pope. Thirty seconds before the Oscar show opened, a director, searching through the audience for a superstar equivalent of Heston, grabbed Clint Eastwood by the arm and pulled him backstage. "I couldn't even find or see the cue cards," said Eastwood later. "And Heston wasn't just a presenter; he was one of the four hosts."

"Clint Eastwood looked as if someone had pushed him from the wings," said *Time* magazine. Eastwood gave his *Dirty Harry* look, hooked his thumbs in his coat pockets, and growled, "This isn't my bag, man." And Heston suddenly burst through the backstage entrance in the Music Center. He ran a comb through his hair, mopped some perspiration off his face, and strode onstage like Moses with his stone tablets.

The superstar had had a flat on the Hollywood Freeway. Heston leaped out of his car and began running down the offramp—a pretty achievement in a tuxedo so tight he could barely sit down. But he made it without a wrinkle or a speck of dust on his shoes.

"Most presenters would crawl to the ceremony if they had to," said a P.R. spokesman for the Oscar ceremony. "It can mean as much as $100,000 more a year from the exposure alone. Why, Ann-Margret was discovered singing a minor medley."

Edith Head, the lady who dressed Hollywood, surrounded by some of her Oscars. More than Bob Hope or Charlton Heston, more than Liz Taylor or Ingrid Bergman, Edith Head had been responsible for the panache of glamour surrounding the Academy Awards. Nominated for thirty-two best costume Oscars, Miss Head was called in to advise the Academy the first year the awards were televised; and she advised the Oscar stars for more than twenty-five years—sometimes recreating dresses for "underdressed" stars only minutes before they went onstage. One year she designed two identical gowns for Joan Crawford—one black and one beige so that Joan had the option of changing in case her predecessor onstage were wearing black like her or vice-versa. "And she needed the gowns," said Miss Head. "She was ready to go onstage in the black when she looked up and saw the same color on a rival. She changed quickly into the identical beige and stole the evening."

Mr. and Mrs. Charlton Heston arriving at the 1971 Oscars—Heston displaying a superbody in a tux that caused the Society of Man Watchers to term his Oscar appearances "one of the world's few sensual and virile monuments left in the male world." Arriving at one awards ceremony in the mid-seventies, Heston was greeted by a chorus of lovely girls in black leotards who chanted "Hubba-Hubba." Heston, who won the Oscar for *Ben-Hur*, became such a fixture on the show that the mere hint of a no-show often threw the Oscar producers into an advanced peptic state. And then there was the minute in 1974 when he arrived late—forcing fellow superstar Clint Eastwood to take on unexpected hosting duties.

Perhaps this interest comes from the enormous audience worldwide. Last year, more than 300 million people saw the Oscar show—or parts of it. It even goes to Nepal on videotape flown direct from Los Angeles. ABC, which has the Oscar contract, is fully aware of this exposure, charging a record $200,000 a minute to advertisers.

The presenter selection process, with its possible conflicts of interest between producers and public relations executives, has never been questioned. But in 1980 a young investigative reporter, Andrew Epstein, completely dissected the stars handing out the Oscars, asking, "How did you get the job? And why?" His conclusions, printed the day before the Oscars, created havoc and panic backstage. Some stars discussed in the article called the *Los Angeles Times*, threatening to stay off the show if retractions were not printed. Epstein's facts, however, held up, and everyone, some of them pouting, made their grand entrances.

Howard Koch, again producer of the show, told Epstein, "Every press agent, manager, and agent I know calls me. Some with good ideas, others to promote someone with a picture opening just to get the exposure." Jack Haley, Jr., a frequent director of the show, said, "You're on your own to cast the show, but I'm constantly besieged by publicists and agents; I've been constantly amazed by some of those they pitched. I'd have thought that some of those people were dead by now."

Sometimes the network carrying the show foists troubled TV stars into the presenters' list. The most blatant example was Robert Blake, whom ABC asked Koch to put on the show. (Blake was then starring in ABC's "Baretta.") "I got a call from someone at ABC," Koch told Epstein. "He said, 'Look, I've never asked you for a favor. . . .' On show day, he [Blake] shows up with a beard and a dirty pair of sneakers. The person from ABC assured me that everything would be okay by the time of the show. That

When it came time for the 1974 curtain to go up, and the backstage crew went on a substitute superstar search, Heston was actually jogging through the dust and muck at the edge of the Hollywood Freeway—the victim of an inopportune flat tire. His going was hindered by rush hour traffic and the cut of his traditionally skin tight tux pants—ready to burst with each of his athletic strides. In the Music Center, Clint Eastwood was too close at hand for frantic producers to overlook, and they shoved him onstage without a word of advice. It was then that Eastwood discovered that he had to open the whole show. His face grimaced, and he finally held up his arms: "This just isn't my bag, man." Several seconds later, like in so many of his movies, Charlton Heston arrived like the cavalry and rescued Clint.

night, he comes in with a big eccentric tuxedo and smoking a big cigar."

Epstein looked a bit deeper and uncovered a bit of Oscarcast nepotism: Presenter Patrick Wayne, for instance, was hosting a syndicated TV show being produced by Marty Pasetta, director of the Academy Award show. "Nobody is going to believe us," said Koch. "But it was my idea to put Patrick on the show, not Marty's. I was in Marty's office one day, saw a picture of Patrick, and thought it would be a good idea to use him. People want to see John Wayne's son. They want to see the son of a great actor." Another presenter, Robert Hays, was starring in *Airplane!*—which was produced by Howard Koch. Likewise Kristy McNichol, also a presenter, was in *Airplane!* (The way the Oscar show was set up, McNichol and Hays, stars of the Koch movie, were also paired as presenters on the show.)

The most infamous "presenter scandal" occurred in 1973 when the Academy, with much fanfare, announced that Mark Spitz would present one of the major awards that year.

The news flashed around the world. A London newspaper doctored an old Spitz swim photograph showing the Olympic swimmer in his quite brief tank trunks holding an Oscar in one hand. A New York newspaper produced an editorial cartoon showing Spitz in a huge pool, holding an Oscar over his head. The caption said, "And now for the best performance by a swimmer doing the breaststroke. . . ."

The decision to have Mark Spitz hand out an Oscar ranks as one of the most blatant examples of misuse of the Oscar show in Academy history. At that time, Spitz had retired from the chlorine and was living the life of a budding movie and TV star in a swank apartment in Marina del Rey. The dashing water baby had just signed a contract with Norman Brokaw, a wizard of cash and hype employed by the world's largest talent agency,

Paramount on Parade. Rock Hudson, John Wayne (while filming his award-winning *True Grit*), Yves Montand, Lee Marvin, Robert Evans, Bernard Donnenfeld, and Clint Eastwood welcome Barbra Streisand to the Paramount lot.

Intercontinental lover Warren Beatty has given the super-puritanical Academy some rough moments as his ladies nearly collided backstage. Rex Reed, for instance, spent a hilarious hour one night tracing the Oscar crew's attempts to keep Beatty and his lady of the moment, Leslie Caron, from getting next to each other. Beatty, an intense actor on and offstage, seems to generally terrorize the Oscar crew with his looks, unpredictability, and way with the ladies.

Grace Kelly kisses her Oscar for best actress in *The Country Girl*, as her co-star William Holden, looks on amusedly. Miss Kelly's gown was designed especially for the Oscar ceremony by Edith Head.

William Morris. The *Los Angeles Times* commented that Spitz was "being merchandised like a chunk of plastic livestock." The water boy had recently signed a multi-million-dollar contract with Schick. And a Mark Spitz poster (showing him grinning in briefs so tiny the poster sold $500,000 worth in gay specialty shops) guaranteed Spitz fifteen cents for each copy sold. Brokaw told *Sports Illustrated* that his soggy client would make TV specials and, eventually, movies, "when the suitable vehicle comes along." It only stood to reason that an appearance on the Oscar show would remind Hollywood (and the rest of the world) that a male Esther Williams was ripe for the picking.

This time, it didn't work. Spitz had already shown up as a lightweight on a TV variety show—his wooden, arrogant manner caused national derision. And the Academy was bombarded with protests over the pending Spitz appearance. Art Sarno, longtime publicist for the Academy Awards, recalled that an equally powerful fuss was made by people within the film industry. What's he have to do with movies? asked the community. And Mark Spitz was forced to stroke his way back to the pool.

On February 15, 1973, Spitz publicly withdrew in special written statements to the *Los Angeles Times*, the *Hollywood Reporter*, and *Daily Variety*. Spitz said, "I told the Academy the honor of being a presenter should be reserved for people who have contributed to the motion picture industry."

Still, William Morris, even in the face of this evidence, continues to claim that Spitz *did* make an appearance on the March, 1972, Academy Awards. A spokesman (Brokaw) told Andrew Epstein: "Uproar? I don't recall an uproar. Mark appeared on the show. I remember this because Mark didn't have a tuxedo—he had plenty of swimsuits though—and we went to a tailor that Howard Koch recommended."

A search of the videotapes of the Oscarcast shows no appearance by Mark Spitz.

But maybe, like streaker Robert Opel's, Spitz' appearance was just too brief to notice.

By 1975 Mark Spitz's motion picture and television career was a national joke. For instance, Bea Arthur, television's "Maude," built a show around the line: "And Mark Spitz will drink a glass of milk on this very stage." And Carol Burnett spoofed the water baby by having Lyle Waggoner in a couple of ounces of tank suit—appearing on a talk show with his own dairy case. But he was still unpasteurized enough in 1974 for the powerful William Morris Agency to wangle an invitation for Mark to present one of the Oscars—a showcase bound to help the agents find the swimmer a movie role. It was announced to Hollywood on February 13, 1974—and retracted only a day later after an industry-wide uproar. It was one thing for Mickey Mouse to hand out an Oscar or, more recently, for Miss Piggy and Artoo-Detoo to serve as presenters. They, after all, were movie stars—however artificial. Bowing out, Spitz told the *Hollywood Reporter,* "I think the honor of being a presenter should be reserved for those who have contributed to the motion picture industry." Ah . . . if only that were so.

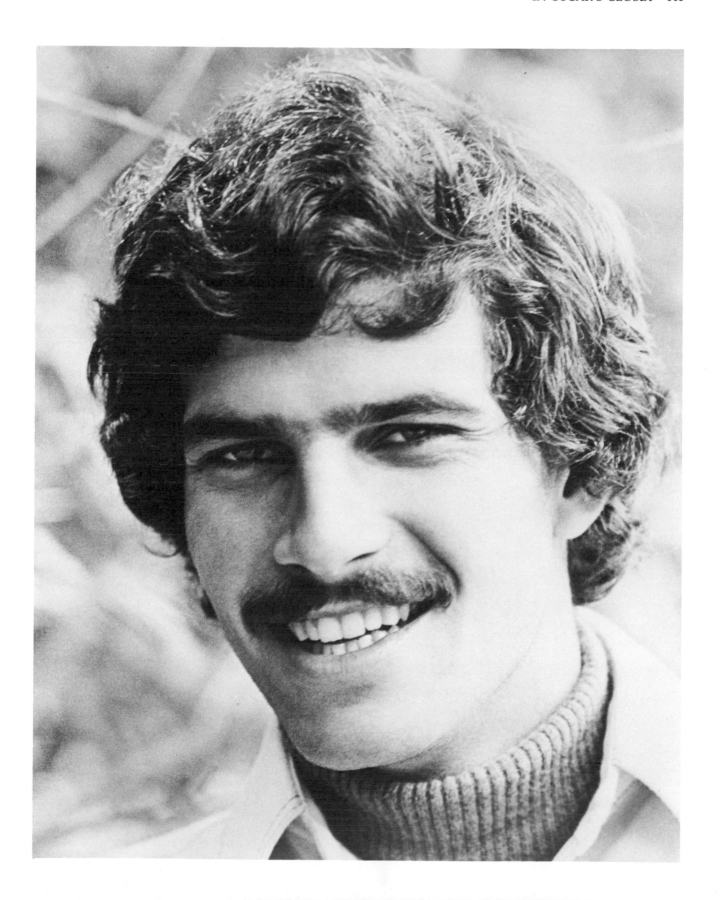

MILKING THE OSCAR TREE

"What's all this fuss over John Wayne's Oscar ads? People have been buying Oscars for at least twenty-five years."
Hedda Hopper.

John Wayne was mighty satisfied as he picked up the afternoon papers on February 27, 1961. A broad grin spread across his face. *The Alamo*, his mediocre tribute to American freedom, was nominated for six Academy Awards, including the big one—best picture of 1960.

Hollywood hadn't wanted the picture made in the first place. But "the big guy" (that's what they called Wayne in those days) had bullied, shoved, and pleaded until several studio financiers gave him the go-ahead. Even then, Wayne had to pour his entire fortune, almost a million dollars, into his opus about Jim Bowie, Davy Crockett (played by Wayne), and other Texas heroes.

In CinemaScope and patriot-color, *The Alamo* opened to reviews that can only be described as "lukewarm" (by Wayne fans) and derisive (by more honest moviegoers). The Duke had directed the film himself so the Hollywood elite said polite things, such as, "It seems like the work of a veteran director not a newcomer," and, "We knew he had it in him."

The voices weren't strong enough for Wayne; somewhere along the line he began to feel that Hollywood owed him an Oscar for *The Alamo*. He had, after all, dreamed of making his personal celluloid testimony for more than a decade. So it galled him when Tinseltown's artistic elite called it a "nice little picture," nice but pale compared to the other masterpieces made in 1960: *Psycho, Inherit the Wind, Exodus, Spartacus*, and others.

Those movies were all part of the town's incessant "Oscar talk." *The Alamo* was not. Wayne decided that the situation was not only unfair—it was downright unpatriotic. Jetting in from Rome, he faced down some reporters at the airport and barked: "This isn't the first time the Alamo has been the underdog. We need defenders today just as they did one hundred twenty-five years ago." But reporters were growing tired of Wayne's blind encomiums on his picture, and the actor saw his remarks twisted out of context.

Hollywood folks just weren't getting the message, so Wayne picked up the phone and called superpublicist Russell Birdwell, the man who had created the hysteria over David O. Selznick's *Gone With the Wind* (using the

Joan Crawford and Humphrey Bogart arriving at Romanoff's for the 1954 nominations telecast.

Scarlett O'Hara search and other techniques). Birdwell was never a man to rate the artistic value of any of the movies he hyped, and Wayne gave him enough money to exceed even the high costs of past Oscar campaigns.

The publicist already knew that an Oscar nomination and perhaps even the Oscar itself could be bought. Who should know better than the publicists? Out of an Academy membership of about 2,000 in 1960, more than 200 were publicists and executives for large public relations companies (200 more were studio executives, 100 were administrators, 150 were producers, 250 were writers, 150 were directors, 175 were "at large" members, 125 produced short subjects, and the rest were actors).

"A few hundred votes, and sometimes as few as twenty-five or fifty, one way or the other, could determine the winner," said Henry Rogers, founder of Rogers and Cowan Public Relations and a veteran of dozens of successful Oscar campaigns. "The Academy Awards are more of a popularity contest than a talent contest," said Rogers. "Whether Hollywood likes to face up to it or not, the voter casts his ballot emotionally, and not critically. Unable to decide which performance he feels is best, he allows his emotions to take over—he has no choice."

John Wayne and Russell Birdwell decided to work this emotion up to a fever pitch. They started with a press release, the likes of which had never been seen before (even in Hollywood). It ran for 183 pages, positively dripped with sugary adjectives, and depicted Wayne as the George Washington of films, storming the celluloid heights for God and country.

Then came the ads—hundreds of them. Every day Hollywood opened up the movie trade papers (*Daily Variety* and the *Hollywood Reporter*), to find new ads, full page and with fist-sized headlines.

The ad campaign didn't stop with asking the Oscar voters to consider *The Alamo*. It soon acquired a bullying tone. And the message was simple: If you don't vote for *The Alamo*, you're not patriotic.

The Hollywood writers, used as they were to such drivel, kept silent at first. But it finally got too bad—even for them. "The implication is unmistakable," said Dick Williams, entertainment editor of the *Los Angeles Mirror*. "Oscar voters are being appealed to on a patriotic basis. The impression is left that one's proud sense of Americanism may be suspected if one does not vote for *The Alamo*."

He made a public appeal, asking Wayne to stop. "Obviously," said Williams, "you can be the most ardent of American patriots and still believe that *The Alamo* is a mediocre film."

John Wayne was just waiting for this signal. He assaulted the Oscar beachhead as if it were Iwo Jima. The ads were doubled and became even stronger. "Oscar will make up his own mind," said one headline. One ad which ran for several days personally attacked columnist Williams, depicting him as a scandal sheet writer.

Williams figured the cost of "*The Alamo* Campaign" at "over $75,000 and probably as much as $150,000." Some Academy officers were insulted; but many more were not. Because it worked. *The Alamo* brought in six nominations. It was listed as one of the five best picture nominees, along with *The Apartment, Elmer Gantry, Sons and Lovers*, and *The Sundowners*. Edged out by the blatant campaign were *Psycho, Sunrise at Campobello, Never on Sunday, Inherit the Wind, Dark at the Top of the Stairs, Exodus,* and *Spartacus*.

The Wayne-Birdwell campaign remains the low point of the Oscar derby to this day. Then and now, it's hard to explain.

Maurice Zolotow, Wayne's principal biographer (*Shooting Star*), believes that Wayne was exhausted and pursued by demons after the *Alamo* experience. "He had gone through a terrible and lengthy journey to get to

"It's up to Oscar" This ad, which ran during the shameless Oscar campaigning of 1961, brought loud guffaws from the tables in Beverly Hills's bistros, since it capped a year-long campaign to gain an Oscar nomination for John Wayne's overlong, overblown film *The Alamo*. But the advertising worked and the film took home a bushel basket of Oscar nominations. There is some evidence that the campaign may not have even been necessary. The Wayne-directed movie was generally respected for his deft handling of the colossal battle footage.

This ridiculous tombstone—predicting the death of Hollywood—appeared in the *Hollywood Reporter* as part of an ad package that intimated that even God considered this film (*The Alamo*) the best ever made. But Wayne and his publicist Russell Birdwell didn't stop with the trade papers. They issued a 200-page press release and strung a banner across Sunset Boulevard which read, "This is the most important motion picture ever made. It's timeless. It will run forever."

HOLLYWOOD ✝

BORN 1907 A.D. – DIED 3000 A.D.

When the motion picture industry's epitaph is written – what will it say?

Will another civilization, coming upon the ruins, find something of worth: a spool of film spelling out a great dream? Or a sequence that merely featured a sex measurement or an innuendo that "got by" the censors?

Will there be left behind, for the ages to come, an enduring screen literature that played a vital role in the twentieth century?

Or do you care?

The sincere and the dedicated do care.

This includes every man and woman who contributed to the making of "The Alamo."

They believe that the motion picture is the greatest force for good or evil the communications sphere has ever known.

The sincere and dedicated throughout the industry have used it for good.

They know that inexorable evolution will some-day, perhaps by 3000 A.D., replace the present-day magic of celluloid in a manner not yet born in the ivory towers of those devoted to the science of obsolescence.

But an obituary will come, an epitaph will be written.

What will it say – or, do you care?

It was the money men who tried to make John Wayne appear to be an actor of great range and enormous reputation. Wayne himself, realizing how closely his world image was built around his own reality, said, "I always play myself—no matter the role. . . . That's the reason I became a star." When John Wayne actually got the Oscar for *True Grit*, it was another chapter in Oscar's continuing book of giving Academy Awards not for performances but for careers. But a couple of years later Wayne actually gave one of the screen's great performances in a much underrated film, *The Shootist*. This time, typically enough, the Academy ignored him.

John Wayne and Chill Wills on the location set for *The Alamo* in Brackettville, Texas. Many Texans and thousands of vacationing Americans turned out to watch as one of the great legends directed his own film. What they found was a man of large humor acting very little like a director and much like the guy next door. It was sad, therefore, when the Oscar campaign made a laughingstock of this achievement. A great fear seems to be abroad during Oscar time—a fear that says advertise or perish.

the place where, finally, the film was up for the Oscar. He was physically and mentally at the end of his tether. He was overwhelmed by debts and everything he owned was mortgaged for the money he had raised to make the film."

If Wayne's own Oscar campaign was deplorable, one of his stars, Chill Wills, made it much worse. Wills had been in Hollywood since 1935, playing his down home, corn pone character in film after film. He decided *The Alamo* was his chance. His personal Oscar campaign even outdid Wayne's, culminating in a double truck ad listing by name hundreds of Academy voters. "Win, lose, or draw," said the ad, "you're still my cousins and I love you all." Groucho Marx replied with his own ad: "Dear Mr. Wills, "I am delighted to be your cousin, but I'm voting for Sal Mineo."

Then Wills decided to call on God. Under a picture of the entire *Alamo* cast, Wills wrote, "We of *The Alamo* cast are praying—harder than the real Texans prayed for their lives at the Alamo—for Chill Wills to win the Oscar. . . . Cousin Chill's acting was great. Your Alamo cousins."

John Wayne, finally waking up to the excess he had helped create, took out a personal ad in the *Reporter* and *Variety.* The actor admitted that the campaign had gone too far, concluding: "No one in the Batjac Organization (Wayne's producing company) or in the Russell Birdwell office has been a party to Mr. Wills' trade paper advertising. I refrain from using stronger language because I'm sure his intentions were not as bad as his taste."

This campaign was excessive but certainly not isolated. For twenty-five years Hollywood press agents, studio executives, and overly zealous agents had been beating tasteless drums to bag both nominations and Oscars. Jennifer Jones was nominated for *Love Is a Many Splendored Thing* thanks to trade paper ads printed in gold ink—specially printed actually; Cecil B. DeMille's cartoonlike *The Greatest Show on Earth* stole the Oscar from *High Noon* after a campaign as noisy as a circus parade; and a golden-worded bit of ballyhoo enabled Lee Marvin's *Cat Ballou* cowboy to take the awards away from Rod Steiger (*The Pawnbroker*), Richard Burton (*The Spy Who Came In From the Cold*), Laurence Olivier (*Othello*), and Oskar Werner (*Ship of Fools*). A similar splash by MGM in 1951 got a best picture Oscar for *An American in Paris,* Vincente Minnelli's frothy ballet film: charming but not truly the best film of the year. That campaign created more injustice than most since the musical beat out *A Place in the Sun, A Streetcar Named Desire, Quo Vadis,* and *Decision Before Dawn.* (In MGM's pre-nomination campaign, the lightweights *Quo Vadis* and *An American in Paris* aced out *Death of a Salesman, The African Queen, Detective Story,* and Hitchcock's *Strangers on a Train.*)

The Academy gets its back up about all this politics every three or four years—fighting back by announcing that the Oscar race is totally unconnected with the massive ad wars.

If only this were true.

Sadly, ruthless Oscar politics are as much a part of the process as the gold statue itself. Joan Crawford once said, "He who barks loudest in the Oscar race gets scratched first and best. Some very talented performers have refused to dirty their hands. And those actors were out in the cold while much inferior actors made the golden circle."

And Crawford should know. She waged not only the most famous campaign for an Oscar; she and her publicist, Henry Rogers, wrote the book.

The year was 1945, and Crawford's career was on the line.

Since 1925, she had been at the top of filmdom's heap; first as the veritable image of the Jazz Age, then as the hard-luck shop-girl-makes-

good of the thirties, and finally as the successor to Greta Garbo and Claudette Colbert at the pinnacle of glamour. She'd married and divorced Douglas Fairbanks, Jr., and Franchot Tone. In 1940 she was the fourth highest paid woman in America.

She had all the laurel leaves of Hollywood success. All but the Oscar. And the fact that she never even won a nomination was starting to gnaw at the edges of her career.

One night, after she read that her arch-rival Norma Shearer was nominated for the fifth time, she turned to her daughter Christina and began spitting out sentences of frustration. "It doesn't matter how brilliant an actor's performance is. The awards are a dole—a reward to the studios rather than a fair vote. If a star had won the award the year before, no one at the same studio has a chance."

She knew what she was talking about; for several years Joan Crawford was not only a member, but as the daughter-in-law of Douglas Fairbanks, Sr., and Mary Pickford, was privy to the intimate machinations of the Academy. (Pickford and Fairbanks were both founders and officers.)

Crawford finally resigned from the Academy in protest after receiving no answer to her official complaints. Nobody denied that she had reason for anger at the Academy and her studio; for fifteen years she had been getting only castoff roles from Norma Shearer, who was married to the MGM boss, Irving Thalberg, and Greta Garbo, who was treated with kid gloves by everyone at Metro. Even when she sparkled in a role, as she did in *Grand Hotel*, the studio saw that its one nomination went to Shearer, Garbo, or Marie Dressler.

There's also no doubt that MGM could have gotten her a nomination and probably an Oscar had they wanted to. By 1935 the Academy of Motion Picture Arts and Sciences had a membership of between forty and eighty (depending on which officer you quote), and the big men associated with the organization frequently made their wishes known (since the Oscar financing came largely from the studios).

Then the roof caved in on most of MGM's big stars, making talk of Oscars a frivolity. Garbo and Shearer suddenly found their pictures turning into flops, and Joan Crawford was one of three big stars labeled "box office poison." (Marlene Dietrich and Mae West were the other two.)

Crawford felt she had one last chance at MGM. She needed strong parts, not the parade of shop girls she'd done for the past five years. She needed to abandon her furs, her wide-eyed, high fashion look. "I need something I can get my teeth into," she told her friend Dore Freeman, then in charge of the MGM still department. "But I don't know if I'll get it."

Crawford was making a fashion program picture called *Mannequin* when she got word that MGM had bought Clare Boothe Luce's study of female bitchiness, *The Women*. Shearer, Rosalind Russell, and Joan Fontaine were already cast, and the rest of the parts had been penciled in. "I want to play Crystal," said Crawford after assaulting Louis B. Mayer in his office. "Why, Joan?" asked Mayer. "That woman is crude, unredeemed."

"But," said Crawford, jutting out the chin in defiance, "it's the best part in the picture. And I can do it." Mayer made Crawford audition for director George Cukor, and he took her. It was to be the last stand in the fifteen-year Shearer-Crawford feud.

Joan and Rosalind Russell stole the picture, and Crawford traded her chit from that film for a chance to play a disfigured beauty in *A Woman's Face*. A year later, however, she found herself back in the rut. "I want out

Garbo! Most critics and the public consider her the greatest actress ever to appear in films. Twice the New York Film Critics—by all standards a fairer jury than the Oscar voters—named her best actress, in 1935 for *Anna Karenina* and in 1937 for *Camille*. The Academy didn't even nominate her for the first, and gave the Oscar to Luise Rainer over Garbo's performance in the latter film. Much later the Academy trotted out one of those "honorary" Oscars and presented it to a nonattending Greta Garbo. Oscar's rejection of Garbo is proof enough that the Academy Awards—during the early decades—were not awards given by peers. They were awards by and for movie politicians. Garbo's peers—when they were actually consulted—gave her unanimous recognition. In 1950 *Daily Variety* polled two hundred veterans of the movie industry and Garbo was named best silent actress, best sound actress, and best all-around actress.

of my contract," she told Mayer. "Now!" The boss finally, after a long fight, agreed to let Crawford go. (He told friends that he felt her career would crumble without MGM's protection.)

A month later Jack Warner grabbed her for a fee of $100,000 a picture, but Joan had tasted, finally, success as an actress. Not just any script would do. "Joan realized," said Dore Freeman, "that this was a comeback for her. What she did would make the difference. She would sink or swim on the strength of one picture."

She could find no script good enough for two years, which is a long time for a film star to be offscreen. Then she read James M. Cain's *Mildred Pierce*. "This is it," she told Jack Warner. "This is the right role." Warner heaved a sigh of relief. Bette Davis had turned it down, so Crawford's decision solved two problems at once.

Mildred Pierce was only a week into production when producer Jerry Wald saw something special in the daily rushes. He smelled an Oscar in the making. He called publicist Henry Rogers, Crawford's press agent, and the Oscar hype of all Oscar hypes was born.

"Why don't you start a campaign for Joan to win the Oscar?" asked Wald.

"But Jerry, the picture's just starting."

"So what?" asked Wald, who told Rogers to call Hedda Hopper and feed it to her as a column item. It worked.

Two days later, readers across America, but most importantly in Hollywood, woke up to this from Hedda: "Insiders say that Joan Crawford is delivering such a terrific performance on *Mildred Pierce* that she's a cinch for the Academy Award." That night Wald went to a Beverly Hills party and had his own item fed back to him. Producer Hal Wallis sidled up to Wald: "Hey, Jerry it looks like Crawford's going to win the Oscar. I don't know where I heard it; I must have read it somewhere."

Henry Rogers, who's called the Henry Kissinger of Hollywood publicists, decided to launch a full-blown Oscar campaign. So he went out to Joan's dressing room at Warners. He broke the campaign to her bit by bit, saying, "I wish I could take credit for this. But it's Jerry's idea. I want your approval to start a campaign right here and now to get people in the industry thinking in advance that you're going to win the Oscar."

Crawford, in full *Mildred Pierce* makeup, raised one eyebrow. "Go ahead, I'm listening."

"If Hedda ran the kind of item she did this morning, I'm sure I can get other columnists to jump on the Joan Crawford bandwagon. Joan, you know as well as I do that members of the Academy vote emotionally. People in our business can be well influenced by what they read and what they hear. Word of mouth has a tremendous advantage. This town is indignant over the way you were treated at MGM. You've cultivated the press all these years, and they love you."

Crawford was silent. She lit a cigarette, and shook her head. "I'm worried about one thing. It could kick back and I could become the laughingstock if it ever got out that Joan Crawford's press agent was plugging her for an Academy Award."

Rogers pulled out a draft of his plan, with all the techniques centered around secrecy and the necessity for all the publicity breaks to seem spontaneous. She reluctantly gave the go-ahead. "It sounds good. But I don't think it can work. I've never been well liked in this business. I've given performances before that I thought deserved Academy consideration, but I never had a chance. People in Hollywood don't like me, and they've never regarded me as a good actress."

Rogers tells the story of this Oscar strategy in his book, *Walking the*

Joan Crawford with co-stars Ann Blythe and Zachary Scott in 1945's *Mildred Pierce*. Crawford had been counted down and out by MGM and all but kicked off the lot by her old boss Louis B. Mayer. The day she left, in fact, there was nobody to say good-bye, and her parking place had already been given to another actress. She managed to cagily coax a contract out of Jack Warner, but voluntarily stayed off the screen for two years before she found a part good enough to revive her career. *Mildred Pierce* it was. Her personal publicist Henry Rogers pitched in—planting rumors about a *Mildred Pierce* Oscar during the first week of shooting. Luckily, the performance in this case matched the campaign. Still, she wouldn't believe she had a chance. "They'll never give it to me," she told friends. "Not to me." So she stayed home Oscar night—even though she was a shoo-in.

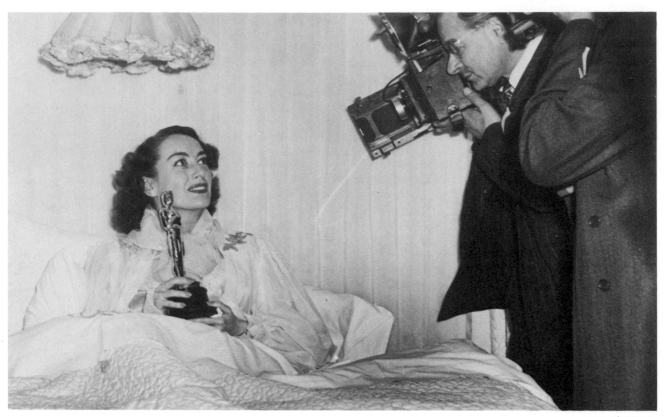

Tightrope: Confessions of a Public Relations Man, a rare and truthful look at the inner workings of movie publicity. Six months after the innocent little sentence in Hopper's column, the Rogers plan had even rebounded back to Warner Brothers itself. Jack Warner, picking up vibes from Rogers' journalistic whispers, told assistants that *Mildred Pierce* is going to be a much more important picture than we originally thought."

There were lines at the box office when the film opened in Los Angeles and New York. The next day Warner ordered the studio to go all out for the Academy Awards, starting a series of ads unprecedented in the eighteen-year history of the Oscar race. Rogers thought Crawford would win; so did Jack Warner and, ironically, Louis B. Mayer.

Only Crawford herself was a doubter.

The day of the awards, Crawford called Rogers. "I can't do it, Henry. I'm so frightened, I know I'm going to lose. They won't vote for me."

"Nonsense," said Rogers. "They love a comeback story. You're going to win. I can feel it."

The actress only shook her head. Then Wald called her. He didn't have to say much. After all, he'd taken a chance on her when nobody else would, casting her in *Mildred Pierce* against the advice of Warner executives and even of his director, Michael Curtiz.

"I'll try," she said. "I'll try." Her dress was laid out; her hair done. But insecurity took over; her iron will failed her for the first time . . . the years and the disappointments had gotten to her. (Crawford was forty-one then—the breaking point for most Hollywood stars.)

She faltered in late afternoon when her temperature soared to 104 and her doctor ordered her to bed.

Crawford's good friend and biographer, Bob Thomas of the Associated Press, wrote about that night thirty years later.

A triumphant Crawford takes her Oscar for *Mildred Pierce* shortly after midnight. Crawford's bedside was mobbed with reporters and stars. Over the years, the rumor grew that Crawford had been perfectly well that night. The truth is that she had a temperature of 104 as she reclined in bed, listening to the Oscar show by radio. But the evening wasn't totally without artifice: her nightgown and wrap were designed by Helen Rose, and a trio of makeup men and hairdressers worked over her face and hair for an hour before she let the photographers in.

"She deserved the prize, she realized. But would they give it to her? They had looked down their noses at her ever since she arrived in Culver City as Lucille LeSueur. But by God, she had showed them! While her arch-rivals at MGM, Norma Shearer, Greta Garbo, and Jeanette Mac-Donald, had vanished from the screen, Joan had returned in triumph. She had dangerously absented herself from the world's theaters for two years, an eternity in the life of a star. It was an arduous time, during which the lack of income and a calamitous third marriage had depleted her savings. She waited and waited, and found *Mildred Pierce*."

At about nine Crawford came downstairs and curled up, in a Parisian robe and gown. So certain was Henry Rogers that he had brought carefully chosen photographers to the house; the radio had been turned on for an hour.

Finally, Charles Boyer, onstage at Grauman's Chinese Theatre announced the nominees: Ingrid Bergman in *The Bells of St. Mary's*, Joan Crawford in *Mildred Pierce*, Greer Garson in *The Valley of Decision*, Jennifer Jones in *Love Letters*, and Gene Tierney in *Leave Her to Heaven*.

When Crawford's name was read as the winner, her eyes turned moist for only a second. Her friends all turned as she looked up and said: "This is the greatest moment of my life."

And no one doubted that she meant it.

The next morning 1,000 telegrams were delivered to Joan's house—with flowers arriving all day. But perhaps the one that meant the most came from her old boss, Louis B. Mayer. And Joan knew HE meant it. He had told his secretary and publicist Howard Strickling that he voted for Joan, not MGM's Greer Garson. Why? asked his secretary. Mayer turned his head away: "Because she deserved it."

Her daughter Christina stayed up with Joan for a while after everyone else left: "She sat holding her Oscar (Curtiz had brought it to her), turning him around to view from every angle. Then we walked down the stairs together, and she placed him all alone in a special little niche at the bottom of the staircase. Mother stepped back to admire him. Turning to me she said with a note of sarcasm: 'I said I wouldn't be there, but I never thought it would turn out like this.'"

That story ended happily but, as Rogers polished his Oscar touch through the next decade, there would be many successes (such as his subtle campaign that helped win the Oscar for Olivia De Havilland for *Hold Back the Dawn*) and some heartbreak.

One of his failures is almost as legendary as the *Mildred Pierce* triumph.

The star this time was Rosalind Russell, an actress as universally liked as Crawford was disliked. Russell had been nominated before, but her producer husband, Frederick Brisson, thought she would never have a better chance than with *Mourning Becomes Electra*, a boring, turgid rendering of Eugene O'Neill's masterpiece.

Brisson went to Rogers, asking him, without Rosalind's knowledge, to do for her what he had so beautifully done for Crawford and De Havilland. There was a bonus if she got nominated and a large bonus if she won. (Some say it was more than $10,000. In any case it was enough to cause his wife to throw up when Russell lost to Loretta Young.)

"I was convinced that a publicity campaign, conceived and executed by the Henry Rogers publicity organization, could result in an Academy Award for my client," Rogers wrote in *Walking the Tightrope*. "Who would be the next person I would touch with my magic wand?"

Rogers tried everything. He bossed fraternities into naming Russell actress of the year, convinced a Las Vegas odds expert to issue odds on all the candidates with Russell the six-to-five favorite, and carefully fed the

Hollywood rumor mill. So successful was Rogers that the annual poll by *Variety* of twenty-five percent of the voters showed that Russell had no competition.

Brisson booked a table at the nightclub, the Mocombo, for dozens of celebrants. And Rogers told his wife to go ahead and spend the $5,000 for new living room furniture (which she did).

As the world knows, it was Loretta Young who said, as she got up, "At Last!"

Roz Russell broke her beads; she had automatically risen to get her Oscar. Thank God for the dark—nobody really noticed.

Rogers got healthily drunk at the Mocombo—remembering only later that even he had gone to sleep during a showing of *Mourning Becomes Electra*.

What all this proves is that the Oscar CAN be bought—nominations for moderate advertising budgets, a major win for megabucks. This, of course, has nothing to do with the Academy and everything to do with the way Oscar is misused.

The stories behind Joan Crawford's award and behind *The Alamo* nominations are the happy side of the story. Far more venal are the recurrent drives by big studios to gain Oscar nominations for films that they, and almost everyone else, know are not Academy Award caliber. The publicity stunts (and they rate no higher title than that) achieve their goal year after year after year in a rotten tradition that stretches back to Oscar's first decade.

Every time this issue rears its head at Oscar time, the Academy issues sanctimonious denials. In 1980, for instance, Academy President Fay Kanin told CBS reporter Steve Edwards, "I seriously doubt that ad campaigns have any effect on voting. At least I would hope not."

Louella Parsons said there was less jealousy afloat over the Crawford Oscar than any other in history. "This is a girl who really worked at acting—year after year after year," said Parsons. And that was Crawford's reputation. She lived on the lot during many of her films, was never known to be a half hour late, and had her lines down a month before shooting. The scene above shows her with Bette Davis in director Robert Aldrich's bizarre suspense drama, *What Ever Happened to Baby Jane?* Crawford called her makeup a "death mask."

Director Alexander Hall and Rosalind Russell on the set of Columbia's *This Thing Called Love*. The film also starred Melvyn Douglas.

Hard evidence through the years makes denials seem ridiculous.

The track record of Twentieth Century-Fox, alone, during the last twenty years is proof enough. Time and time again that studio has succeeded in hoisting dismal but expensive films into the Academy's golden five. Each time it happens several excellent films are frozen out. For example, Fox's *Cleopatra* got a passel of nominations (including best picture) at the expense of *Hud* and *Irma La Douce*. *The Sand Pebbles*, same studio, made it, sacrificing *Blow-Up*, *Morgan*, and *The Professionals*. And in 1969 a Fox spending spree managed to squeeze the disastrous *Hello, Dolly!* into the five best picture nominations in a year that shamefully shut out Peter Fonda's *Easy Rider*, *They Shoot Horses, Don't They?*, *The Prime of Miss Jean Brodie*, *Bob & Carol & Ted & Alice*, *Goodbye, Columbus*, and *The Sterile Cuckoo*.

The classic case of the "Twentieth Touch," however, was the vehement campaign they waged for *Doctor Doolittle*, a 1967 film that even the boys in Fox's back rooms knew was a disaster. "The eighteen million dollar turkey," they called it.

The "*Doctor Doolittle* Oscar Caper" is particularly special because Twentieth Century-Fox got caught with their votes down. A brilliant journalist and writer named John Gregory Dunne was taken to the studio's corporate bosom to paint the studio in golden tones.

They had no way of knowing he was an asp of truth.

Dunne followed the movie from its first edited frame to its last bought vote, then put it all together in a volume called *The Studio*, which is now a text in some film schools. So thoroughly was the studio's dishonest reaction to a bad picture revealed that many Hollywood executives go into a cold sweat for fear it could happen again. Public relations men describe their careers as "before Dunne," and "after Dunne," with the latter resembling Joseph Goebbels' P.R. plan for Hitler.

The journalist hadn't dug too far before he uncovered the fine hand of Rogers, Cowan, and Brenner—the same (only Brenner is gone). And their hand showed up first in a splashy but highly inconsequential announcement in the *Hollywood Reporter* that another R.&C. client, Bobby Darin, was going to unveil the *Doctor Doolittle* songs at a Red Cross gala for Princess Grace.

John Gregory Dunne was such a hale-fellow-well-met that he found himself on a plane aimed at Minneapolis—the site of *Doctor Doolittle*'s sneak preview. Across the aisle was Warren Cowan of Rogers and . . . "The picture, as befitted its 18 million dollar budget, was scheduled to be the studio's major contender in the Academy Award race," wrote Dunne, who sneaked a nice look at the early master plan for *Doolittle* publicity. On the list was a plan to manufacture and distribute (free) Pushmi-Pullyu cuff links and tie clasps. (*Doctor Doolittle* disappeared so quickly that it's hard to remember, but Pushmi-Pullyu, I believe, was a singing-dancing llama that dueted with the film's star, Rex Harrison.) The master plan also included plans for wax figures in Madame Tussaud's Wax Museum and a "*Doctor Doolittle* Day" at thousands of schools across America which would apparently free the students to see Rex and Pushmi.

The people who haplessly wandered into the *Doctor Doolittle* preview in Minnesota didn't exactly groan as the film wound through the projector. But none of them wandered out singing the Pushmi-Pullyu song either. It was not much better at a preview in San Francisco.

Bosley Crowther and the New York critics finally dipped their pointed quills into it coming up with blood. "The youngsters should enjoy it and the intermission was thoughtfully inserted at just about the right place," wrote Crowther in his paper, the *New York Times*.

Time magazine warned that "size and a big budget are no substitutes for originality or charm." And even the trade paper *Daily Variety* which, to quote Dunne, "depends on advertising from the studios," said, "the pic suffers from a vacillating concept in script, direction, and acting."

This in no way dampened Fox's campaign to buy the Oscar nomination.

Dunne got this down in black and white. Texts of memos from studio publicist Jack Hirschberg state, "The following has been decided regarding our Academy Award campaign for *Doctor Doolittle*. Each screening will be preceded by champagne or cocktails and a buffet dinner in the studio commissary. *Doctor Doolittle* is the studio's prime target for Academy Award consideration."

Hirschberg then provided a breakdown of all the Academy branches, organizing the showings to accommodate all of them.

"The studio's Academy Award exploitation plan for *Doctor Doolittle* was highly successful," wrote Dunne. "Despite mediocre reviews and lukewarm box office returns, the picture garnered nine nominations and won two Oscars."

Again, *Doctor Doolittle*'s purloined votes were the Academy's loss—in prestige and objectivity. To get *Doolittle* nominated, the Oscars had to overlook *In Cold Blood, Cool Hand Luke, Two for the Road, Barefoot in the Park, The Dirty Dozen, The Whisperers,* and *Thoroughly Modern Millie.*

These traditions continued into the seventies (although big budget films suddenly went out of Oscar fashion in 1978). In 1974, *The Towering Inferno* took a best picture nomination away from *Alice Doesn't Live Here Anymore* and *A Woman Under the Influence.* In 1975, *Jaws* made it into the golden circle instead of *Shampoo.*

The communications explosion in Hollywood has given the big producers and publicists even more toys. Pay TV reaches an estimated ninety percent of the Academy's eligible voters. And movies (such as *Breaking Away*)

Paul Newman, here in *Cool Hand Luke*, has been the classic victim of high-priced Oscar hype, starting in 1958 when the heavy United Artist's campaign for David Niven in *Separate Tables* outranked him and continuing through the sixties when U.A.'s expensive ballyhoo for Rod Steiger buried his work in *Cool Hand Luke*. By 1973, when Newman's bravura work in *The Sting* was eligible, a new generation of media sexy actors had appeared so Redford got the nomination instead. Since that year his work has fallen below Oscar class—but he may get his recognition after all as a director. (But again, Redford is fast outpacing him.)

Rex Harrison and Twentieth Century-Fox's singing parrot mug the camera in a peppy scene from *Doctor Doolittle*—one of the films for which Fox bought a place on the best picture list through advertising and champagne buffets for Oscar voters. As Ezra Goodman pointed out in his *The Fifty Year Decline and Fall of Hollywood*, the Oscars "can certainly be rigged promotionally. In order to give *Doctor Doolittle* a place on the list, the Oscar voters had to ignore *Othello, The Pawnbroker,* and *A Patch of Blue.*

In Germany on the set of Stanley Kramer's *Judgment at Nuremberg*. Montgomery Clift was nominated as best supporting actor, but the Oscar voters gave the award to George Chakiris for *West Side Story*.

that have been made available to pay TV have fared better than average in preliminary voting. Exploitation like this can make even the preview for a nominated movie into an important trump card. The Theta Cable shows those trailers upwards of fifteen times a day until it's almost subliminal advertising going directly to Oscar voters. (Several scenes of Bette Midler's *The Rose* remain engraved on the Academy's collective psyche.)

Some of the campaigns become so dangerously crude that they backfire entirely.

In 1961 Montgomery Clift's overt advertising undoubtedly cost the troubled actor his final chance at the Oscar. Not only did the ads capitalize on *Judgment at Nuremberg*, they tried to make hay from Clift's ill and depressed appearance. Since all Hollywood knew how sick he was, the implication was, "Vote for Clift now—it's your last chance."

Joan Crawford said it best: "Why suddenly expect the process to be fair—it didn't even start out that way."

Clift sprawled across the cement of the Rome train depot in an agonizing scene from *Indiscretion of an American Wife*, produced in Italy by David O. Selznick. Vittorio De Sica said Clift was the only decent thing about the film: "A cerebral actor with emotions playing on his face the way music plays on a fine violin."

7 | GOLDEN IDOL

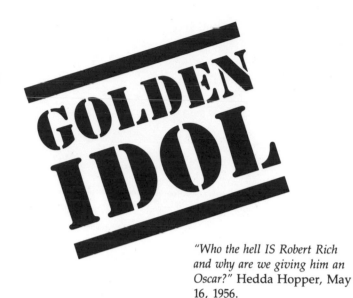

"Who the hell IS Robert Rich and why are we giving him an Oscar?" Hedda Hopper, May 16, 1956.

Titian-haired Deborah Kerr said the name first: "And the winner for writing is . . . Robert Rich."

All through the ermined and tuxedoed crowd in Grauman's Chinese Theatre, America's most famous heads craned to catch a glimpse of Hollywood's hottest new writer. Grace Kelly, Carroll Baker, and Rock Hudson—all aware that this wunderkind could easily write their next picture—glanced toward the writer's contingent, an anonymous mass of penguin suits.

Time was suspended for the usual number of seconds. But, finally, a handsome young man dashed toward the stage and into the spotlight of instant fame.

"Why that's Jesse Lasky, Jr.," said Hedda. "What's going on?"

Lasky was asking himself the same question as he tugged down his black tie and smoothed the lines of his custom tux. He tried to practice the words of his speech but his mind kept wandering to the $64,000 question: "Who IS Robert Rich?" The thought had been bugging him for twenty-four hours—ever since the Writers Guild had told him he'd probably have to go up and claim the Oscar for his fellow writer. The Hollywood gossip underground—perhaps the most accurate gossip fountain outside the CIA—had already decreed that Rich would walk off with the award for his dazzling screenplay for *The Brave One,* an RKO film that was nominated for three Oscars.

But the gossip began and ended with that bit of information. "No, I've not met him," said the president of RKO to Lasky's question. Then, the day of the awards—just as Lasky was about to give up on finding a single personal tidbit about the phantom writer, a man called up the Writers Guild, claiming he was Robert Rich. His wife, he said, was going to have a baby that very day, and he had to be at the hospital with her during what promised to be a difficult delivery.

Well that's a start, thought Lasky, and it was great comfort as he walked onstage toward Deborah Kerr, took the Oscar in his well-tanned hand,

Al Jolson stood far back in the wings watching Larry Parks portray him in this scene from *The Jolson Story* (1946), then turned to a friend with tears in his eyes. "This guy's a genius," said Jolson. "He's caught the essence of me yet he's added that sense of tragedy—his performance is making a statement about me."

Twenty years after Dalton Trumbo won an Oscar for his script *The Brave One*, he finally received the award from Academy President Walter Mirisch—shown here offering the golden idol at the writer's deathbed. This was one of the few injustices of the blacklist era that was finally corrected. The Academy knew then—as it knows now—that Trumbo also earned a second Oscar for his original story used by Paramount for *Roman Holiday*. The man whose name Dalton Trumbo used for *Roman Holiday*, Ian McLellan Hunter, admitted long ago that he was only passing on the writer's story to Paramount in exchange for $40,000—money that kept a roof over Trumbo's head during the blacklist years.

received a kiss from the actress, and then mumbled something about Rich's predicament, adding that his "good friend was attending the result of another creative effort. . . ." And the ordeal was over.

Lasky tucked the Oscar into the trunk of his sports car—ready for delivery to the safe at the Writers Guild.

But the saga of Robert Rich was only starting—Lasky found that out the morning after. The first phone call came at about 9 a.m. "Mr. Lasky," said the secretary at the Guild, "we have checked all the lists here for an address—or even a phone number—and Robert Rich isn't even a member." Now what? "Better call the Academy," Lasky said. For the next four hours his phone rang like a repeater rifle: the Associated Press, the *Los Angeles Times*. . . .

"Jesse Lasky, Jr., accepts award for non-existent writer," said a headline in the *New York Times*. "Who Is Robert Rich?" asked the *Chicago Tribune*, which included a statement from the Academy saying, "We have no records on him beyond the fact that his fellow writers voted for him."

Hedda Hopper didn't bother with the telephone. The morning after, she had the limo whisk her out to RKO pictures, where the first serious Rich hunt began. The brass there told Hedda that their producers had not actually met Robert Rich either. The phantom scribe had submitted the original script through a major Hollywood agent; RKO had bought it, sent a sizable check to the bank, and made the picture—so they said.

The same day, Hedda barged through the doors of the agent's office— a man whose phone had been tolling all day. "Bug off," he said tersely. "Case closed."

The Oscar was sent immediately back to the Academy; Robert Rich was temporarily erased from the record books, and the mystery faded into Hollywood-past . . . but not before it brought a touch of sweet revenge to a screenwriter banished from Hollywood, during the Communist hunt that had hit movieland in 1950.

His name was Dalton Trumbo, the brilliant writer of *Kitty Foyle, Thirty Seconds Over Tokyo*, and *Our Vines Have Tender Grapes*. HE was Robert Rich, the creative genius behind a ghost name, forced to adopt a "front" in order to create for a Hollywood that had blacklisted him.

Winning was "bitter-sweet," he said later. "Sitting in another country and seeing my work win was frustrating for me personally, and tragic for Hollywood as a whole," Trumbo said to close friends.

On February 6, 1957, the Academy board, alarmed by the number of past nominees and winners being called to Washington in the Communist hunt, passed a rule that stated: "Any person who, before any duly constituted Federal legislative body, shall have admitted that he is a member of the Communist Party (and has not publicly renounced the Party) or shall have refused to respond to a subpoena to appear before such a committee or body, shall be ineligible for any Academy Award so long as he persists in such a refusal."

"We never meant it to be taken literally," said an Academy leader from the fifties—talking off the record and laughing nervously. "We were only protecting our rear. How could we give Oscars to people all the studios were blacklisting? How could we? Anyone else in our shoes would have done the same thing."

The Robert Rich Affair quickly became cause célèbre of the entire period, a rallying point for the supporters of the blacklist—as well as its foes. There were several reasons for this. First, Trumbo/Rich was a solid member of "the Hollywood Ten" (see Appendix), a group of Hollywood writers and directors who may or may not have been Communists, but who refused to say and went to prison for their stance. Second, Trumbo quickly became the most successful (and richest) of scores of writers who used ghost names to continue their careers as Hollywood screenwriters. And finally, Trumbo became such a successful ghost writer (for such future Oscar-laden films as *Spartacus, Exodus, The Sandpiper*, and *Papillon*) that his fame and the humor of the "Rich Affair" were the first holes in the dike built by the town's ultra-conservatives.

It didn't seem so funny, however, in 1957 when Oscar formed its own blacklist. "The name of the game was UnAmericanism, and the referee was blowing the whistle on everyone," wrote Jesse Lasky, Jr., in his book, *Whatever Happened to Hollywood?* "With a prevalence of witches, the only problem was: Which witch to hunt? That not-too-bright young producer who had risen too quickly; that story editor who hired only guess-what-kind-of-writers? The actor who got the part you were up for?"

Screenwriter Philip Dunne, himself a former Oscar nominee (*How Green Was My Valley*), saw the Academy's blacklist rule as a simple outgrowth of the general Hollywood red scare. "The list expanded from the ten to the several hundred, from suspected Communists to their suspected sympathizers, to their defenders." In his 1980 autobiography, *Take Two*, Dunne tells of the slow spread of the fear until there was even "a gray list, consisting of people who could be hired, but just to be on the safe side, better not."

The loyalty oath originated as soon as word spread through the Academy that blacklisted writer Michael Wilson was sure to be nominated for his 1956 movieplay, *Friendly Persuasion*. (Wilson had won the Oscar in 1951 for his *Place in the Sun* script.) The loyalty rule was quickly enacted, and *Friendly Persuasion* was nominated for its screenplay on the provision that Wilson's name be omitted from the ballot.

The next ghost writer didn't appear in the nomination ranks until late 1958—when the gossip mill again predicted that a non-existent writer,

Nathan E. Douglas, was an almost certain winner for co-scripting *The Defiant Ones*, a racial blockbuster starring Tony Curtis and Sidney Poitier. An obscure voice on the telephone informed several Academy directors that Nathan E. Douglas was none other than Ned Young, a blacklisted writer who, for personal reasons, had taken the Fifth Amendment before the House UnAmerican Activities Committee.

The Academy took immediate steps to rescind the rule—after high level diplomatic meetings between *Defiant Ones* writers Harold Jacob Smith (a real name) and Nathan E. Douglas/Ned Young. Over cheesecake and coffee at the Brown Derby, the Henry Kissingers of the Academy told Douglas/Young they'd let him take home the Oscar if he won. But only if he promised not to embarrass Oscar by publicly announcing that Douglas was only a "ghost."

So Oscar shucked his loyalty cloak.

And Robert Rich finally got his Oscar—from Academy officers who took it to Dalton Trumbo's bedside in 1975. (The screenwriter was critically ill with cancer.)

Ned Young is still listed as Nathan E. Douglas on the official Academy rolls. The Academy maintains that Young or someone acting in his behalf would have to petition for the change and present an affidavit from the producers of *The Defiant Ones* stating that Douglas is, indeed, Young—a fact the Academy is fully aware of.

If this misconception is mildly damaging to film researchers, the case of *The Bridge on the River Kwai*, one of the landmark films of all time, is far more serious. The film walked off with seven Oscars in 1957, including best picture, best actor (Alec Guinness), best direction (David Lean), best cinematography (Jack Hildyard), best editing (Peter Taylor), best scoring (Malcolm Arnold), and best screenplay (credited to Pierre Boulle, the author of the book that preceded the film).

There's no doubt that Alec Guinness is Alec Guinness, that Lean is Lean—etc. But nobody that has ever read about the making of the movie believes that Pierre Boulle wrote the screenplay. Super writers Carl Foreman and Michael Wilson, both blacklisted, wrote the script, working almost a year on it. "Well, ALL Hollywood knows that," sniffed Hedda to a BBC interviewer in 1964. "All Hollywood."

"I owned the rights to *Bridge on the River Kwai* all along," says Carl Foreman. "I was going to write and produce the film version through an agreement with Alexander Korda (a famed British producer), but the British market was glutted with World War II prisoner of war stories, and the financing fell through. Foreman trekked back to America with his rights. Sam Spiegel, an independent producer for Columbia, agreed to produce, including in the agreement an unwritten condition that Foreman and Wilson remain anonymous.

"At the time, I never thought for a minute that Pierre Boulle would retain screenplay credit for eternity. The film became legendary, as you know. And everyone in Hollywood knew I wrote it with Wilson. That knowledge was what broke the blacklist for me and a number of others."

Foreman, who has come back big as a producer-writer-director on such films as *Born Free*, *The Guns of Navarone*, and others, expresses only mild annoyance at the deception. Others are angrier. Henry Rogers, founder of the huge Hollywood P.R. firm of Rogers and Cowan (which handles Foreman), says it's a shaft. "Pierre Boulle had nothing to do with the screenplay. Mild pressure that has been put on Spiegel and the Academy has had no effect. Spiegel does not want to admit he succumbed to subterfuge—at least that's the way it seems."

Officials at the Academy maintain that "rules are rules. Unless we get

A mourning Sidney Poitier cradles the dead Tony Curtis in the final scene from Stanley Kramer's *The Defiant Ones*, which inadvertently ended the Academy's "loyalty oath" during the blacklist period. The Oscar committee, already embarrassed by the "Robert Rich" affair, knew that Nathan E. Douglas, nominated for writing *The Defiant Ones* script, was actually writer Ned Young using a "front." Oscar brass met with Young, asked him not to embarrass them, then withdrew the "I am not now, nor have I ever been" pledge from the list of Academy Award requirements. But the men in charge forgot to change the credits on the Oscar record. So it's Nathan E. Douglas, who never existed, whose name is on the Oscar.

Alec Guinness, William Holden, and James Donald on the set of *Bridge on the River Kwai*, the film that broke the blacklist. Winner of the New York Film Critics Award, the Golden Globes, and the Academy Award, the film was so critically and financially successful that all Hollywood suddenly had a reason to break the blacklist—so they could hire Carl Foreman, one of the authors of the screenplay. Foreman, who had himself purchased the property from French novelist Pierre Boulle, collaborated with fellow blacklistee Michael Wilson to author the script. But Columbia Pictures gave the screenplay credits to Boulle, who admittedly doesn't write in English and employs a translator for his own works. When it became public knowledge that Foreman and Wilson were the authors, the anti-Communist scare came to an end.

When Larry Parks returned to Hollywood after agonizing through this appearance on the House Un-American Activities Committee stand, the derogatory headlines greeted him. "Jolson Sings Again," read the *Hollywood Citizen*. "A Stool Pigeon Sings Too Late," read a line over Hedda Hopper's scathing column. Parks was finished from that moment—unjustly tarred and feathered by zealots. Only in the seventies were the records set straight—too late for Parks.

Oscar nominee Adolphe Menjou who bought his own ticket and a new London suit to voluntarily testify about his former friends before H.U.A.C. Menjou's list included more than twenty-five fellow Oscar nominees and several winners.

affidavits giving Foreman and Wilson credit—there's nothing we can do about it." The Writers Guild tells the same story. "We can only go by the film's official screen credits," says Alan Rivkin, a longtime official of the Writers Guild. "I may know it was Foreman and Wilson; you may know it's Foreman and Wilson; the whole Academy can know that. But we're helpless until the credits are officially changed." Spiegel has routinely refused to discuss the matter—officially.

An even wilder legend has grown into Wagnerian proportions, involving a brilliant little comedy, *Roman Holiday*, probably written by Ian McLellan Hunter. William Wyler, producer of the film, says there's no doubt about the authorship—"It's Hunter."

Problem is: Dalton Trumbo (aka Rich) told a UCLA film professor, Dr. Howard Suber, that he (Trumbo) had written the Audrey Hepburn movie through an agreement that allowed Wyler to use Hunter's name.

The legend emerged while Suber and Trumbo were driving back from a radio broadcast in the seventies. "I had begun to feel that Trumbo might have written the film after a major director made a slip about Trumbo winning two Oscars under other names. So I phrased a question to him this way: 'Did William Wyler know that you had written *Roman Holiday*?' Trumbo didn't actually answer me. But further on down the road, he said: 'You bastard! Who told you?'"

In actuality, it appears that Hunter wrote the script which won an Oscar. But the story illustrates the uncertainty and confusion which are legacies of the blacklist. Dr. Suber, who has devoted fifteen years to studying the list, has explained, "A number of people who WEREN'T blacklisted, now claim they were—it's all acquired a glamorous patina with age."

The Academy is closer than it thinks to the blacklisted writers; fifteen writers (certified as having been officially blacklisted) account for seventeen nominations and eight Oscars) (see Appendix).

The era also took painful toll from the careers of a number of Oscar winners and nominees in acting categories—most notably Larry Parks (best actor nominee for *The Jolson Story*), who found his career permanently destroyed after his appearance before H.U.A.C.—where he "named names" but was still driven from Hollywood in a typhoon of hatred. It was about Parks that Hedda poisonously penned: "Who cares about that one little actor? He should have fessed up when he was first asked instead of crawling under fear of a subpoena or jail term."

But the post-Oscar experiences of four actresses—Lee Grant, Gale Sondergaard, Anne Revere, and Kim Hunter—best symbolize the ravages of the period.

Lee Grant, who finally netted the best supporting actress award in 1975 for *Shampoo* (after four nominations) tells it this way: "As I stood there with the Oscar in my hand, I heard applause within the applause. I understood then. They KNEW. They knew, and they were letting me know."

By then, the long ordeal of Lee Grant had been over for some time. But in 1952, the year after her triumphant screen debut in *Detective Story* (for which she was nominated), she found herself hounded out of films, out of TV, and off the radio. And it all had nothing to do with her personal politics. She was, however, married to suspected Communist writer Arnold Manoff. Worse, she was a close friend and student of another Communist suspect, well-known character actor J. Edward Bromberg.

The blacklist pressure may have contributed to Bromberg's fatal heart attack. Grant ordered flowers and held a memorial service. Later she found herself on the blacklist.

"She was just a seventeen-year-old kid with a tremendous career before her," said TV star John Henry Faulk, who wrote a classic volume on the

blacklist (*Fear on Trial*). "She was a fighter, though. She just decided it wasn't going to get her down, by damn. She was aimin' to whip 'em." That she was! She stood up at an emergency meeting of the American Federation of Television and Radio Artists and began pointing to members scattered around the room. "You turned on us! So did you! And you! And you!" she yelled to members who had been feeding facts and figures to the House UnAmerican Activities Committee, nearly all of them false or fabricated.

Lee Grant didn't get a single job in American films for seventeen years.

Then, finally, after an attorney worked for five years to prove her innocence, her name was taken off the list—with a letter from Washington D.C. and a very mild apology. Then came *Terror in the City, In the Heat of the Night, Buona Sera, Mrs. Campbell, Plaza Suite,* and eventually the Oscar.

"I rushed into films as if I'd never had an acting job in my life," says Grant. "I was high on acting. Since the blacklist got so little mass publicity, nobody really knew where I'd been—or even that I'd been gone. I had limitless energy and staying power."

Now, in the eighties, Lee Grant has not only come all the way back, she's surpassed herself, directing and writing her own film.

"But that's not to say that there haven't been permanent legacies. No matter how successful I am now—I remain paranoid, afraid that it all might crumble again like it did after *Detective Story* in 1951.

"Suddenly I couldn't remember anybody's name; still can't. That comes directly from the years when I trained myself daily NOT to remember the names. I wanted to forget the names of friends so that I wouldn't even be able to give them names—if they asked me." The actress leaned out of her lush rambling house above the Pacific Ocean. "It's not easy to feel the fear

John Garfield and Lana Turner, two fine actors who were destined never to get an Oscar, in a bleakly lighted scene from *The Postman Always Rings Twice.* Tay Garnett, the film's director, knew there was only one actor who could duplicate the range required by the James M. Cain character. Several years later Garfield, one of the biggest names to be blacklisted, died of a heart attack the night before he was to testify before H.U.A.C.

The most iron-willed of the blacklist survivors is actress Lee Grant, virtually the only one of the three hundred blacklistees who has not only come back but has surpassed herself—winning an Oscar for *Shampoo* and becoming one of the industry's few woman directors. (Her *Tell Me a Riddle* was released to great acclaim in late 1980.) But for seventeen years, beginning with 1951 when Lee Grant was nominated for her first Oscar, the actress couldn't get a decent job in films or television. Her great error was holding a memorial service for her blacklisted teacher and mentor J. Edward Bromberg.

well up inside your chest over something that happened twenty-five years ago."

The day the actress finally walked back onto a Hollywood sound stage, she found her past waiting for her. "One of the men I had faced down years before was featured in the film where I had the lead. The door opened; he stepped in. Our eyes locked. He came slowly over; then introduced himself.

"That's how this thing ended for most of us—with a slow, drawn-out whimper."

The afternoon sun added a shading to Lee Grant's eyes and highlighted her blond hair. The lady who's back on top was silent for a second. Then she said: "You know, that was the way the blacklist worked—not by some sinister design, but by omission. For instance, a producer would say, 'Let's hire him, or her,' and somebody else would say, 'Wasn't she involved in something back there? I don't exactly know what.' The only thing they knew was that there was some dim background. And since this town never wants even the hint of trouble—the blacklist is continued. For some people it still continues."

Of those still under the shadow, Gale Sondergaard, the legendary winner of the first Oscar ever given for best supporting actress, is another notable casualty—a waste of Oscar-caliber talent.

Sondergaard, who has made at least three total comebacks in Hollywood, has remained under such a pointless shadow that not even the greedy money men of TV have taken the cue.

Her first resurrection happened ten years ago on the old Warner Brothers lot where Gale achieved her legendary position among the screen's character actors. "I was out here at the Mark Taper in *Uncle Vanya*, and Robert Wagner came backstage one night. He talked to me about his series,

'It Takes a Thief,' mentioning a guest shot for me. I would be following an appearance by Bette Davis, and it seemed appropriate."

Sondergaard agreed and drove out to the lot several days later. As her car came up to the gate, Murray, a guard from the old days, came personally down to greet her. It was like a scene out of *Sunset Boulevard*. "Miss Sondergaard," he said, leaning into her car, "it's great to have you back—don't stay away so long." It was the same in the wardrobe department. The girls dropped their work and gathered around the actress—who had made *Anthony Adverse, The Life of Emil Zola*, and twenty others on the lot in the decade from 1935–45.

"When I got on the Wagner set, they had managed to wind up the shooting early, and they asked me to come back the next day for an early take."

Gale Sondergaard lingered in the big empty stage (where *The Jazz Singer* started talking movies in 1927) and walked down a staircase. Bob Wagner caught her eye, and she began to talk—"You know this is the first time I've been on a Hollywood sound stage in twenty years. They were aghast. I had to sit down and explain it all."

But the comeback didn't take—Sondergaard, wife of director Herbert Bieberman, a blacklisted artist who went to prison for taking the Fifth, had become one of the blacklist's main targets.

It was six years until the next call came, from the producers of *Return of a Man Called Horse*. It was the same story; Sondergaard was lionized, welcomed back, and critically acclaimed once again as one of Hollywood's great ones.

Again, it was a useless exercise. "It's her age," said a producer at CBS. "She's simply too old now." To prove them wrong, the actress climbed up the comeback road still a third time in 1980. She took the central role in a new Broadway play, *Goodbye, Fidel*. It lasted only a few weeks—but long enough for the *New York Times* to call her "a bright, vibrant oasis in a year of dismal drama." The actress packed up her things and returned, again, to Hollywood.

In 1978 Gale was brought back by the Academy as one of the centerpieces for the "Fiftieth Birthday of Oscar," joining such relics of the golden age as Jane Powell, who sang a fluttery waltz, and Cyd Charisse, who modeled period costumes from Oscar's past.

The crowd of oldtimers roared. And fan mail poured in again to Sondergaard's agent. She's moved from the mansion in the Hollywood Hills now—down to a more modest compound in fading Echo Park which was fashionable in the thirties—the era when she was a Hollywood rage, so popular that she was the original choice for the wicked witch in *The Wizard of Oz*.

Her 1936 Oscar for *Anthony Adverse* sits in a special niche in the hall not far from a picture of the early Sondergaard in a red dress and monkey-fur coat walking on Herbert's arm at the world premiere of *The Life of Emil Zola*. "You ask me what's exciting," she said with a glance at the photo and a smile that could erase time. "That was exciting—a proud, brief moment."

"I have no bitterness about what *they* did. I don't know who *they* are even. *They* was a system—a force that was there—a force grabbing everybody and pulling them down."

Evidence now shows that Parks and Sondergaard were the era's ultimate casualties. But the most bizaare victim of Oscar's flirtation with the blacklist was a movie, *High Noon*—the ultimate Western masterpiece and the creation of director Fred Zinnemann and blacklistee Carl Foreman.

In Academy history only the loss of *Citizen Kane* to *How Green Was My Valley* created as much uproar. And the screams started the minute Cecil

Gale Sondergaard as captured by Lawrence Durrell during her glamour period—about 1945. She was such an adept character actress that, by 1936, she was one of a handful of performers for which the Academy created new best supporting categories, and she won the first one for *Anthony Adverse*. She created an entire genre—the svelte, sexy, and gorgeous villainess, and she was the original choice for the witch in *The Wizard of Oz*—a part she surrendered rather than make herself ugly. From the minute her husband, director Herbert Biberman, was named as a possible Communist Party member, Sondergaard's career was over. Only in 1970 when Robert Wagner talked her into a guest shot on "It Takes a Thief" did she return to a Hollywood soundstage.

Gary Cooper had been a screen hero, tried and true, for twenty years when he made *High Noon* and faced down the street demons. But his biggest victory came offscreen when he faced down a furious Hollywood establishment to back writer Carl Foreman only days after he was blacklisted. Foreman, who had left the *High Noon* set to appear before H.U.A.C., found himself out of a job at Columbia Pictures and tried to salvage his living by forming his own production company. "Sign me up," said Cooper. "And use my name publicly."

B. DeMille's potboiler, *The Greatest Show on Earth*, won best picture honors over the now classic Western.

No other story in Oscar's history reveals the basic and pervasive fear of the Academy's block voting and the occasional courage of the creative forces who choose to fly against this withering headwind of disapproval.

This time, the hero of the shoot-out is the same on and off the screen—Gary Cooper.

Even the setting was unlikely—sleepy Sonora, California, a city far enough into Northern California for the town folks to be wary of those city slickers, the moving picture people. Gary Cooper reported to the set in the fall of 1951 as the second choice for the lead. (Producer Stanley Kramer had asked for Gregory Peck but was turned down flat.) From his first cup of coffee with the crew, Cooper knew he had landed smack in the middle of a covey of cinema's young turks: Kramer, who was becoming known for producing "message pictures"; Foreman, who'd written the scripts for *Home of the Brave* and *Cyrano de Bergerac*; and Zinnemann, whose major works until then had pitted man against his conscience.

It was a congenial crew—almost had to be in isolated Sonora. But bits and pieces of gossip about the anti-Communist developments back in Hollywood began seeping in.

Suddenly it was brought home in the gut when Foreman's name was added to the growing list of suspects that was being assembled by the House UnAmerican Activities Committee in Washington (a list that was leaked to the press before some committee members got a copy).

Foreman got the dreaded summons, went to Washington, took the Fifth, and was blacklisted as soon as he finished *High Noon*.

Foreman arrived back on the set frightened but inspired. He put his script back into the typewriter. Slowly, on those dusty days on the set,

The cover of *Time* magazine given to Cooper after he starred in *Mr. Deeds Goes to Town* which revealed Cooper as one of the finest and deepest actors in the business. Typically for the Academy, he wasn't even nominated for this film but won the Oscar instead for the one-dimensional *Sergeant York*. Cooper's fate somehow became personally entwined with that of the Oscars—both when he made a spectacular comeback in *High Noon* and on the night when James Stewart broke down while accepting an Oscar for his friend and revealed that Cooper was dying.

TIME

THE WEEKLY NEWSMAGAZINE

GARY COOPER—JOHN DOE
He made the cover.
(Cinema)

Jean Arthur and Gary Cooper in Cecil B. De Mille's *The Plainsman*. Cooper played Wild Bill Hickcock, a far cry from his Oscar-winning portrayal as Will Kane in Stanley Kramer's *High Noon*.

Foreman began crafting *High Noon* to fit the McCarthy era like a Saville Row suit fits the newest member of the House of Lords. Foreman used words instead of scissors, building a poem about fear.

"So much of the script became comparable to what was happening," said Foreman decades later. "There are many scenes taken from life. One is a distillation of meetings I had with partners, associates, and lawyers. And there's the scene with the man who offers to help and comes back with his gun. 'Where are the others,' he asks? 'There are no others,' says Cooper."

Cooper, Kramer, and Zinnemann all knew about the subtle shifts. They agreed—even to the point of leaking the strategy to Columbia's boss, Harry Cohn, a bitter foe of the H.U.A.C. and the blacklist.

One day shortly near the end of shooting, Cooper wandered over to Foreman and said, "Thanks. This is a good one." He shook the writer's hand and headed back to his dressing room.

Cooper seemed anxious to give Foreman even further support, but the gesture was wordless, an unspoken promise.

The writer was puzzled but forgot about it back in Hollywood where all hell broke loose when Hedda Hopper and John Wayne demanded publicly that Foreman be fired and that, as Hedda wrote, "He never be hired here again."

The next day, Kramer, in a frantic attempt to salvage Foreman's investment in the Kramer Company, publicly announced he was disassociating himself from the beleaguered writer. Foreman was never to forgive Kramer even though the producer revealed it was either cut bait or lose the entire company, including Foreman's own investment. The bitterness continues into the eighties.

Kim Hunter, here with Vivien Leigh in *A Streetcar Named Desire* made perhaps the most sensational ingenue splash in the history of the industry as Tennessee Williams's troubled young heroine. Everybody wanted to sign her, and she walked off with the best supporting actress Oscar in a hands-down contest. Six months later her name was engraved in granite on the blacklist. She was never to make an adequate comeback.

The day Kramer sliced free his close friend, Foreman got a call at home—late in the evening. "How's it going?" It was Gary Cooper. The writer explained that, since he owned some properties himself (including *The Bridge on the River Kwai*), he was going to form his own company. "Count me in—now. Use my name," said Cooper. "I mean it."

Foreman waited a couple of minutes then called another Hollywood pal, publicist Henry Rogers. "What should I do?" he asked. Rogers, fast emerging as the most important public relations man in town, told him to set a press conference and come out in the open with it.

The announcement made page one of *Daily Variety* and the *Hollywood Reporter*. Cooper, several others, and Rogers himself were named as members of the board. But somebody had tipped off Hedda before press time. Rogers' switch phones at home were jammed before the P.R. whiz got home. First on the line was the acid voice of Hedda: "Now I know why I got mad at you years ago," she said. (Hedda had long ago boycotted Rogers.) "You're just no good. You've got yourself mixed up with that Commie bastard Carl Foreman. That washes you up in this town. I'm going to see to it that you're driven out of business."

The next couple of calls came from John Wayne, Ginger Rogers, and Ward Bond—all members with Hedda of the right wing Motion Picture Alliance for the Preservation of American Ideals, an organization of more than a thousand actors, writers, and directors.

So many calls came through in that six hour period that Rogers began to realize that they had been staged. "It was," he said later, "a calculated plan of terror."

At this point in the action *High Noon* was still in post production, but Cooper and Zinnemann, by their tacit support of Foreman, had made the

Hollywood establishment a mite skittish about the movie.

Cooper had given his word, confirmed it, and then taken off into the wilds of Montana—fishing. The first morning, Cooper and another pal, Ernest Hemingway, were casting for trout when a Western Union man showed up at the stream—a fistful of telegrams in hand. One was from Warners—they wanted to break his contract, using an outdated "morals clause." And there were threats from Louis B. Mayer and producer Walter Wanger.

The hero of *Sergeant York* and *Meet John Doe* hiked back to the lodge and got the long distance operator.

"Carl—"

But Foreman stopped him. "I know. Nobody can hold up against this . . . not even you."

Cooper admitted defeat—not even his broad shoulders were strong enough to fight the political current. "But he was the only big one who tried," said Foreman. "The only one."

Henry Rogers, in his own hot box, got a call from the biggest agent in town. "He said he'd have to pull his clients if this kept up. He told me to back down. But I didn't . . . refused. But I was scared." So Rogers held on, giving up only after Foreman himself made him do it. "Nobody can hold out against all this . . ." Foreman told Rogers. "I'm giving up."

A couple of weeks later Foreman packed up his typewriter and his family and moved to England—where he stayed until *The Bridge on the River Kwai* restored his career and then some.

Meanwhile, *High Noon* made money so quickly and won critics so completely that it squeezed out seven nominations, including best picture. Over at the Academy, the rafters of that twenty-five-year-old institution were shaking with the aftershock that a sizable list of past winners was banished from Tinseltown. Back-fence gossip made the membership painfully aware of the subtle propaganda written into *High Noon*. "A great film but mighty political."

The nervousness increased when the New York Film Critics named *High Noon* best picture of 1951.

Luckily for everybody, a circus soap opera, *The Greatest Show on Earth*, became the biggest box office hit in twenty years, taking in $12 million in only a year. A good excuse, right? The voters had often (too often, some said) named economic movies over artistic triumphs. It was to be so again. Cecil B. DeMille walked off with the best picture Oscar on the back of an elephant and a train wreck, the movie's only touch of excitement.

Later, when the smoke cleared, only the loss of *Citizen Kane* a decade earlier drew as much rancor from critics and movie fans.

The one choice everybody agreed on was Gary Cooper as best actor.

It is important thirty years later to see that the Academy was not an actual participant in these sorry episodes. Actress Lee Grant prefers to call the Academy just another victim. "At first, it looked like this was going to be permanent. The fear became THE reality."

Dalton Trumbo seems to have written the last word: "When you who are in your forties look back with curiosity at that dark time, as I think occasionally you should, it will do you no good to search for villains. There were none. There were only victims."

Lloyd Bridges, Katy Jurado, Gary Cooper, and Grace Kelly in *High Noon*.

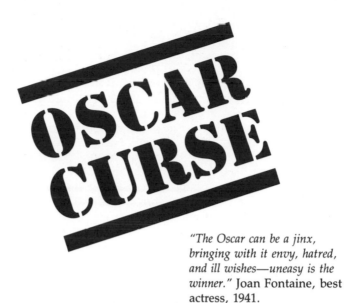

8 OSCAR CURSE

"The Oscar can be a jinx, bringing with it envy, hatred, and ill wishes—uneasy is the winner." Joan Fontaine, best actress, 1941.

A human storm broke over Rod Steiger's shoulders. Mikes were jammed into his exhausted face. Flashbulbs blinded him. A pack of rapacious journalists yelled at him, bullied him with questions, dared him not to answer. Hands yanked at his satin lapels; cords from a dozen TV cameras wound around his legs.

Suddenly, he was a prisoner of fame—caught in a hornet's nest of unreality. It was, he would remember, exactly like the crowd scene from *Day of the Locust*. But he would only remember that after he was hemmed in by the gilded bars of international stardom. But at the time, in April of 1968, it was only the slightly bitter hangover after a hefty taste of sweet victory. Within the space of three months, Steiger had won the top acting prizes of the National Society of Film Critics, the New York Film Critics, the Golden Globes, and the British Film Academy.

And now the Oscar! It had been five minutes since he bounded toward the stage, and it had gone by in slow motion. First, Audrey Hepburn languidly read the nominees: "Warren Beatty, Dustin Hoffman, Paul Newman, Spencer Tracy." Then the words, "Rod Steiger, *In the Heat of the Night*." Then the roar. Wave after wave of shouts . . . because Steiger was an "inside winner, an actor's actor." Probably no single winner since Paul Muni and Laurence Olivier had as much respect from his peers.

Steiger tightened his longshoreman's fist around the Oscar and rubbed it across his wrist in a gesture that seemed to ask, "It's real, isn't it?"

He'd had it almost in his hand two years before for *The Pawnbroker*. That year, even the guys in Vegas said he'd win. But Lee Marvin, another guy who came up the hard way, took home the prize for the lightweight *Cat Ballou*. But even as an "also ran" Steiger was boosted into the golden circle whose names are above the title. With *In the Heat of the Night* he broke the bank.

So Steiger shrugged off the clamoring mob, hoisted his Oscar up over his head, and smiled across the room at the gossip columnist. "Oscar curse—what's that? Not for me." He sailed out to his limo, hanging ten on a wave of glory.

Valerie Perrine and Rod Steiger on the set of *W.C. Fields and Me,* which contains one of Steiger's great performances. When the critics crucified it, Steiger went into such a depression that he "stayed in bed for days—sometimes weeks. It seemed like there was no force strong enough to get me out." Steiger is perhaps the classic victim of the Oscar curse, a syndrome that stems from "too much, too soon" given to winners the morning after. "I suddenly felt like a ball player who'd hit a home run and turned around to find the stands empty," said Steiger.

The gossip columnist just smiled, twisting one ruby red lip into a sneer. "Just wait, mister, just wait."

During the next decade Rod Steiger had little time and no inclination to look back. His salary soared to $750,000 a picture, and his tough guy mug became one of the ten best known in the world.

He traded his Oscar chit for chances to play the greatest roles in history: Mussolini, Lucky Luciano, and that Waterloo of parts, Napoleon (in the multi-million dollar *Waterloo*). But the Oscar propulsion ran out—as it always does. Steiger faced his fiftieth birthday a physical wreck (he needed open-heart surgery), an artistic casualty, (critics were blasting his performance in *W.C. Fields and Me*), and a personal victim (his third marriage had just crumbled in a bitter court confrontation).

"I was scared to death, and couldn't work," he said. "To get out of bed and brush my teeth was a big accomplishment. 'The bed is death,' I used to say to myself. 'Go ahead, lie here and talk to yourself, but the goddamned bed is going to kill you.' "

It was there, in his solitude, that Steiger looked back over the decade to Oscar night, 1968, when the columnist asked him about "the Oscar curse" and then folded her arms to wait.

"From the minute you get off the stage, it seems they're looking for you to fall," says George Kennedy, who won his best supporting Oscar the same year (for *Cool Hand Luke*). "There was a guy waiting for me behind the curtain. 'Hey, George,' he said. 'Do ya think it'll be a jinx for you?' He didn't so much as say congratulations or good going. Then I heard that question over and over and over again during the next few weeks. What a bunch of bunk."

Kennedy's beef is on target.

The so-called Oscar curse was invented during the Academy's early days by that mama of all columnists, Louella Parsons. To Louella, whose spun-sugar view of Hollywood allowed for all superstition, the jinx was born on a Tinseltown Ouija board—like some celluloid black cat. "Beware, beware," Louella cautioned many a dewy-eyed winner, "the Oscar will get you if you don't watch out."

This was just so much emotional claptrap, of course. But the Oscar curse is real, and it was born in that era. It was born of greedy agents who priced their Oscar winning clients out of existence. It was born of studio bosses who shoved their Oscared stars into quickie films designed merely to cash in on the Academy's largess. And, in some cases, it was born of the stars themselves as they turned piggish and "high hat."

"I don't know if it should even be called a jinx," says Rita Moreno, an Oscar winner who's tasted of the curse. "But the award can quickly be turned into a downer by people who try to cash it as a promissory note. That is the curse."

Rita's own victory over the burden an Oscar places on a career is telling because it took her almost twenty years to climb out of the shadow that was cast on her by the statue.

Her flirtation with the Academy Awards began on April 9, 1962.

It was a banner year for the Oscars—a hundred million fans would watch the ceremony through new TV hookups, and the largest contingent of superstars since the 1940s were jammed into the Santa Monica Civic Auditorium.

While Greer Garson and Natalie Wood were having their hair done in Beverly Hills, Rita, then a moderately successful ingénue, flew into Los Angeles from Manila—tourist class. She blew her savings on a Paris gown, picked up her mom, and joined the crush of cars heading toward the searchlights.

© A.M.P.A.S.

Greer Garson and James Cagney with their best actor and best actress awards for 1942. Cagney received his Oscar for his portrayal of George M. Cohan in *Yankee Doodle Dandy*, and Miss Garson received best actress for her role in *Mrs. Miniver*.

Like many other stars, Rita Moreno learned painfully that Oscar holds a two-edged sword. Her best supporting actress award for *West Side Story* brought her acclaim but also a demeaning stereotype in the minds of producers as a Latin spitfire. All she was offered were tawdry duplicates of her "Anita" role. George Chakiris, who won best supporting actor for the same film, also suffered. His production company hustled him into a string of quickies and his reputation declined. Young performers in particular are easy prey for a greedy system.

The next two hours slipped by in a daze as Rita Moreno sat in a row awash with mink, Dior, and custom-cut tuxedos.

Then the envelope—THAT envelope. "And the winner is, for *West Side Story*, Rita Moreno."

She gave her mother a hug; ran the fifty yards to the stage; took her Oscar, shook it a little, and started to cry.

Then she rushed back to the airport, boarded a midnight flight for Manila, and disappeared from Hollywood sound stages for seven years. Her Oscar turned back into a pumpkin, and her career was back at the starting point.

Louella could hardly wait to list her as the latest victim of the curse.

In reality, Rita Moreno's problems proved to be more scientific and more intriguing than those invented by the columnists. She rolled the dice—took a gamble on a hunch. She should not, she decided, doom herself to play and replay the Puerto Rican spitfire character until she became a Hollywood stereotype (such as Judy Holliday's dumb blonde or Yul Brynner's bald and macho Oriental—career traps that grew directly out of Oscar victories).

"It wasn't easy," said Moreno. "I was terrified at first. I knew I had to get out of town because there was too much temptation here. I could have taken any of those spitfire roles and made a bundle. Luckily I was so demeaned—I mean it's really demeaning after you've won the Oscar to be offered the same role over and over again. They only wanted me to drag out my accent-and-dance show over and over again. And boy was I offered them all—Gypsy fortune tellers, Mexican spitfires, Spanish spitfires, Puerto Ricans—all those 'Yankee peeg, you steel me peeple's money' parts.

"The only thing I could do was turn my back on it."

Rita was luckier than most Oscar winners—she'd been dancing and singing on Broadway since she was thirteen. So, when she finished her Manila quickie, she bought a ticket for New York.

Oscar's history certainly boasts of more success stories—rescued careers and quick fortunes—than it does of reversals. But evidence of Oscar backlash goes as far back as the era when Luise Rainer won two awards in a row (1936 and 1937) and then virtually never made another decent film . . . and her career quickly became a curiosity—a Hollywood footnote.

Some veteran stars like Joan Fontaine continue to speak of an Oscar jinx. "The Oscar was a marvelous concept of some very responsible people," says Fontaine, who was named best actress in 1941 for Alfred Hitchcock's *Suspicion*.

"It was supposed to be an event to make our business more dignified. But it quickly became just another monetary spectacle." Fontaine feels—has always felt—that the Oscar hangover comes from the massive publicity that comes with the territory. "In the forties, and still today, winners of the Oscar seemed like members of royalty suddenly elevated to the throne. You suddenly have international recognition, preferential treatment. Naturally, there is many an ill-wisher, many a doubter."

Fontaine would have more than her share of this because of a backstage feud with her sister, Olivia De Havilland—an incident that fills the single largest file in the motion picture Academy's own biography files.

"They are gunning for you after you win. If you fail for any reason to see the press on the set, you've suddenly gone 'high hat.' And the critics are so hard on you that they seem to be in a hurry to tear you down from that supposed high place that the Oscar won for you.

"Everybody is jealous—especially the producers and directors because the Oscar winner is suddenly the one they want to see. And producers are

Rod Steiger in his role as *The Illustrated Man*, one of the bizarre but daring series of films he made after winning the Oscar for *In the Heat of the Night*.

used to being top dog."

Indeed, in Fontaine's case David O. Selznick, who had called Joan the "hardest woman in Hollywood to get a performance out of," quickly took public credit for building her to her Oscar peak. "She could have become a top star no place else but at Selznick," he wrote in a letter. "I nurtured her."

"Then I got typed," Fontaine states. "One critic for the *Saturday Review* said I could probably only play simps. But my simping became suddenly more expensive—Selznick charged a lot more for my services . . . then I had a publicity glut—my picture was everywhere at once."

Joan was photographed in fifty different suits for Easter P.R. in 1943, was decked in twenty fur coats for Sunday supplements, and modeled hair styles especially for blondes. The Selznick flaks made certain that entertainment editors were sick and tired of Fontaine within three years.

Meanwhile, Selznick loaned her out, using her as a made-to-order simp in movies like *Jane Eyre*.

"An Oscar can damage irreparably one's relations with family, friends, co-workers, and the press—certainly the press."

In recent Academy history, nobody has taken more Oscar aftershocks than Rod Steiger . . . and from all sides.

For five years after his best actor award, he rode the Oscar high with all the trimmings—the media blitz, the six-figure salary, and, he says, the chance to try his greatest acting challenges.

"It's like any other contest. You're number one for awhile. Then you slip to number two. Then number three. Then it's every man for himself." Eighteen months after his win, Steiger's face was spread across the slick double-page spreads of a dozen magazines. "Let us Now Praise the Famous Me," said a headline in *Esquire* magazine. And a London tabloid, in a rare case of the sillies, proclaimed Rod and then-wife Claire Bloom as "The King and Queen of Hollywood," even painting British crowns over their Technicolor faces.

Steiger traded his Oscar for chances to make a wide range of films—from the bizarre *Illustrated Man* to *The Sergeant*, a frank and daring exploration of macho homosexuality. In this, Steiger veers sharply off the course usually followed by Oscar winners. Normally, winners happily kiss their statuette and then sign multi-million dollar pacts to make routine box office films. They then ride their Rolls-Royces into the sunset of Beverly's top hills.

A prime example of the cash-in is Lee Marvin from Steiger's own generation of winners. Marvin, after showing tour de force performances in *Ship of Fools* and *Cat Ballou* in the same year, consigned himself to forgettable movies. For consolation he has taken home massive paychecks. " 'Just toe the mark and say the lines.' That's Bogart's line, and, in the long run, he's right," Marvin said recently. He pulls a million a movie, and, he says, "I'm satisfied."

But Steiger forsook the millions and plowed into highly experimental waters. Some critics feel he will reap rewards in cinema history books for his troubles. One of his movies, *No Way to Treat a Lady*, has become another of the medium's "flawed classics" and *Happy Birthday, Wanda June* is on its way.

"Suddenly it began to dawn on me that I felt like a ballplayer who had hit a home run in an empty ballpark."

He'd also coasted through his third marriage (and a bitter, publicized suit for half of Steiger's supposed $2.4 million a year), through the two expensive failures (*Waterloo* and *W.C. Fields and Me*), and through open-heart surgery. He was face-to-face with both physical and artistic mortality. "Confronting death is a big shock to the ego," Steiger said. "It scares the shit out of you." When the critics turned on him, he was hit in a somewhat more private part of the anatomy. "I felt like I was under seige on the set of F.I.S.T.; I was in the midst of terror. I didn't think I could even remember my lines."

But the actor knew his Oscar honeymoon was over long before that. "It was over the minute I did a film that didn't do well." It was during his year of researching Napoleon's final days that he began to feel that Oscar glory (and Hollywood fame for that matter) could well be compared with the Parisian fickleness that dogged the French emperor.

Steiger, in spite of it all, views the Academy Awards with a mixture of slight disdain and awe. "It becomes a fad every April. I respect their decisions. But then I don't even like to lose a tennis game. When I was up for *The Pawnbroker* and lost, that ceremony goes by in a haze. And did I have to lose to *Cat Ballou?*"

Maybe some of the actor's awe harks back to his experience with *The Pawnbroker*. "Winning that nomination was an enormous help in getting directors to listen to me when I feel a scene isn't going right," he told an interviewer at the time. "The year I was nominated happened to be Hollywood's year. When *The Sound of Music* wins an Academy Award, you know its Hollywood's year. The year before, England walked off with the honors so Hollywood had to say, 'Wait a minute. This has got to be Hollywood's year.'

"If you've given a performance that you believe is good, there's nothing the matter with taking pride in the recognition an Academy Award symbolizes. I didn't kiss anybody's ass to get it. And its main value is that it protects an actor's position and power. It helps him in the tactical maneuvers that you have to have—if you want to keep your self-respect."

In 1980 the Oscar curse began lifting for Steiger—with five of his pictures going into release within a seven month period, ranging from *The Chosen* with fellow winner Maximilian Schell to a Nazi occupation film, *The Lucky Star,* with Louise Fletcher (also a former winner for *One Flew Over the Cuckoo's Nest* in 1975).

Oscar's prestige, in any case, has never been in question. Its economic worth to an actor is another thing.

A London tabloid fixed the value of Julie Christie's Oscar for *Darling* (1965) at $10 million. "That's what she'll get during the next ten years," said a columnist, writing under a headline: "OCAR For Julie." Estelle Parsons found that her fee had been multiplied by ten the day after she won for *Bonnie and Clyde.* And George Kennedy freely admits that his supporting Oscar for *Cool Hand Luke* made him Hollywood's richest character actor.

The "cash value" of an acting Oscar was a taboo subject during the Academy's first three decades. But the fifties changed all that when the studios began the dubious tradition of massive, national post-Oscar campaigns that are now routine.

Laurence Olivier and Joan Fontaine in *Rebecca.* This was Fontaine's second film for director Alfred Hitchcock. She received an Oscar for her role in Suspicion (1941) and was nominated for her role in *Rebecca.* Her loan-out fee jumped after the Oscar but not her pay. Selznick held her contract as well as her money.

In 1940 Joan Fontaine's official loan-out fee jumped from $25,000 to $100,000 after she was nominated for *Rebecca.* A year later, after her Oscar-winning film *Suspicion,* Selznick Studios, which held her contract, began charging as much as $200,000 per picture. "I never saw a cent of those increased fees," says Fontaine, who continued to receive $12,500 a week (her pre-Oscar paycheck). The inflation chased off producers who otherwise might have used Fontaine. And she describes the futility and frustration of the post-Oscar blues in her caustic book about Hollywood, *No Bed of Roses.* "I sat idle for six months after *Suspicion.* He (David Selznick) was trying to get the highest bid for my services . . . but that was only common practice then." Selznick also used his own Oscar inflation scale when he loaned out Ingrid Bergman, Jennifer Jones, and others in his stable of stars.

In the thirties and forties stars were often "rented" by their home studios to rival producers, and it was no secret that an Oscar moved a star into a higher rent district. Fontaine feels these salary hikes have contributed greatly to the post-Oscar syndrome: "It gave people a chance to say—or at least think—is she worth it? If the picture was a success, fine. If not, this was the first step back down."

Oscared stars of the fifties began talking about salary gains as early as the morning after—with the stakes going higher every year. Civil court records give plenty of examples.

Marlon Brando got $75,000 for *A Streetcar Named Desire* and took a whopping post Oscar jump to $1.2 million for the Technicolor turkey, *Mutiny on the Bounty,* in 1962. His fee was scaled downward in the late sixties but was up again to about $1.5 million for *The Missouri Breaks* after his second Academy Award for *The Godfather.*

William Holden was in the moderate price range for *Sunset Boulevard* and *Stalag 17,* but joined the ranks of the millionaires after his Oscar for the latter film.

Such inflation filtered on down in descending value, depending on the award. Dorothy Malone, for instance, was taking home about $90,000 a year from her contract with Universal in 1955. She had been in Hollywood for ten years by then, having been spotted by a talent scout in an amateur play at Southern Methodist University. First she tried RKO where the bosses felt she was their answer to the girl next-door. (MGM had Donna Reed, Fox had Jeanne Crain, etc.) Films like *The Falcon and the Coeds,* and *Too Young to Know* quickly put her to sleep.

Dorothy Malone presenting Ivan Tors with the best special effects award for the third in the James Bond series, *Thunderball*. Tors is perhaps best known for his long-running TV series, "Sea Hunt."

Then she tried Warners. There her hair was lightened to "blondine" and she was draped on the arms of a succession of screen cavalry lieutenants, who fought off the Indians and romanced Dorothy in their tight Helen Rose uniforms. Then she landed a steamy role in *Battle Cry*, where she tempted Tab Hunter while changing in a butterfly chair.

Universal, her new studio, relegated her back to junk. "By 1955, I was spending more time in Dallas, my hometown, than I was in Hollywood. It was more challenging for me to do public relations for an insurance company and a Texas airline than to play the roles they gave me."

She decided to give it one more try. In late 1955 she hired a press agent and bleached her hair platinum for sexy "other woman" parts. The change was instantaneous and breathtaking, and she was penciled in as Robert Stack's sister in *Written on the Wind*.

The 1956 best supporting actress Oscar for *Written on the Wind* resulted in instant salary inflation. From her pre-award $90,000, Malone's salary jumped to $125,000 in 1956, to about $160,000 in 1958, to $164,000 in 1959. By then the Oscar honeymoon had waned and her salary headed down: to $98,170 in 1960, $58,013 in 1961, and $32,456 in 1962.

It's an old Academy Award story in Hollywood, as greedy agents and studio bosses push their winning stars to higher salaries and shove them into quickie movies or TV shows. The star is rarely at fault, but the results usually mirror the eventual salary drop that hit Dorothy Malone.

"The day after you do a picture that loses money," says Rod Steiger, "your price heads back down." Steiger's per-picture pay jumped from about $100,000 to "at least $350,000" after his Oscar for *In the Heat of the Night*. The actor was paid about a million dollars for the disastrous *Waterloo*. After that his prices nosedived. But he has now survived the Oscar blues and scored

This classic shot of Julie Andrews and *The Sound of Music* children in the Austrian Alps circulated so widely that it came back to Julie by typing her almost forever in the saccharine image of the Rodgers and Hammerstein heroine. The image has dogged her steps, greatly limiting and binding an actress of incredible range, much as the gift of sweetness and light typed Doris Day a decade earlier.

again with *The Amityville Horror.* "You suddenly become the latest fad," said Steiger. "I went to the top and stayed there for awhile. Then I did some pictures that weren't so lucky. Then I made one picture for less than my salary—suddenly people were asking me to take the lesser fee regularly."

When an Oscar winner fails it's usually a big failure; a million dollar failure. The Hollywood executives, who seem to see the Oscar as a sort of golden four-leaf clover, soon feel that a winner can sprinkle Oscar dust on even the dreariest of films. "Executives suddenly lose their perspective with a big Oscar winner," said Bosley Crowther of the *New York Times.* "The safeguards they normally have fail to operate. Disasters easily follow."

The Oscar often creates an artistic and economic Peter principle for these stars—they rise to their level of least effectiveness. Then the fall—sometimes reaching proportions of a Greek tragedy.

This is what happened to Julie Andrews—who won the Oscar for her cloyingly sweet performance in *Mary Poppins.* Neither she—nor the big studio movies she represented—have been the same since. Twentieth Century-Fox rushed her into *The Sound of Music* and then watched in amazement as that movie, a mild Broadway success, became the most successful film in history. (It overtook *Gone With the Wind* after it was out for only a month.) It seemed that Julie could do no wrong, and the Fox brass offered her the moon to make the splashiest musical ever made. It was such a sure thing that they decided to call it simply *Star!* No explanation needed. Right? I mean, after all, this was Julie Andrews—folks in Calcutta, for chrissakes, were going to see her four and five times. Even the sacred cows were neglected for a couple of days.

But *Star!* waltzed into the box office records as a musical *Cleopatra.* And Julie plummeted from Oscar superstardom to the stages of Vegas where

A spoonful of sugar almost turned Julie Andrews's film career into a pillar of salt. The actress, shown here with Dick Van Dyke and friends in *Mary Poppins*, and with Christopher Plummer in *The Sound of Music*, won her Oscar for the Disney film *Mary Poppins*. And she won it, in large part, because of the movie community's outrage that Audrey Hepburn had been cast by Jack Warner in the role Andrews originated in *My Fair Lady*. At one Oscar banquet the actress held up a plaque and said, "Thank you, Jack Warner." The Academy Award for *Mary Poppins* and the nomination for *The Sound of Music* put Julie Andrews on a pedestal. From that moment on the studios decided she could only appear in tuneful, bloated productions—ignoring the range she had shown in *Torn Curtain*, *Thoroughly Modern Millie*, and *The Americanization of Emily*. It was with considerable bitterness that she found audiences wouldn't accept her as a three-dimensional woman.

they gave her $250,000 a week to sing, sweetly, the songs from *Mary Poppins*.

In early 1980 Julie reported to a Hollywood sound stage to make a film intriguingly titled *S.O.B.*, which was written by husband Blake Edwards and is about, he says, an actress who won an Oscar for Peter Pan and then did utterly different parts—and is trying to find her way back. Poetic justice, some say.

Julie Andrews' Oscar story, however, is hauntingly familiar. It echoes all the other Oscar cash-ins throughout Hollywood history. Again, the industry's normal artistic and economic safeguards were lowered at half-mast in deference to an Oscar, allowing Julie's career and Fox's product to soar past the failsafe mark.

But it all started back in August of 1964 when *Mary Poppins* opened in New York City. One of the drooling reviews in the *Hollywood Reporter* summed up the hysteria: "This is the kind of film and the kind of performance that creates not fans but evangelists." Which is precisely what happened. Out in Foggy Bottom, Alabama, and Shenandoah, Iowa, women's clubbers told their friends who told their friends that here finally was "a gal you can take the family to see—ALL the family."

Miss Andrews, as she was called by then at Fox, had already finished *The Sound of Music*, which opened only a few days before the Oscar ceremony. Here is the way the *Hollywood Reporter* welcomed it: "This lady is not just a great star. She is not just an ordinary film personality. She is a whole, whirling galaxy. Once there was Mary Pickford, then there was Garbo, now there is Julie."

This would seem silly were it not for the fact that Hollywood reads the *Hollywood Reporter* as gospel . . . they take it seriously. It's the first thing Bogdanovich reads as he heads off the racquetball court. Cher carries it to her fanny tightening class, and Ryan O'Neal scans it while he's pumping iron. So what did this mean? Julie Andrews had just become a box office saint.

Miss Andrews, then twenty-nine with only three films behind her, was rushed into *Hawaii* to the tune of $700,000 and her pick of co-stars. When she jetted to the islands, she couldn't have known that James Michener's poem to the tropics would be her last truly successful film of the seventies.

In quick succession, *Star!*, *Darling Lili*, and *The Tamarind Seed* bombed at the only place it counts—the box office.

"I think *Star!* failed because the public wasn't very happy with seeing me in drunken scenes," she told writer Charles Higham. "It was very hard for me to play drunk scenes. I had to force myself to do it, but I think it worked. Then the public refused to accept me as a spy, and that disappointed me awfully," she said about *Darling Lili*, which is fast becoming a critical success in cult cinema circles. "I was a victim of typecasting. I can't knock *The Sound of Music* and *Mary Poppins* because they gave such an awful lot of pleasure to a lot of people. But that kind of exposure puts you into the greatest danger. I won an Oscar for *Mary Poppins* and then went into the most successful musical up to that time. Now I can see that I was too quickly bracketed in one category. And I couldn't escape."

She was also a victim of the Oscar hangover. Because she won and was so quickly nominated again for *The Sound of Music*, film executives felt they could hardly just put her into a little, well-made movie. They had to show her rising full-blown in CinemaScope conch shells like Venus rising from the sea. So she quickly sank.

It looks like she's going to have the last laugh. Those who have seen the rushes for *S.O.B.* say that Andrews gives it right back—in the gut.

George Kennedy, who won for *Cool Hand Luke*, found that his Oscar truly made his fortune. "My fee increased about ten times overnight." The same thing was true for Estelle Parsons, who won the Oscar for *Bonnie and Clyde*. Kennedy, however, has become somewhat of a legend by parlaying his Oscar into increasingly lucrative roles. "They can't seem to do one of those disaster films without me," said Kennedy, who avoided the Oscar curse by making steady gains rather than jumping into more daring waters.

Which is where she had to take it.

Scores of Oscared actors have played the money game and won permanently fat paychecks—Holden, Sinatra, Ernest Borgnine, and Gene Hackman to name only a few. Hackman's win for *The French Connection* led directly to the $1.3 million superagent Sue Mengers got him when he replaced George Segal in the disastrous *Lucky Lady*.

Among those who took Oscar and ran with it to monetary Himalayas, George Kennedy is somewhat of a legend. "Here's an actor who won thirteen years ago," said a major agent. "He hasn't made an economic stumble since."

"My salary was multiplied by ten the minute I won," says Kennedy, who went to the Oscar ceremony thinking he would lose to Michael J. Pollard in *Bonnie and Clyde*. "We weren't supposed to win. I wasn't thinking about it, even. My performance in *Cool Hand Luke* had already changed things for me. People were saying, 'Hey this guy can do something besides kill people.'

"Everything changed for me after the Oscar. I got a certain figure for *Cool Hand Luke* and a new figure for everything that followed. But the happiest part was that I didn't have to play only villains anymore. In that film (*Cool Hand Luke*) I was able to show the compassionate side of the character. The Oscar flooded this with attention. I began to get roles that were sympathetic. Now, three out of four roles offered to me are likable characters."

Like many Oscar winners, Kennedy began feeling the winds of change even before the nominations were announced: "I was working on *Bandolero* with Jimmy Stewart, Raquel Welch, and Dean Martin. Stewart went to the producers and told them the word was getting around about *Cool Hand*

Ernest Borgnine was not a victim of the Oscar curse, but neither was his career simply "made" by his Oscar-winning portrayal of *Marty*. Since *Marty* was a character role, the Hollywood of the fifites didn't know how to cope with him.

© A.M.P.A.S.

Luke. Then he asked that my name be put above the title. In some ways that means as much to me as the Oscar."

Kennedy shares the belief of many when he says, "You would be hard pressed to find one example to prove that the Oscar, by itself, can hurt you."

But he admits that some salary demands that are heaped on Oscar's shoulders can cause trouble. "When a star's salary jumps to superstar level—the next big, big step above my level—the salary jump can backfire.

"It has nothing to do with whether a star like Rod Steiger (or Julie Andrews) is a good actor. The real question is, 'Does he or she have enough charisma and luck—that's a lot of it—to justify a million dollars?' "

Kennedy, who's piloted the *Concorde*, ridden the steamer in *Death on the Nile*, polished off *The Brass Target*, and been shaken apart in *Earthquake*, has seen a "lot of winners price themselves right out of existence. But that has nothing to do with the quality of an actor's performance."

The cash registers have been ringing since the first Oscar ceremony, when inexpensive ingénue Janet Gaynor's salary tripled in the late twenties. Some examples: Cagney, $140,000 a year before Oscar, $362,000 after; Wallace Beery, $75,000 before, $200,000 a year after; Claudette Colbert, $100,000 before, $350,000 after; Katharine Hepburn, $120,000 before, $206,000 after; Victor McLaglen, $50,000 a year before, $165,000 after.

There is another form of "Oscar cash-in"—a more subtle and perhaps more damaging misuse of an Academy Award. Since the thirties, Hollywood's money men have never been able to resist herding the winners through projects that are designed to cash in, quickly and bigly, on the prestige of an Oscar. "Almost the morning after I won for *Charly*, a film I had to hand-guide through production, I was descended upon by the same myopic Monday morning quarterbacks who hadn't wanted to make the movie in the first place," said Cliff Robertson, who won the best actor award in 1968. "In all cases, their creative credentials had not improved over the weekend. They came up with a lot of money and a lot of junk."

This post-Oscar stampede toward the box office has resulted in some notable career casualties. Susan Hayward, for instance, never made a single critically successful film after winning for *I Want to Live!* Bette Davis had to flee to England and fight Jack Warner for decent roles after being nominated four times and winning twice. And Jose Ferrer was rushed through an insipid series of films after his win for *Cyrano* and his nominated triumph in *Moulin Rouge*.

But the career disasters inflicted on Luise Rainer and on Dorothy Malone, although two decades apart, are perhaps the most typical. Both emerged from the semishadows to national prominence and both were pushed almost out of the business by greedy producers and agents.

It was Rainer's post-Oscar problems that caused Louella Parsons to coin the term "Oscar jinx" in the first place. Louella was trying to endow the Oscar with an emotional power and superstition, while the Rainer problems were really a case of striking too quickly and too many times while the Oscar was hot.

The "Luise Rainer Affair" reeks of *Sunset Boulevard* and has become one of the prime skeletons in Oscar's closet. Rainer, an actresss who was brought to MGM from Vienna to compete with Garbo, hit it so big and disappeared so completely that an erroneous folk tale has grown up around her name.

The story goes that Luise Rainer, who some said was more beautiful than Garbo, refused to sit on Louis B. Mayer's lap when she asked him to renegotiate her contract after the Oscar. So, say the snipes, Luise was quietly set out in the MGM sun to wither and die.

According to another legend, the "Viennese Teardrop," as she was called, was systematically destroyed by the Mayer regime after Thalberg died. (Rainer was a Thalberg creation.)

The real story of Luise Rainer, the first woman to win two Oscars in a row, has remained buried in a slag heap of gossip—perhaps because it reveals a highly unflattering portrait of the Academy Awards during their golden era.

Stripping away the decades shows that Luise Rainer, and her two Oscars, were a political accident, an accident that was a powerful symptom of Oscar's ills in the mid-thirties.

The week Rainer was nominated for *The Great Ziegfeld* in the winter of 1936, the Academy was at its weakest point—hundreds of actors (virtually every big name in town) and hundreds of writers had quit, enraged over the organization's domination by the Hollywood establishment (see Chapter Three).

It was a complicated problem. But, in a nutshell, actors, writers, and directors felt that the Academy had sold them out during the National Recovery Administration's attempt to deal with Hollywood's growing labor problems. The Academy, by default, had supported producers' demands for control of agencies and salaries.

In any case, the Academy of Motion Picture Arts and Sciences was crippled. The period is clouded in secrecy, but even Academy officers admit that more than half the members had resigned. Some estimates place the membership at "several hundred." But many others say frankly that it was only a handful. Frank Capra, who became Academy president in 1936, says, "The membership was down to fifty, and even that was fast eroding." Director Walter Wanger, who succeeded Capra as president in the early

The term Oscar curse was invented for Luise Rainer, here with William Powell and appearing as Anna Held in *The Great Ziegfeld*, which brought Rainer the first of two Oscars in a row. (The second was for playing a creaky Chinese peasant in *The Good Earth*.) MGM publicists liked to say that Miss Rainer's sixty-second scene on the phone was studied, dissected, and shown to acting classes around the world. And this may have been true: it seems more likely, however, that the scene was used to effectively show how NOT to handle a short bit. The writer Dalton Trumbo used to tell his colleagues, "Don't take the Oscars so seriously. . . . After all, they gave two of them to Luise Rainer."

forties, says the size of the organization bottomed out at forty.

In any case, only a handful of people were involved in the process that selected candidates for the award . . . which pitted Luise against Irene Dunne, Gladys George, Carole Lombard, and, much closer to home, Norma Shearer. Rainer's part was so small in *The Great Ziegfeld* that she would be classed as a supporting player today. And Shearer's vehicle, *Romeo and Juliet* was hand picked for her by husband Irving Thalberg. If ever a part was designed to win the Oscar, it was this one. Voters would have easily taken the bait, too, except for Oscar's weakened condition. Metro-Goldwyn-Mayer generally, and Louis Mayer and Irving Thalberg specifically, had kept a stranglehold on Oscar voting since 1927 when Mayer called together a "few of his closest friends" to create the Academy of Motion Picture Arts and Sciences. Not only did he pay for the organizational dinner, he grandly lent his personal attorney to draft the bylaws.

It paid off! The lion's share of Oscars and nominations during the first decade quickly turned to outright greed. MGM won 153 nominations and 33 Oscars during the first decade. Only Paramount (the other behind-the-scenes power in the Academy) was close, with 18 Oscars and 102 nominations. Warners took only 71 nominations and 15 Oscars, Columbia counted 43 nominations and 10 Oscars, and Fox had 54 nominations and 13 Oscars.

The claim has often been made that MGM naturally made better and more pictures during this era and deserved its lion's share. But records show that Warners released 441 pictures during the same decade—almost as many as MGM, which launched 464. MGM's iron grip on the Oscar race was blatant enough for Joan Crawford to show friends internal studio memos which frankly discussed who should win in each race. "They just

passed the best actress around from studio to studio like a dole," Crawford told her daughter Christina. "It's just another form of power to them."

This began to change, ever so slightly, in 1935 when almost every big star in Hollywood boycotted the ceremony. Stars such as Jeanette Mac-Donald, James Cagney, and Robert Montgomery stayed on the phone for days before the awards, convincing their fellow artists to stay away. The same stars—bolstered in 1936 by hundreds more—further urged writers and actors to refuse to even mail in their ballots. And no matter what the Oscar apologists say, this left the decision in pitifully few hands. Ordinarily the voters would have tossed the statue to Norma Shearer without a second thought. So Luise Rainer's first Oscar probably came to her by default.

The first Oscar merely led to the second through still another set of political circumstances. Frank Capra and the Academy officers, trying frant-ically to bring the Oscar race back into perspective, opened the vote to about 14,000 extra players and writers in Hollywood. And it was this huge group that chose Rainer's performance in *The Good Earth* over Garbo's in *Camille*. Rainer, a self-effacing newcomer, was far better liked, generally, than Garbo, Irene Dunne, Janet Gaynor, and Barbara Stanwyck. And she had the publicity from the previous year on her side.

Insiders at MGM say that THIS is the real story behind Luise Rainer's sudden fame and sudden fall. "They never planned for her to win in the first place," said a former MGM publicist. "You must remember that 'they' wanted to decide what to do with whom. So they didn't treat her as a winner."

In Rainer's own words: "For my second and third pictures I won Acad-emy Awards. Nothing worse could have happened to me." James Robert

Robert Donat and Ronald Ward on the set of *Goodbye, Mr. Chips*. The film was made in England by MGM and Donat received an Oscar for his per-formance. This was something, since among the contenders in 1939 were Clark Gable for *Gone With the Wind*, and Laurence Olivier for *Wuthering Heights*.

Dorothy Malone was able to weather the Oscar curse mainly because she was rescued by the juiciest role in the television series *Peyton Place*. Starring with Ryan O'Neal, Mia Farrow, and Barbara Parkins in a top-rated show gave Malone the exposure she failed to get from the second-string productions her agent signed her for.

Parish, probably MGM's most qualified scholar, said, "She won unprecedented audience sympathy. Almost by default, she was considered a dramatically versatile actress. Today, her acting technique in those films seems more mannered monotony than versatility. Compared to other actresses of more enduring qualities, such as Ingrid Bergman, Luise seems simply not of flesh and blood." (Parish's fresh insights are from his encyclopedic work, *The MGM Stock Company*.)

Two years later Rainer was a has-been, having finished three hasty pictures so dreary that they don't even show up on "Movies 'Til Dawn"— *The Emperor's Candlesticks, Big City,* and *Toy Wife*. "I was just a piece of machinery with no rights," said Rainer. "They completely abused me. I was catapulted into the position of being a box-office attraction. Nothing could have been worse."

Enough of that callous, commercial attitude toward the Oscar remained twenty years later to relegate Dorothy Malone to the same fate. But there was one difference between the two: Dorothy's performance on the set of *Written on the Wind* was so sensational that gossip was already giving her the Oscar even before the nominations were made.

Her agents got the word also. She was bound, body and soul, to the huge MCA organization. And MCA had nepotistic ties to Malone's contract company, Universal. "The word got out so quickly on my work in the film that I was grossly overworked when I went to get the Oscar. Both the studio and my agents rushed to cash in. They put me into every dog made that year."

She made an incredible fifteen films in eighteen months—all of them quite forgettable: *Quantez, Tip on a Dead Jockey, Warlock, The Last Voyage,* and

Frank Sinatra, here in *The Manchurian Candidate*, experienced the Oscar curse in reverse. He'd been fighting for his career when he got the role of Maggio in *From Here to Eternity*. Oscar night he became probably the most popular winner in the history of the ceremony, and a whole city was touched when the actor grabbed his Oscar and walked out onto the empty Beverly Hills streets . . . to savor his triumph in solitude. It was his rebirth.

Sidney Poitier, here in *Buck and the Preacher*, won an Oscar for *Lillies of the Field* much to the surprise of every Johnny-come-lately producer in town. The audience roared its approval as Poitier became the first black to take a best actor award, but the next morning Poitier found that he still couldn't get financing for *To Sir, With Love*. His Oscar couldn't be traded for a single dime of financing: in fact, Poitier had to star with no salary and carry the movie hat in hand to distributors. When the film made more than ten million dollars its first month out, Hollywood finally stood up and took notice.

The Fast and the Furious being some of the "better" ones. "If somebody had just been honest with me and said, 'Let's wait and get some really good parts,' or if they'd just stopped to think about it. But I had very bad advice and am quite bitter about it. I was in the top fifteen box office stars the three years before the Oscar. It was pretty much downhill afterwards."

It took a TV series, "Peyton Place," at another studio (Fox) to put Malone back in the mainstream of Hollywood. But the momentum was gone. The actress eventually moved back to Dallas where she has become a TV freelancer and a star of regional theater.

Even when the award isn't waved before the faces of producers as a bargaining tool, it can cause career aftershocks for many winners by forever identifying them with the role or type of role for which they won the Oscar. History is full of examples: Gloria Grahame, who became typed as the bad girl with the heart of gold; Charles Coburn, who was forever locked into his dotty old man character; and Hattie McDaniel, who was forced to repeat her Southern mammy time and again just to keep working.

Gale Sondergaard became welded to her performance as the archetypal villainess; Audrey Hepburn was linked to the wide-eyed gamine; Shelley Winters is still making money off her portrayals of blowsy women far beyond their prime. Donna Reed, Frank Sinatra, Ernest Borgnine, and Red Buttons have all built careers off the typecasting shoves given them by their Oscar wins.

"When Red Buttons won the Oscar for *Sayonara*, his career was at a standstill," said his agent Martin Baum. "That Oscar and the way the industry reacted to it gave him a whole new career—now he's done twenty films and goes back to Vegas as a highly paid headliner."

Baum has learned the hard way about the other side of Oscar typing: when client Sidney Poitier became the first black performer to win the best actor Oscar (for *Lilies of the Field* in 1963) the industry seemed to view the win as a "one time thing—unlikely to be repeated," said Baum. And Poitier's Oscar came as a real surprise to the big movietown bosses. The "in money" was on Paul Newman for *Hud* or maybe Albert Finney for *Tom Jones*.

Hollywood's myopic bosses felt the city had done enough by tossing him a bone. "We tried for months, unsuccessfully, to get financing for Sidney's next picture, *To Sir, With Love*, but nobody was interested," said Baum. "Finally, James Clavell agreed to write the script for nothing and to direct for only a percentage of the film. Sidney had to work at no salary just to prove himself all over again—and that was all after the Oscar." *To Sir, With Love* of course went on to earn $50 million worldwide.

"The only real change in my career was in the attitude of newsmen," said Poitier. "And they started to query me on civil rights and the Negro question incessantly. Ever since I won the Oscar, that's what they've been interested in—period." (Hollywood apparently decided that one Oscar was enough. Poitier has never been nominated again, even for *In the Heat of the Night* which brought an Oscar to his co-star, Rod Steiger.)

A year after his Oscar, Poitier turned the final print of *To Sir, With Love* over to Columbia Pictures. The brass there looked at the print, were frightened of it, and put it on the shelf for more than a year. Poitier threatened to go public, however, and Columbia sneaked it in two locations: an art theater in Manhattan and a theater in Westwood near the University of California at Los Angeles. The sneak in Los Angeles was given no ballyhoo and no advertising. The opening titles simply rolled onto the screen after the first show of the evening. First, there was stirring among the packed student audience. But the English rock star Lulu's rendition of the title song became hypnotic. When Poitier appeared on the screen, the student

Maggie Smith as the unforgettable bohemian in George Cukor's *Travels With My Aunt*, found the dark side of Oscar's rainbow after she won her second Oscar as best supporting actress in *California Suite*. (Her first Oscar was for *The Prime of Miss Jean Brodie*.) After the second Oscar, the actress didn't receive a single offer for more than a year. Ironically, she had played a disenchanted British nominee in the Neil Simon farce, complaining at one point that acting doesn't win Oscars—"What I need is a dying father."

audience cheered. There was a near riot of approval when Poitier made his first breakthrough as a black teacher trying to win over a classroom of London toughs.

But there was only one representative from Columbia Pictures at the showing, and nobody passed out rating cards. The studio released it anyway. It was an instant worldwide hit. It was so popular that Columbia hired the men of Gallup Poll to find out why. The answer turned out to be Sidney Poitier. That only served to rankle the Columbia brass. When Oscar time rolled around again, *To Sir, With Love* was not nominated, not even for the title song—one of the major film hits of the troubled decade that began in 1968. Poitier was likewise passed over for Columbia's silly tearjerker *Guess Who's Coming to Dinner* which earned an Oscar for Katharine Hepburn.

Another of Baum's clients, the British actress Maggie Smith, hasn't had a single film offer of any kind since she won her second Oscar for *California Suite* in 1979. She was named best actress of 1969 for *The Prime of Miss Jean Brodie*. "Maggie's Oscars have, I think, typed her as a quote—actress—unquote," Baum said. "Those awards clearly typed her as a great actress—but not necessarily as a leading lady. They'll probably call when they have a part for a quote—great actress—unquote."

This type of industry reaction to the Oscar stretches far back to the early decades of the award and was firmly entrenched when a newcomer named Anne Baxter won the best supporting actress award in 1946.

She was a dark horse if there ever was one. Hollywood's smart money wasn't riding on Baxter as the ballots went out. For one thing, Baxter was still a starlet—a girl who would be gilded and groomed at the express whim of Twentieth Century-Fox, following a pattern that had been set for Alice Faye and Betty Grable. For another thing, Baxter, only twenty-two,

Anne Baxter won her Oscar for a character role in *The Razor's Edge*, a fact which probably saved her from the Oscar curse. "The studio (Twentieth Century-Fox) didn't know what to do with me: I was an ingenue who'd won the Oscar for character parts. That was a very lucky condition because I played roles that would never have gone to me had I fit the usual studio mold."

was up against four heavyweights: Lillian Gish, Ethel Barrymore, Flora Robson, and Gale Sondergaard, winner of the first supporting actress award ten years earlier.

"So when Fox found I had won the Oscar for *Razor's Edge*, they put me in a very special position. You see, the part I played, Sophie, was an alcoholic and on drugs—every bit a character part. I was twenty-two and labeled a 'character actress.' Fox had been used to calling for a 'Betty Grable script' or an 'Alice Faye script.' They really didn't know what to do with me."

While the studio was trying to read Oscar tea leaves, they loaned Baxter out to that old Oscar veteran, MGM. Then somebody got sick and she took over a part in *Walls of Jericho*. "Secretly, I was delighted," Baxter said. "To me, every part was a character part. Ironically, my Oscar kept me from being typed. Those were the days of ironclad stables of stars. If you played wives—you played wives forever. I managed, through a series of crazy flukes, to keep from falling into the Hollywood mold." Consequently, her forty-year career has included such diverse experiences as *All About Eve*, *The Ten Commandments*, and scores of star performances on television. "Along the way, I've been directed by Lewis Milestone, Billy Wilder, Otto Preminger, Fritz Lang, Mervyn LeRoy, and Cecil B. DeMille. Some of that I owe directly to Oscar."

Many others failed to make that leap over the artificial barriers in the minds of casting agents. Dean Jagger, Edmund O'Brien, Celeste Holm, Teresa Wright, Wendy Hiller, George Sanders, and Ed Begley all stayed in the supporting mold. And Donna Reed, Shirley Jones, Martin Balsam, Jack Albertson, and Eileen Heckart all turned to TV to get roles as good as the ones that won them the Oscar.

Oscar typecasting is a trap that can be avoided only by deft maneuvers.

No one knows this better than Estelle Parsons who, after a long Broadway career of great depth, won the 1967 best supporting award for *Bonnie and Clyde*. Miss Parsons, Broadway's woman of a thousand faces, played the hysterical and silly Blanche—the dramatic fulcrum for Warren Beatty's "Clyde" and Faye Dunaway's "Bonnie."

"I must have been offered dozens of Blanche parts in the years right after the Oscar," said Parsons. "For that matter, I still get those offers. My salary went up immediately; there was a lot more interest in me by the press and my name went up over the title."

Parsons routinely turned down carbon copies of the hysterical Blanche. "There were suddenly a lot of people who wanted me to trade on the award—some of them people who should have known better. I could have cashed in on it big. But who wants to do the same part over and over again? I made a pact with myself early on never to play the same role again—and I haven't." After a second tour de force in 1968's *Rachel, Rachel* (for which she got a second nomination), the actress had to turn from movies to TV, where she played "challenging" roles on "The Defenders," "The Nurses," and "Medical Center." She turned to Broadway for *Miss Reardon Drinks a Little* and *Miss Margarida's Way* and to regional theater where she played Lady Macbeth.

Parsons says she has few hopes that the chances in films will change for her and for many others of Oscar caliber: "The kind of work I do is found much more often in TV than in films. Films have become very stereotypical lately. They're not as interesting as TV, which has far more 'good actress' parts—and besides what I'd really like to do is a standup routine in Vegas. To hold my own there would be a *real* challenge."

If today's best supporting awards are no guarantees to challenging work, the situation may have been far worse in the big studio years. Thelma Ritter, for instance, was nominated seven times for playing basically the same character. And she never got a really good film role.

In 1941 Mary Astor, who had just won the best supporting actress award, found her illusion about the Oscar's mystique dashed from the minute she reported for her new Metro contract. "I was offered a long-term contract at MGM with its secure income plus a forty-week year—great security for an aging actress," she said. Suddenly, coming off a career high that included not only the Oscar but the female lead in *The Maltese Falcon*, Astor found that she was "a piece of property and typed for mother roles. Even the people at the studio started calling me 'Mom.'"

Astor got her lifetime studio pass and her key to the dressing room on a Friday morning; Friday afternoon they called her and told her to be in makeup at 8 a.m. Monday. "You'll play Susan Peters' mother," they told her. No script, no instructions. "Oh yeah," said the voice on the phone. "The script isn't out of mimeo yet—don't worry, you'll get one."

"And that's what's happened to the power and the glory of the Oscar?" Astor asked herself. "And how long will it be before another *Maltese Falcon* comes along? Or a play on Broadway? Oh, shut up, Mary, and be happy; you've got that check coming in every week."

Of all the morning-after stories about the Oscar, few are more poignant than the one told sadly by Beverly Hills realtor Elaine Young—former wife of Oscar-winner Gig Young, who, in an apparent murder-suicide, shot himself to death after killing his new wife of three weeks in 1978.

"For Gig the Oscar was literally the kiss of death, the end of the line. It was a case of the old saying, 'Be careful what you wish for—you may get it,' " said Miss Young. "You know what Gig truly, really wished for—he wanted, at least once, to be given a chance to star in a good movie; his own movie. He wanted to be more than just supporting in somebody else's film.

Faye Dunaway has played leading roles in films covering a wide spectrum from *Bonnie and Clyde* to *The Eyes of Laura Mars*, but she received acclaim and an Oscar for her portrayal of the neurotic television producer in Sidney Lumet's *Network*.

Jane Fonda and Michael Sarrazin in an agonizing scene from *They Shoot Horses, Don't They?* In one of Fonda's finest performances, she drifted through the Depression-era film as a victim of society doomed from the start of the film. But as important as Fonda was to the film's artistic success, Gig Young, as a marathon-dance barker, was more so. By serving as the very incarnation of society's evils, the actor spit his lines out through the celluloid, demonstrating a thespian range that had been hidden for twenty years under a bushel of Hollywood drivel. But the movie was not all smooth going . . . Fonda and other cast members made it clear from the start that they felt Gig Young was over his head (although they changed their minds as soon as the first dailies came in).

"He started out as a strong dramatic actor—did you know that? Then he turned to comedy—after that, he couldn't get out of his own way. He supported Doris Day; he supported James Cagney; he supported Clark Gable. And finally he supported Jane Fonda in *They Shoot Horses, Don't They?*

"What he was aching for, as he walked up to get the Oscar for *They Shoot Horses, Don't They?*, was a role in his own movie—one they could call, finally, a 'Gig Young movie.'"

She calls him an "actor's actor." And the record bears this out; when his name was announced as the winner in 1970, the audience of his peers gave him a roar that hadn't been heard since the fifties—the kind of roar that greeted Ingrid Bergman or Susan Hayward.

But he made only two pictures after the Oscar, supporting chores in *The Hindenburg* and *The Killer Elite.*

"Look over Oscar's record for the futile exercises in shallow honor," says Miss Young. "There you'll find Oscar's ultimate sadness."

Gig Young's victory in the Oscar race was both the best thing that had ever happened to him . . . and the worst. For years Gig Young had been fighting to gain recognition as an actor and star in his own right rather than being just a second fiddle to Doris Day, Clark Gable, Tony Randall, James Cagney, and others. *They Shoot Horses, Don't They?* seemed to be just that chance. But it was not to be. The Oscar only welded Gig Young forever to his own personal purgatory as a supporting player . . . a great one, but a second fiddle nonetheless.

APPENDIX
ACADEMY AWARDS COMPENDIUM

Gene Kelly in the "Broadway Melody" number from *Singin' in the Rain*. Considered to be one of Hollywood's best musicals, the film received no Oscars.

Kill 'Em by Silence

Films listed in the American Film Institute's Top Twenty which were not even nominated by the Academy of Motion Picture Arts and Sciences. The A.F.I. polled 35,000 to determine the list.

The General, 1927. Buster Keaton finished this classic comedy in time to qualify it for the first Academy Awards. But by then he was at MGM, which had an iron grip on the newly formed Academy. Louis B. Mayer saw no reason to nominate Keaton for a film that was made for another distributor. And that was that. The comedy plays for laughs against a bittersweet panorama of the Civil War.

The Crowd, 1928. King Vidor's silent masterpiece about the futility and fear of life in the faceless big city. It was the first film to deal with the loss of identity in the urban canyons, and was ahead of its time in treating the monetary crisis of the lower middle class. Louis B. Mayer, Vidor's boss and the man who founded the Academy, let it be known that a nomination for "best director is sufficient." So *The Crowd* was overlooked in the name of splashiness and melodrama: *Wings, Seventh Heaven*, et al. Five people did the final voting, and Vidor says he lost because Mayer maintained that the film was not financially successful enough to win. So the director's prize went to a lion of Hollywood society, Frank Borzage for *Seventh Heaven*.

City Lights, Charlie Chaplin, 1931. The silent clown was at his height in this film which capped twenty years of comedy work. But the film was just that—silent. Once sound came in, the Academy became its immediate slave. There was little chance of a nomination. The Oscar was happy with the sappy *Skippy* or the forgettable *East Lynne*.

King Kong, 1933. It's hard to imagine today, but the Academy blindly nominated ten films and still managed to exclude this fantasy-horror classic. Merian Cooper, a dashing pilot in World War I who became the genius of adventure films, produced *King Kong* for RKO. That was the rub. RKO knew it had a breakthrough film on its hands, but lacked the political moxie to break into the Oscar race. Had it been made at MGM, it would probably have won.

Modern Times, 1936. Charlie Chaplin's masterpiece of the thirties, *Modern Times*, met all the qualifications for nominations—it even made money, about $2.5 million worldwide. But it failed to pull even a single nomination—not even for cinematography or art direction. There was certainly room for it on the 1936 Oscarlist—which included such junk as Jean Harlow's *Libeled Lady* and Deanna Durbin's teenage soprano opus, *Three Smart Girls*. Charlie just wouldn't play the Oscar game.

Singin' in the Rain, 1952. A film that spoke in music's international language and became an instant hit in America, France, England, Germany, and Japan, it was cut adrift to face the Oscars when MGM decided that *Ivanhoe* had to be nominated or it would not make back its cost. So *Ivanhoe* it was. MGM also had other pictures in the fire for best art direction (*The Merry Widow*) and best cinematography (*Million Dollar Mermaid*)—both categories in which *Singin' in the Rain* might have won. The film was also a major box office hit—which worked against it in the bastardized Oscar politics of the fifties. Then, studios felt hits did not need Oscar help but flops like *Ivanhoe* did.

Psycho, Alfred Hitchcock, 1960. *THE* horror classic of all time. Hollywood was aware of the film's stature from the minute it was released to both box office success and critical acclaim. 1960, however, was firmly locked into the habit of lavish, even shameful, Oscar campaigning. Hitchcock considered the ads demeaning and pointless. So *Pyscho* lost its place in the nominees to John Wayne's trivial film, *The Alamo*, which had at least $100,000 in advertising.

Janet Leigh and John Gavin in Alfred Hitchcock's black-and-white masterpiece, *Psycho*. No Oscars.

Big Winners

Hundreds of films have bagged one, sometimes two, Oscars. But a select group of movies have won three or more—and three seems to be the demarcation line. Here, alphabetically within their categories, are those films:

Eleven Oscars: *Ben-Hur.*

Ten Oscars: *West Side Story.*

Nine Oscars: *Gigi, Gone With the Wind.*

Eight Oscars: *Cabaret, From Here to Eternity, My Fair Lady, On the Waterfront.*

Seven Oscars: *The Best Years of Our Lives, Bridge on the River Kwai, Going My Way, Lawrence of Arabia, Patton, The Sting.*

Six Oscars: *All About Eve, An American in Paris, The Godfather, Part II, A Man for All Seasons, Mrs. Miniver, A Place in the Sun.*

Five Oscars: *The Apartment, Around the World in 80 Days, The Bad and the Beautiful, Doctor Zhivago, The French Connection, How Green Was My Valley, In the Heat of the Night, It Happened One Night, The King and I, Mary Poppins, Oliver!, One Flew Over the Cuckoo's Nest, The Sound of Music, Who's Afraid of Virginia Woolf?, Wilson.*

Liza Minnelli and Oscar winner Joel Grey as they appeared in director Bob Fosse's award winning film, *Cabaret*. It was Fosse's directorial debut in the film medium.

Four Oscars: *All The President's Men, Anthony Adverse, Barry Lyndon, Butch Cassidy and the Sundance Kid, Cleopatra (1963), Hamlet, The Heiress, High Noon, The Informer, The Lost Weekend, Marty, Network, Sayonara, The Song of Bernadette, Spartacus, A Streetcar Named Desire, Tom Jones.*

Three Oscars: *Casablanca, Cavalcade, Cimarron, Darling, The Diary of Anne Frank, Elmer Gantry, Fiddler on the Roof, Gentleman's Agreement, The Godfather, Grand Prix, The Great Ziegfeld, Hello, Dolly!, How the West Was Won, Hud, Jaws, The Life of Emile Zola, The Lion In Winter, Love Is a Many-Splendored Thing, Midnight Cowboy, Miracle on 34th Street, Rocky, Roman Holiday, The Rose Tattoo, Seventh Heaven, The Story of Louis Pasteur, Sunrise, Sunset Boulevard, The Thief of Bagdad (1943), To Kill a Mockingbird, The Towering Inferno, Treasure of the Sierra Madre, Yankee Doodle Dandy.*

Roger Corman alumnus Jack Nicholson won acclaim for his performance in Roman Polanski's thriller, *Chinatown*.

Big Losers

Classic films that were heavily honored in the nominations, but left out in the cold by the final voters.

Film	Nominations	Oscars
Mr. Smith Goes to Washington (1939)	11	1
Citizen Kane (1941)	9	1
For Whom the Bell Tolls (1943)	9	1
Since You Went Away (1944)	9	1
Johnny Belinda (1948)	12	1
Quo Vadis (1951)	8	0
Giant (1956)	10	1
Mutiny on the Bounty (1962)	7	0
Becket (1964)	12	1
The Sand Pebbles (1966)	8	0
Airport (1970)	10	1
Chinatown (1974)	11	1
The Turning Point (1977)	11	0

Forgive Us Our Sins

Still today wives can be heard luring their husbands to the suburban movie theater with the soothing call, "Well, it must be good—it *was* nominated for an Oscar." By its very presence within Oscar's golden circle, the most mundane film acquires the trappings of legend, cinema to be savored to the last inch of celluloid. How often have you seen this phrase tagged onto the ad for an unlikely looking TV movie, "Nominated for an Oscar"? Alas, a best picture nomination is hardly a guarantee—Oscar's golden circle is littered with at least a ten percent ratio of turkeys. Here are some of the most flea-bitten dogs from Oscar's golden lists.

Bad Girl, a bit of sentimental slop starring Sally Eilers and James Dunn, probably owed its place on the best picture list to the social and financial position of its director Frank Borzage, who had won the first directing Oscar for *Seventh Heaven*. Bizarrely, Borzage beat out King Vidor but more tragically Josef Von Sternberg for this bit of clap-trap (with the *Bad Girl* helmsmanship judged better than Von Sternberg's *Shanghai Express*). The plot of *Bad Girl* revolved entirely about the difficulties a young couple have in finding the right doctor for their soon-to-be born child. The husband finally takes to the boxing ring to find the cash for that special pediatrician. The key line in the film comes when the boxer shows up at the doc's office to plunk down the cash. The dad looks around, mugs the camera a bit, and says, "Gee, Doc, you got a swell dump here." Hopefully, you'll never be called on to see this one. It's so obscure that *Movies On TV, Halliwell's Film Guide*, and *The New Encyclopaedia of Film* don't list it at all. One of the few places it appears is on Oscar's proud master list.

Here Comes the Navy, nominated for best picture in 1934, features a young James Cagney changing from a cocky ne'er-do-well into a cocky Navy hero—with ho-hum support from Pat O'Brien and Gloria Stuart. Lloyd Bacon provided what direction there was, and studio boss Jack Warner let the Oscar people know that this was HIS personal selection for the finest film of 1934. In order to nominate such drivel, Oscar's cozy little selection committee had to slight such giants as King Vidor's *Our Daily Bread, Of Human Bondage* with Bette Davis and Leslie Howard, *Twentieth Century* with Carole Lombard and John Barrymore, *Death Takes a Holiday, The Count of Monte Cristo*, and Marlene Dietrich's *The Scarlet Empress*.

Three Smart Girls, nominated for best picture in 1936, made a star out of shrill-voiced Deanna Durbin, who played one of three teenage girls who bring their parents back together—a feat they supposedly accomplish by merely singing. "A movie idiotically tuned in on happiness," wrote the *New Yorker* while Graham Greene described it as "laundered and lavendered." Nobody—least of all the film's producer Joe Pasternak—pretended it was a good film. But it sure made money—two million dollars in the first six months, thereby insuring itself a nomination. While rushing out to nominate this frippery, the Academy by-passed *Show Boat, The Petrified Forest* with Bogart and Davis, Erroll Flynn's *Charge of the Light Brigade*, Lillian Hellman's *The Children's Hour, The General Died at Dawn*, and Fritz Lang's *Fury.*

Test Pilot, nominated for best picture in 1938, was a jerky little melodrama starring Gable and Tracy as, you guessed it, test pilots and Myrna Loy as their soft-hearted stay-at-home. With most of the action taking place in airfield coffee shops and most of the dialogue centering on "how dangerous it is up there," the film is quite a yawner when it appears on the late show. And it beat out Hitchcock's *The Lady Vanishes, Angels With Dirty Faces, The Dawn Patrol*, and Selznick's *The Adventures of Tom Sawyer.*

Anchors Aweigh, a pleasant musical with Kathryn Grayson, Gene Kelly, and Frank Sinatra, had no business on the Oscar list in 1945—when movies were just entering an era of postwar realism. But Louis B. Mayer of Metro-Goldwyn decided it would make the list—and make the list it did, although MGM had to sacrifice its own far superior products *The Picture of Dorian Gray, National Velvet*, and *Our Vines Have Tender Grapes.* Consider the films sacrificed to gain this soprano-eaten epic a place on the top five: *G.I. Joe, Love Letters, Keys of the Kingdom, Leave Her to Heaven, The Clock*, and *A Song to Remember.*

Five Films Which Shouldn't Have Won

Mrs. Miniver, best picture, 1942; director, William Wyler. This was a propaganda film greatly sweetened by the talents of Greer Garson and Walter Pidgeon. But many find it unwatchable today—bathed as it is in the school of the crying towel. That's not the point, of course. *Mrs. Miniver* defeated such fine films as *The Magnificent Ambersons, The Pride of the Yankees*, and *King's Row.* The vote is excusable, taken as it was in 1943, the darkest year of the war for England, where the film was set.

An American in Paris, best picture, 1951; director, Vincente Minnelli. Rabid fans of the movie musical will defend the selection of this frothy poem to Gershwin and Paris. And it IS a fine musical, although not as fine as *Singin' in the Rain* or *Bandwagon*, which weren't nominated. In another year it might have been an obvious champ. But in 1951 it triumphed over *A Streetcar Named Desire, A Place in the Sun*, and *Quo Vadis. The African Queen, Detective Story*, and Hitchcock's *Strangers on a Train* were not nominated.

The Greatest Show on Earth, best picture, 1952; director, Cecil B. De Mille. When this tawdry soap opera about the circus plays on TV even children turn it off. With a silly script and even sillier acting by Betty Hutton, James Stewart, and Charlton Heston, the movie beat *High Noon, The Quiet Man*, and *Moulin Rouge. Come Back, Little Sheba, The Bad and the Beautiful*, and *Viva Zapata* weren't even on the Academy's list of five. But the vote was taken at the height of the McCarthy era, and the obvious winner, *High Noon*, was caught up in the House UnAmerican Activities furor (because of its scriptwriter, Carl Foreman). Hedda Hopper personally campaigned against it.

Oliver!, best picture, 1968; director, Carol Reed. An overblown musical valentine to Dickens and Victorian England, *Oliver!* was pleasant entertainment, little else. The acting was turgid, cartoonish. The script could have been written in 1920. But the film beat out *Romeo and Juliet, Funny Girl, The Lion in Winter,* and *Rachel, Rachel,* any one of them better than the winner. Even finer films, *2001: A Space Odyssey, Faces,* and *The Heart Is a Lonely Hunter* weren't even nominated.

Rocky, best picture, 1976; director, John Avildsen. Just when critics said "box office voting" was over, the Academy gave this entertaining bit of hokum its highest award. *Rocky,* a fairy tale about a losing boxer who is turned into a winner, was quite inferior to all of its fellow nominees, *All the President's Men, Network, Bound for Glory,* and *Taxi Driver.* Not nominated were *Marathon Man, The Front,* and *The Last Tycoon.* One rule of Oscar voting held true: given a choice between intelligent plot and raw emotion, the Academy almost always chooses the latter.

LEFT

Rocky, a low-budget loser-becomes-winner opus, walked off with best picture over heavyweights like Sidney Lumet's *Network*.

RIGHT

Barbra Streisand as Fanny Brice, her Oscar winning role in *Funny Girl*.

Thank You, Very Much
(Literate Acceptance Speeches)

Barbra Streisand, for *Funny Girl* (best actress): "Hello, gorgeous."
Meryl Streep, for *Kramer vs. Kramer* (best supporting actress): "Holy Mackerel!" and "I can't hear your questions over my heartbeat."
Loretta Young, for *The Farmer's Daughter* (best actress): "At last!"
Edith Head, for *Roman Holiday* (best costume design): "I'm going to take it home and design a dress for it."
Jane Wyman, for *Johnny Belinda* (best actress, playing a deaf mute): "I accept this very gratefully for keeping my mouth shut; I think I'll do it again."
Dimitri Tiomkin, for *The High and the Mighty* (best musical score): "To all those who helped me get where I am: Brahms, Bach, Beethoven, Richard Strauss, Johann Strauss. . . ."
John Wayne, for *True Grit* (best actor, playing a one-eyed sheriff): "I should have put on that eye patch years ago."
Lee Marvin, for *Cat Ballou* (best actor): "I think half of this belongs to a horse somewhere out in the Valley."
Mercedes McCambridge, for *All the King's Men* (best supporting actress): "I just want to say to all beginning actresses: Never get discouraged. Hold on! Just look what can happen."

LEFT

Jack Nicholson as he appeared in *Five Easy Pieces*.

RIGHT

Liv Ullmann.

In Whose Opinion?

Select comparisons between the New York Film Critics Awards (an unbiased body) and the Academy Awards.

Best Film	New York Critics	The Oscars
1968	*The Lion in Winter*	*Oliver!*
1969	*Z*	*Midnight Cowboy*
1970	*Five Easy Pieces*	*Patton*
1971	*A Clockwork Orange*	*The French Connection*
1972	*Cries and Whispers*	*The Godfather*
1973	*Day for Night*	*The Sting*
1974	*Amarcord*	*The Godfather, Part II*
1975	*Nashville*	*One Flew Over the Cuckoo's Nest*
1976	*All the President's Men*	*Rocky*

Best Actor		
1968	Alan Arkin, *The Heart Is a Lonely Hunter*	Cliff Robertson, *Charly*
1969	Jon Voight, *Midnight Cowboy*	John Wayne, *True Grit*
1972	Laurence Olivier, *Sleuth*	Marlon Brando, *The Godfather*
1973	Marlon Brando, *Last Tango in Paris*	Jack Lemmon, *Save the Tiger*
1974	Jack Nicholson, *Chinatown*	Art Carney, *Harry and Tonto*
1976	Robert De Niro, *Taxi Driver*	Peter Finch, *Network*

Best Actress		
1967	Edith Evans, *The Whisperers*	Katharine Hepburn *Guess Who's Coming To Dinner*
1968	Joanne Woodward, *Rachel, Rachel*	Katharine Hepburn, *The Lion in Winter* Barbra Streisand, *Funny Girl* (tie)
1969	Jane Fonda *They Shoot Horses, Don't They?*	Maggie Smith, *The Prime of Miss Jean Brodie*
1972	Liv Ullmann, *Cries and Whispers*	Liza Minnelli, *Cabaret*
1973	Joanne Woodward, *Summer Wishes, Winter Dreams*	Glenda Jackson, *A Touch of Class*
1974	Liv Ullmann, *Scenes from a Marriage*	Ellen Burstyn, *Alice Doesn't Live Here Anymore*
1975	Isabelle Adjani, *The Story of Adele H.*	Louise Fletcher, *One Flew Over the Cuckoo's Nest*
1976	Liv Ullmann, *Face to Face*	Faye Dunaway, *Network*

Richard Burton in the role of Thomas Becket.

Al Pacino as Michael Corleone in *The Godfather*.

Oscarless

Some artists have been Oscar bridesmaids so often that they've become a cause célèbre for Academy critics—and many say the circle of Oscar losers is more illustrious than the winners list.

Richard Burton: Seven nominations. In Hollywood films since 1952 (*My Cousin Rachel*), Burton has been the victim of Oscar trends or voter sentimentality in almost every case. His performance in *The Spy Who Came in from the Cold* should have easily defeated Lee Marvin's broad charade in *Cat Ballou*; his portrait of the man without hope in *Who's Afraid of Virginia Woolf?* is one of the great acting feats of the decade but lost to Paul Scofield's *A Man for All Seasons*; even Burton's role in *Anne of the Thousand Days*, not one of his best, was still a head higher than John Wayne's *True Grit*. Ex-wife Liz Taylor believes "they had to go out of their way to deny him the Oscar for *Who's Afraid of Virginia Woolf?*"

Deborah Kerr: Six nominations, including 1953's *From Here to Eternity*, which should have won her the Oscar. But Paramount Pictures launched a dazzling and expensive campaign for Audrey Hepburn, who took home the Oscar for *Roman Holiday*, a frothy comedy. As Anna in *The King and I*, it was a tossup between her and Ingrid Bergman who won for *Anastasia*. In 1960 she was certainly better than Liz Taylor, the winner for *Butterfield 8*. The British actress was too good an actress and too weak a box office star. That tells the story in an era when the Oscar was tossed to stars who made money, not to actresses who made fine films.

Al Pacino: Five nominations, from *The Godfather* to *Dog Day Afternoon*. During the 1979 Oscar ceremony, a kaleidoscope of Pacino's career flashed across the screen as Jane Fonda announced him as a nominee for *And Justice For All* (not one of his best roles). "Jeesus," said a reporter for the *Los Angeles Times*, "what-a-range." Pacino, along with DeNiro, has shown a range unequaled in modern cinema. (DeNiro has an Oscar for best supporting actor, *The Godfather*.) Pacino's most deserved nomination came from 1974's *The Godfather, Part II* which was neck-and-neck with Jack Nicholson's *Chinatown*. But the Academy being the Academy, voters bypassed them both to choose Art Carney for the obscure *Harry and Tonto*.

Shirley MacLaine: Five nominations, starting with *Some Came Running* in 1958. The very last of the big studio stars, Shirley MacLaine reported to MGM when the studio was breaking apart at the seams. And it was blatant studio politics that sunk Shirley's chances in 1958. MGM threw its weight behind Liz Taylor for *Cat on a Hot Tin Roof* (although Susan Hayward won). The studio did it a second time in 1960 when she should have been a shoo-in as the lost heroine in *The Apartment*. MGM, trying to squeeze the last drop out of Liz Taylor, helped her win for the dismal *Butterfield 8*. Luckily, MacLaine's a perennial—with the recent *Being There* and *The Turning Point* to her credit.

Montgomery Clift: Four nominations. The classic Hollywood outsider, Montgomery Clift gave Oscar-class performances at least ten times——ranging from *The Search* (one of his nominated roles) to *Freud*, a fine but flawed portrait of the father of psychoanalysis. Clift was oriented to New York and to Broadway—a fact which counted him out in the opinion of many Oscar voters. Bogart's *The African Queen* outpolled Clift's dazzling performance in *A Place in the Sun*. (The maudlin tribute to Bogie also aced out Brando's *A Streetcar Named Desire*.) And there is little doubt that he should have won for *From Here to Eternity* in 1953, but the film's studio, Columbia, threw its votes to Burt Lancaster—in the same film.

And Monty was defeated by the wooden William Holden for *Stalag 17*. (But Holden was really winning for *Sunset Boulevard*—which was over-sighted several years earlier.) "What do I have to do to prove I can act?" he asked a New York critic.

Greta Garbo: Three nominations. Garbo! The classic victim of studio poli-tics. The actress of the thirties, she was nominated for *Anna Christie* in 1931, for *Camille* in 1937, and for *Ninotchka* in 1939. In 1931 and 1937 Garbo would have won easily if MGM had not rigged the races against her. In 1931 MGM production chief Irving Thalberg delivered the studio votes on a platter to his wife Norma Shearer, the winner for *The Divorcee*. It was the same in 1937 when the studio commanded its members to vote for the winner, Luise Rainer, for *The Good Earth*. MGM prexy Louis B. Mayer virtually ruled the Academy with an iron hand from 1927 until 1935, so he must have been somewhat responsible when Oscar failed to even nominate Garbo for *Queen Christina*, *Anna Karenina*, and *Mata Hari*. Fortunately for her, Garbo could have cared less. It was the Academy's reputation that took the body blow.

Martin Sheen: As battle-weary soldier in Francis Ford Coppola's *Apoca-lypse Now*, Sheen carried a massive acting load. But his gift was con-trolled, taut, almost invisible. For his trouble, he got a heart attack, lost two years out of his life, and watched Oscar voters go for the rampant overacting of Al Pacino in *And Justice for All*, the shouting and posturing of Jack Lemmon in *The China Syndrome*, and the wooden thunderbolt Roy Scheider, reprising his own *Jaws*—but with tap shoes instead of a harpoon.

Thelma Ritter: Credited with rescuing more dismal films than any actress in Hollywood, Ritter was nominated for six Academy Awards and never won. Like Gig Young (who eventually won), Ritter disappeared into the fabric of a film, while the melodramatic school took home the Oscar ba-con. Fluttery Josephine Hull in *Harvey* copped it from her in *All About Eve*, Gloria Grahame's wide profile of an actress in *The Bad and the Beautiful* beat out Thelma's *With a Song in My Heart*, and young Patty Duke in *The Miracle Worker* aced out Ritter's performance in *Birdman of Alcatraz*.

Eleanor Parker: This versatile actress, who looked and acted completely differently in almost each film was nominated for *Caged*, *Detective Story*, and *Interrupted Melody*. In many ways her work in *Home from the Hill* and *The Man with the Golden Arm* was even better. While she was under con-tract to MGM, the studio shoved her through a series of Technicolor bombs designed to cash in on her beauty rather than her talent. The Oscar eluded her.

Kirk Douglas: He was so fine in *Champion* that he seemed destined to rank with the legendary Oscar actors. His portrait of a driven fighter was a hard act to follow. But he did it—first as a sharkish studio head in *The Bad and the Beautiful* and then as Vincent Van Gogh in *Lust for Life*. Both brought him best actor nominations. Also of Oscar class, but unnomi-nated, were *Spartacus*, *Young Man with a Horn*, *The Devil's Disciple*, *Two Weeks in Another Town*, and *Detective Story*. While the other actors of his generation got Oscars—Lancaster, Peck, and Borgnine—Douglas was beaten by histrionics: Broderick Crawford in *All the King's Men* won in 1949, Cooper beat him in 1952 with *High Noon*, and Yul Brynner got the award that truly belonged to Douglas (for *Lust for Life*) in 1956.

Cary Grant: The debonair Grant has made even life look easy, so why not acting? In this respect he has been his own worst enemy—Oscarwise. "I play myself beautifully," he has said again and again. The town came to

Martin Sheen.

Joanne Woodward.

Warren Beatty.

Basil Rathbone and Nigel Bruce.

Burgess Meredith.

Fred Astaire.

believe it. But Grant remains the champ of America's comic actors—with more range than Dreyfuss and more subtlety than Lemmon. He never cared about the Oscar particularly and maintains that the institution was fine "back in the days when it was still just a party—a chance for some fun." His two nominations— in 1941 and 1944—were for *Penny Serenade* and *None But the Lonely Heart*. But he could easily have been picked for *The Awful Truth, His Girl Friday, Indiscreet, Topper, Bringing Up Baby, The Philadelphia Story, Arsenic and Old Lace, To Catch a Thief,* and *North by Northwest.*

Irene Dunne: With her abundance of natural talent, she was forced to choose between opera, musical comedy, and films. This was 1922, and she became discouraged after flunking (but with grace) an audition for the Metropolitan Opera. She went into a road company of *Irene,* then into *Showboat* as Magnolia. A studio contract followed and her first Oscar nomination came for 1931's *Cimarron*. Other nominations were for *Theodora Goes Wild, The Awful Truth, Love Affair,* and *I Remember Mama*. Twice she was beaten by the maudlin overacting of Luise Rainer, the Viennese Teardrop. She naturally lost to Vivien Leigh in *Gone With the Wind*. The Oscar she deserved for *Cimarron* went to the hammish Marie Dressler. And Jane Wyman in *Johnny Belinda* was judged better than Dunne in *I Remember Mama*. She could have easily been nominated for *The Mudlark, Penny Serenade,* and *Anna and the King of Siam.*

Basil Rathbone: Although acknowledged in his own era as one of the three finest actors in films (the others being John Barrymore and Paul Muni), Oscar politics were weighted against him. First of all, he was the screen's greatest villain in a town where bad guys rarely win. Second, Rathbone was the man the studios sent for whenever their limp-throated stars had to look good. He was a sort of artistic crash cart that saved matinee idols from tripping over their handsome faces. In spite of scores of roles that should have gotten him the Academy's nod, he was nominated only twice: for *Romeo and Juliet* in 1936 and for *If I Were King* in 1938 (he won neither year). He could have been picked as well for *Robin Hood, The Mark of Zorro, Anna Karenina, A Tale of Two Cities, Captain Blood, Garden of Allah, Dawn Patrol, David Copperfield, Tower of London,* and *Confession*. He grew wealthy from the Sherlock Holmes series, but, at the end of his career, ungrateful Hollywood put him into movies such as *Hillbillies in a Haunted House* and *The Ghost in the Invisible Bikini* (sadly, he played the ghost, a pale shadow of himself in those final films).

Agnes Moorehead: Arguably the finest all around actress in Hollywood's history, she began her film career playing Kane's mother in *Citizen Kane* and exited in a gothic film, *Dear, Dead Delilah*. She was another actress so skilled that she disappeared deep within her celluloid characters. She was nominated five times and in several cases she was without doubt the best supporting actress of the year. She never won. For instance in 1942 her work in Orson Welles' *The Magnificent Ambersons* was easily better than Teresa Wright's work in the soapy *Mrs. Miniver*. She likewise was better in *Mrs. Parkington* (1944) than the showy Ethel Barrymore in *None But the Lonely Heart*. Ironically, she reaped more honors for her work as Endora, Elizabeth Montgomery's mother in "Bewitched." And she could have done that one on the phone.

Others: Eddie Albert, Jean Arthur, Fred Astaire, Carroll Baker, John Barrymore, Warren Beatty, Barbara Bel Geddes, William Bendix, Charles Bickford, Dirk Bogarde, Charles Boyer, Jeff Bridges, Billie Burke, Dyan Cannon, John Cassavetes, Charles Chaplin, Lee J. Cobb, Gladys Cooper, Tony Curtis, Marlene Dietrich, Robert Duvall, Clint Eastwood, Peter Falk,

W.C. Fields, Albert Finney, Errol Flynn, Nina Foch, Henry Fonda, Lynn Fontanne, John Garfield, Judy Garland, Ann Harding, Barbara Harris, Richard Harris, Miriam Hopkins, Leslie Howard, John Ireland, Danny Kaye, Sally Kellerman, Gene Kelly, Shirley Knight, Alan Ladd, Elsa Lanchester, Angela Lansbury, Piper Laurie, Gertrude Lawrence, Carole Lombard, Alfred Lunt, Marsha Mason, Joel McCrea, Adolphe Menjou, Robert Mitchum, Marilyn Monroe, Don Murray, Mildred Natwick, Paul Newman, Merle Oberon, Peter O'Toole, Jack Palance, William Powell, Tyrone Power, Robert Redford, Paul Robeson, Edward G. Robinson, Flora Robson, Mickey Rooney, Gena Rowlands, Rosalind Russell, Peter Sellers, Jean Simmons, Kim Stanley, Barbara Stanwyck, Gloria Swanson, Franchot Tone, Lana Turner, Liv Ullmann, Robert Vaughn, Clifton Webb, Tuesday Weld. . . .

Paul Newman.

An Oscar by Any Other Name . . .

The Academy Awards have made a name from giving best acting awards to those who in no way gave the best performance in their given years. Oscar is a gentleman of tradition and sentiment—qualities more highly prized by the voters than dramatic ability. But every once in a while even Oscar has gone too far. A few of those include:

Katharine Hepburn, best actress for *Guess Who's Coming to Dinner* in 1967. The only actress with three best acting awards, Hepburn probably won in 1967 because of the maudlin nature of the integration soap opera—with extra brownie points because she had nursed her friend Spencer Tracy through his last film. Any one of her four competitors could have legally qualified as best actress of 1967; Hepburn could not. Her fellow nominees: Anne Bancroft, *The Graduate*; Faye Dunaway, *Bonnie and Clyde*; Audrey Hepburn, *Wait Until Dark*; and Dame Edith Evans, *The Whisperers*. This was one of the years which make you wonder about the taste of the average Oscar voter.

Henry Fonda.

Elizabeth Taylor, best actress for *Butterfield 8* in 1960. The headlines on Los Angeles' tabloid newspapers screamed "LIZ DYING" the day Oscar voting started. It threw them into a panic. This might be, they thought, the last chance to give Liz her Oscar—which, arguably, she deserved for *Cat on a Hot Tin Roof* in 1958 or for *Suddenly, Last Summer* in 1959. She barely survived; flew into town while still an invalid and walked up to get her Oscar leaning heavily on Eddie Fisher's arm. Again, Liz was the sole nominee who obviously did not deserve the Oscar. Her competitors: Melina Mercouri, *Never on Sunday*; Shirley MacLaine, *The Apartment*; Greer Garson, *Sunrise at Campobello*; and Deborah Kerr, *The Sundowners*. Not even nominated were: Jean Simmons in *Elmer Gantry*, Janet Leigh in *Psycho*, and Wendy Hiller for *Sons and Lovers*. Even Taylor says, "I won it because I almost died."

Peter O'Toole.

Lee Marvin, best actor for *Cat Ballou* in 1965. By 1965 Marvin had turned in more than fifty films, almost singlehandedly carrying such movies as *Pete Kelly's Blues, The Comancheros,* and *The Killers* of 1964. The Oscar voters were just itching to give him an Academy Award. *Cat Ballou* was a change of pace for Marvin, and he was capable of carrying the satirical cowboy. But this was NOT the best performance of the year. Rod Steiger was the odds-on critical favorite for *The Pawnbroker*. (In fact, voters committed another miscarriage two years later when they gave Steiger the Oscar he should have gotten for *The Pawnbroker* and thereby denied it to Warren Beatty in *Bonnie and Clyde*.) Runner-up to Steiger was Richard Burton in *The Spy Who Came In From the Cold*.

James Stewart, best actor for *The Philadelphia Story,* 1940. This is one of the Academy's classic cases of a "better late than never" Oscar. Stewart had certainly earned the Academy Award for *Mr. Smith Goes to Washington* in 1939. But the competition—including Clark Gable for *Gone With the Wind*—was stiff, and the winner, Robert Donat for *Goodbye, Mr. Chips,* was Stewart's equal. The voters picked 1940 to set the record straight. It must have been hard to pick a winner that year—a year of classic performances: Charles Chaplin, *The Great Dictator*; Henry Fonda, *The Grapes of Wrath*; Raymond Massey, *Abe Lincoln in Illinois*; and Laurence Olivier, *Rebecca*. Not nominated were William Holden, *Our Town*; Herbert Marshall, *The Letter*; Charles Boyer, *All This and Heaven Too*; and Errol Flynn, *The Sea Hawk.*

LEFT

Bette Davis and Leslie Howard in *Of Human Bondage.* Some believe if the film had been made at Warners, rather than RKO, Davis would have received an Oscar.

RIGHT

Eddie Fisher and Elizabeth Taylor attend an awards ceremony during their brief and stormy marriage.

Bette Davis, best actress for *Dangerous,* 1935. A guilty conscience Oscar. In 1934 Bette Davis *had* given the best performance of the year in *Of Human Bondage,* which created an entirely new type of screen heroine—the bitch without redemption. Davis had made that for RKO and not her home studio, Warner Brothers. Therefore, neither RKO nor Warners put her on their lists. So she wasn't even nominated. The Oscar voters-at-large raised a ruckus, gaining the right to vote for Davis as a write-in. Even then, the Warners brass sent out a memo hinting to voters that a vote for Bette was not a vote for Warners. Claudette Colbert got the Oscar. The Davis fever was raging so furiously in 1935 that they would probably have given her the Oscar for reading the phone book. Fellow nominees—Elizabeth Bergner, *Escape Me, Never*; Katharine Hepburn, *Alice Adams*; Miriam Hopkins, *Becky Sharp*; Merle Oberon, *The Dark Angel*; and Claudette Colbert, *Private Worlds*—all had bigger challenges than Bette. Bergner, Oberon, and Hopkins were never to get an Oscar.

Ingrid Bergman, best supporting actress for *Murder on the Orient Express,* in 1974. Ingrid Bergman walked out to the end of the stage after getting her Oscar and directed the Academy's attention to Valentina Cortese, the actress who actually deserved the Oscar for *Day for Night.* Charles Champlin, entertainment editor of the *Los Angeles Times,* called the gesture a high point of the Oscar decade. The Bergman Oscar, her third, is typical of the sins committed in the name of best supporting performances—because the voters, having to choose between established names and dazzling newcomers, almost always pick the old favorites. Other examples are: Helen Hayes who won for *Airport* over Karen Black in *Five Easy Pieces*; George Burns in *The Sunshine Boys* over Chris Sarandon in *Dog Day Afternoon* and Brad Dourif in *One Flew Over the Cuckoo's Nest*; and Jason Robards for *Julia* over Peter Firth in *Equus* and Mikhail Baryshnikov in *The Turning Point.*

The Godfather and the Academy

Paramount's saga of the underworld establishment was planned and partly filmed as one sprawling chronicle (and that was the way it came to network television). Although it was released as two films, *The Godfather* in 1971 and *The Godfather, Part II* in 1973, many film critics view it as a whole unto itself. Following that line of thinking, *The Godfather* has accounted for more nominations—21—and has launched more Oscar-class stars than any project in film history.

The Alumni

Actors: Marlon Brando, best actor, 1972; Robert De Niro, best supporting actor, 1974. Al Pacino, best actor nominee, 1974; James Caan, Robert Duvall, and Al Pacino, best supporting actor nominees, 1973; Michael V. Gazzo and Lee Strasberg, best supporting actor nominees, 1974; Talia Shire (Coppola's sister) best supporting actress nominee, 1974.

Direction: Francis Ford Coppola, nominee for best direction, 1972; Oscar winner in 1974.

Production: best picture, 1972; best picture, 1974—Albert S. Ruddy, producer.

Writing: Mario Puzo and Francis Ford Coppola, best screenplay, 1972; best screenplay, 1974.

Technicians: Anna Hill Johnstone, nominee, best costume design, 1972; Bud Grenzbach, Richard Portman, and Christopher Newman, nominees, best sound, 1972; William Reynolds and Peter Zinnen, nominees, best film editing, 1972; Dean Tavoularis, Angelo Graham, and George R. Nelson, winners, best art direction, 1974; Theodora Van Runkle, nominee, best costume design, 1974; Nino Rota and Carmine Coppola, best original dramatic score, 1974.

Joiners

The Academy of Motion Picture Arts and Sciences has grown from less than a dozen members in 1927 to 4,306 in mid-1980. But it's been a

Al Pacino and Robert Duvall in *The Godfather*.

bumpy ride—the Academy has gone in and out of fashion over the decades. For instance, by 1932 about 1,200 had signed up. Then came the attempt by the studios to use the organization as a company union. Actors, writers, and musicians resigned by the hundreds. Frank Capra says the Academy was down to forty people in 1936. The long climb back finally hit its stride in 1970 when the membership went above 3,000.

The Branches

Actors: 1,072 members, ranging from June Allyson to Vanessa Redgrave to Shirley Temple Black. There was some hesitation during the late sixties—when the anti-Academy movement became chic—but now most of the "new Hollywood" belongs, including: Jane and Peter Fonda, John Cassevetes, Michael Douglas, Peter Bogdanovich, and Dustin Hoffman.

Directors: 212 members, ranging from King Vidor to Hal Ashby; from Roman Polanski to Steven Spielberg; from Martin Scorsese to Jack Webb.

Executives: 228 members, including the longtime studio bosses and the new moguls such as Alan Ladd, Jr., Sherry Lansing, and David Begelman.

Musicians and composers: 222 members, ranging from Marvin Hamlisch to disco wizard Paul Jabara; from the ageless Hoagy Carmichael to Italy's Riz Ortolani. Others are Irving Berlin, Anthony Newley, Leslie Bricusse, and Burt Bacharach.

Also: Art directors, 220 members; cinematographers, 103 members; film editors, 162 members; producers, 274 members ; writers, 356 members; short subjects, 194 members; public relations directors, 189 members; sound technicians, 215 members; members at large, 260.

Lastly, the Academy now carries 599 on its non-voting associates list—a highly significant number since that list is a purgatory for Academy members who have been out of the swim too long. The longer that list grows, the closer the Academy comes to true representation of Hollywood today. The Academy, however, has found it impossible to retire any of its "name" actors—no matter how retired—so the actors branch is crammed with antiques.

Surprising Members

Dustin Hoffman: Now forty-three, Hoffman is considerably wiser about the commercial ways and means of Hollywood. But back when he was about thirty-three, and was passed over for *Little Big Man, Papillon,* and *Straw Dogs,* Hoffman was Oscar's bitterest and most public enemy. He called it a cruel charade—pointless and patently unfair. Hoffman was nominated for *Lenny, Midnight Cowboy,* and *The Graduate.* The actor had a brief lull in the late seventies with the minor flops *Agatha* and *Straight Time.* And sometime during that plateau he decided to play the Academy's game—winning the big one for *Kramer vs. Kramer* in 1980. Oddly enough, *Kramer vs. Kramer* showed only a couple of Hoffman's dazzling dramatic skills.

Peter Bogdanovich: A director-writer who went Hollywood quick, Bogdanovich is a deputized critic of the Academy Awards. His incisive journalism in 1977 was the only credible commentary on the fiftieth birthday of the Oscars. Virtually every other article wallowed in glowing, sentimental slop. He had been nominated for *The Last Picture Show* but has not been nominated since, in spite of virtuoso work on *Paper Moon* and *What's Up, Doc?* His mild jabs at Saint Oscar may have contributed to these oversights.

Marlon Brando: He refused to take his 1972 Oscar for *The Godfather,* sending a sometime Indian maiden, Sacheen Littlefeather, to turn it down. He'd sent a five page speech along with her. She never read it—but stated simply that Marlon was shunning the Oscar because of the country's treatment of the Indians. The Academy expected a cancellation. Instead Brando simply renewed his membership with no comment—leaving his Oscar in the vaults.

Give Me Your Tired Plots, Your Clichés

Only certain types of films win Oscars — the same tawdry few favored by Hollywood's money men for seven generations. Musicals, obvious comedies, tepid war movies, an occasional message movie — Oscar has been a dull creature of habit. And to the great detriment of the Academy's image, new genres are routinely shut out (for instance, violence, *Straw Dogs;*

George C. Scott in his best-actor role as General George S. Patton, Jr.

outer space, *2001: A Space Odyssey*; and "new wave," *Easy Rider*). Here is a partial scoreboard of Oscar-winning genres.

War: *Wings, All Quiet on the Western Front, Mrs. Miniver, The Best Years of Our Lives, From Here to Eternity, The Bridge on the River Kwai, Patton,* and *The Deer Hunter.*

Musicals: *Broadway Melody, The Great Ziegfeld, An American in Paris, Gigi, West Side Story, My Fair Lady, The Sound of Music,* and *Oliver!*

Comedy: *It Happened One Night, You Can't Take It With You, The Apartment, Tom Jones, The Sting,* and *Annie Hall.*

Melodrama: *Cavalcade, Grand Hotel, Mrs. Miniver* (a war soap opera), *Casablanca* (likewise), *The Greatest Show on Earth* (a circus soap opera), *All About Eve* (a Broadway soap opera), *Gone With the Wind,* and *Rocky* (a boxing soap opera).

Crime: *The French Connection, The Godfather,* and *The Godfather, Part II.*

Crusading Films: *The Lost Weekend, Gentleman's Agreement, In the Heat of the Night, One Flew Over the Cuckoo's Nest,* and *Kramer vs. Kramer.*

Adventure: *Around the World in 80 Days, Ben-Hur,* and *Lawrence of Arabia.*

Performance Genres

Prostitutes with Hearts of Gold: Shirley Jones, *Elmer Gantry*; Janet Gaynor, *Seventh Heaven*; Judy Holliday, *Born Yesterday*; Elizabeth Taylor, *Butterfield 8*; Susan Hayward, *I Want to Live!*; Donna Reed, *From Here to Eternity*; Jo Van Fleet, *East of Eden*; Lila Kedrova, *Zorba the Greek.*

Adulterers: Norma Shearer, *The Divorcee*; Simone Signoret, *Room at the Top*; Helen Hayes, *The Sin of Madelon Claudet*; Gloria Grahame, *The Bad and the Beautiful*; Julie Christie, *Darling.*

Mental Disturbance: Fredric March, *Dr. Jekyll and Mr. Hyde*; Joanne Woodward, *The Three Faces of Eve*; Ronald Colman, *A Double Life*; Emil Jannings, *The Last Command*; and Jack Nicholson, although feigned, in *One Flew Over the Cuckoo's Nest.*

Biographies: George Arliss, Disraeli; Charles Laughton, Henry VIII; Paul Muni, Louis Pasteur; Spencer Tracy, Father Flanagan; Gary Cooper, Sergeant York; James Cagney, George M. Cohan; Luise Rainer, Anna Held; Patty Duce, Helen Keller; Alice Brady, Mrs. O'Leary of Chicago; Anthony Quinn, Paul Gauguin; Paul Scofield, Sir Thomas More; Katharine Hepburn, Eleanor of Aquitaine; Barbra Streisand, Fanny Brice.

And, regardless of genre, it helps greatly to die before the end of the picture: Emil Jannings, *The Last Command*; Fredric March, *Dr. Jekyll and Mr. Hyde*; Wallace Beery, *The Champ*; Victor McLaglen, *The Informer*; Spencer Tracy, *Captains Courageous*; Robert Donat, *Goodbye, Mr. Chips*; Ronald Colman, *A Double Life*; Laurence Olivier, *Hamlet*; Broderick Crawford, *All the King's Men*; Jose Ferrer, *Cyrano de Bergerac*; Yul Brynner, *The King and I*; Alec Guinness, *Bridge on the River Kwai*; Susan Hayward, *I Want to Live!*; Simone Signoret, *Room at the Top*; Elizabeth Taylor, *Butterfield 8*; Donald Crisp, *How Green Was My Valley*; Teresa Wright, *Mrs. Miniver*; Anne Baxter, *The Razor's Edge*; Gloria Grahame, *The Bad and the Beautiful*; Frank Sinatra, *From Here to Eternity*; both Red Buttons and Miyoshi Umeki, *Sayonara*; Burl Ives, *The Big Country*; George Chakiris, *West Side Story*; Shelley Winters, *The Diary of Anne Frank*; Melvyn Douglas, *Hud* and *Being There*; Ethel Barrymore, *None But the Lonely Heart*; Paul Scofield, *A Man for All Seasons*; Marlon Brando, *The Godfather*; Jack Nicholson, *One Flew Over the Cuckoo's Nest*; Peter Finch, *Network*; Vanessa Redgrave, *Julia*; Ben Johnson, *The Last Picture Show*; Christopher Walken, *The Deer Hunter.*

Pardon Our Oscar

Oscar history is loaded with oversights, embarrassing winners and nominees, and lapses of taste. But occasionally, the Academy Award voters outdo even themselves. Here are a few:

The *Scenes from a Marriage* Affair: The critical elite on both coasts was bowled over by a three-hour Ingmar Bergman film, *Scenes from a Marriage*. It appeared to be an Oscar shoo-in for best direction, best picture, best actress, and best editing. But the preliminary ballots (containing the 350-or-so pictures eligible) went into the mail without the Swedish film. A furor erupted. Directors including Frank Capra and George Cukor ran ads in the trade papers begging the Academy to put the film onto the preliminary list. Gregory Peck, then Academy president, ruefully explained that a highly technical point excluded *Scenes from a Marriage*. The saga, as it turned out, had been first shown as a television movie in Sweden in 1973. It was the date of the film that excluded it rather than its origin as a television show. The controversy became a rage as the final Oscar voting neared. The Academy board of directors, however, would not back down. Finally Charles Champlin wrote: "As it stands, the luster of the top awards in many categories will be tarnished because Bergman's brilliantly observed and superbly executed drama was not on the ballot. It is crazy and unfair to the winners and losers alike and a seemingly needless blow to the credibility and prestige of the Academy Awards."

Barbra Streisand in director Gene Kelly's *Hello, Dolly!*, a box-office disaster.

A Penny for Your Expensive Turkeys: Or, how Twentieth Century-Fox bought nominations for three disasters (*Doctor Doolittle*, *Hello, Dolly!*, and *Star!*) by trading on studio politics, waging shameless ad campaigns, and wooing the Oscar voters with expensive food and very private screenings. It all started in 1967 when the brass at Twentieth released *Doctor Doolittle* to widespread derision and apathy. This overproduced children's film wasn't one of the top twenty films of 1967, much less a member of the top five. John Gregory Dunne has shown in his book *The Studio* how Fox waged the *Doctor Doolittle* campaign voter by voter as if they were fighting street-by-street in a besieged city. Each of the Academy branches had an entire series of private showings, preceded by a buffet dinner and followed by a midnight champagne supper. Further, Fox mailed out copies of the record, ran a massive ad campaign, and even held a telephone campaign. Worse for history, the studio used its clout in the branches to see that its own *Two for the Road* was dropped from the preliminary cinematography and editing lists. Never mind that the editing and photography on *Two for the Road* were excellent while *Doctor Doolittle* was only mediocre in those areas. *Doctor Doolittle* needed the Oscar nominations to help it at the box office, and Fox saw that the film got them. The studio P.R. department did the same thing in 1969, gaining the musical dud *Hello, Dolly!* nominations for best picture, best cinematography, best art direction, best sound, and best editing. The film sacrificed in this outburst of corporate greed was *2001: A Space Odyssey*, which had dazzling photography, superlative art direction, and was one of the best two or three films of the year. The Academy's reputation is still suffering from that one.

Music? That's Just Noise: The Oscar case against *Saturday Night Fever*. In 1977, *Saturday Night Fever* gave the movies a new type of hero— the daytime loser who becomes a prince by night—and a new star, John Travolta. It made so much money so fast that even the Academy couldn't ignore it. (The Academy can overlook ANYTHING but a hit.) The Hollywood voters tossed the film a prize bone—a best acting nomination for John

Lee Grant, once blacklisted, is now active in both performing and directing.

Travolta. But the Academy's music branch excluded it from competition in any of its categories. The score, in fact, was counted out before the quarterfinals. "They could have played any music during those scenes," said a spokesman for the music branch. "We have to consider the appropriateness of the music to the plot." The Gibb Brothers, better known as the BeeGees, had created an entirely new score for the disco movie, a score that fit the action in a subtle manner. Nobody who saw John Travolta walking through the opening song, "Stayin' Alive," doubted the power of the new song or the score as a whole. But did the music voters even see *Saturday Night Fever*? Probably not. To exclude the BeeGees, the music branch had to nominate *Mohammad — Messenger of God*. The nominees for best song were laughable: "The Slipper and the Rose Waltz," "Someone's Waiting for You," "Candle on the Water," "Nobody Does It Better," and "You Light Up My Life," the winner. "Stayin' Alive" became the theme for a new generation, while "You Light Up My Life," an international hit, came from a stupid film that was purposely written to go under the song.

The Little Red Oscar

The Oscar races became so intertwined with the anti-communist movement in Hollywood that the Academy drafted a loyalty oath required of all nominees. But many of those blacklisted, officially, had been nominees and winners throughout Academy history. Here is a partial list of blacklisted nominees and winners.

John Garfield, twice nominated, died of a heart attack the night before he was to appear before the House UnAmerican Activities Committee.

Gale Sondergaard, winner of the first best supporting actress award, and a later nominee, was blacklisted and could not get a job in Hollywood from 1950 until 1970.

Anne Revere, a best supporting actress winner and a nominee two other times, was never able to recover from her H.U.A.C stigma.

Kim Hunter, Oscar winner as best supporting actress in *A Streetcar Named Desire,* was unjustly implicated and kept off the screen from 1953 until 1965.

Lee Grant, four times nominated and the winner of best supporting actress for *Shampoo,* was blacklisted, resulting in her being kept out of the industry for seventeen years.

Oscar-Class Writers who were on the blacklist: John Bright, one nomination; Sidney Buchman, one nomination, one Oscar; John Howard Lawson, one nomination; Dalton Trumbo, one nomination, one Oscar under the pseudonym "Robert Rich" and another uder the "front" of Ian Hunter; Donald Ogden Stewart, one nomination; writer Howard Koch, one nomination, one Oscar; Lillian Hellman, two nominations, Dashiell Hammett, one nomination; Alvah Bessie, one nomination; Albert Maltz, one nomination; Abraham Polansky, one nomination; Carl Foreman, one nomination, one Oscar under the name of Pierre Boulle; Michael Wilson, one Oscar, one nomination, one nomination disqualified due to the loyalty oath; Waldo Salt, two nominations, one Oscar; Ned Young, one nomination, one Oscar, both under the pseudonym "Nathan E. Douglas" and still listed incorrectly in the Academy records.

Oscar Brass

The Academy of Motion Picture Arts and Sciences, buffeted as it was by the political currents in Hollywood, has eaten up its presidents—making many of them victims of Oscar's general ill will. Below is a partial list—annotated.

Douglas Fairbanks, Sr., 1927–1929. Doug lent his position as Hollywood social leader to the Academy's first stumbling years. His main accomplishment was, appropriately an Oscar for his wife, Mary Pickford—one of the first victories for politics rather than acting ability.

William C. De Mille, 1929–1931. The selection of Cecil's brother kept the helm of the Academy firmly in the hands of the studio executives. A popular choice, De Mille was a screen behind which Louis B. Mayer and others turned the Academy into a company labor union.

M.C. Levee, 1931–32. A man who left no discernible record one way or the other.

Conrad Nagel, 1932–1933. Nagel, a popular actor and Hollywood social figure, was the lamb sacrificed by the Mayer clique as it tried to block the actors, writers, and directors out of legitimate labor unions.

J. Theodore Reed, 1933–1934. A president who went down in history as the unfortunate helmsman the year the Academy's producers tried to shove wage and agent controls through the new National Recovery Administration. More than 1,500 members resigned during this period.

Frank Lloyd, 1934–1935. The Academy fell apart during this regime, dropping from more than a thousand members to less than a hundred.

Frank Capra, 1935–1939. Capra, the director of *The American Dream,* was elected only once and then declared Oscar emperor until 1939. There were forty members when he took over, Capra has written. And those forty weren't all gung-ho. Capra forced the Academy to drop out of the labor union business and went about the task of saving the organization. "I had to beg the guilds to let me send them ballots," says Capra. "It was touch and go for awhile."

Walter Wanger, 1940–1945. He guided the Academy through the war years and maintains the organization had "less than fifty active members" during most of that time. (Bette Davis was elected president in 1941 but quickly resigned when she found she was only "a figurehead for the producers.")

Jean Hersholt, 1945–1949. Hersholt moved the Oscar voting into better artistic waters—and that meant recognition and votes for the increasingly fine British product. When *Hamlet* was named best picture, the producers had already pulled all of their cash out of the Oscar ceremony and were ready to gut the Academy. It was touch and go again.

Charles Brackett, 1949–1955. The man who turned to TV in order to pay for the Oscars, and thereby created the publicity-glutted monster we know and love today. The first TV rights were bought for $100,000 a year. Now the price is near $2 million.

George Seaton, George Stevens, B.B. Kahane, Valentine Davies, Wendell Corey, and Arthur Freed, 1955–1967. Uneventful but lucrative years as Oscar grew successively bloated on television cash.

Gregory Peck, 1967–1970. Along with Charles Champlin, Peck is the man who's done the most to bring Oscar voting into the space age. He worked steadily to update bylaws, weed out aged voting members, and increase the voting itself, which many believe was down to forty percent of Academy membership in the early sixties.

Daniel Taradash, Walter Mirisch, and Howard W. Koch, 1970–1977. All

Patty Duke won an Oscar for her portrayal of Helen Keller in *The Miracle Worker*.

Julie Christie.

have slowly but surely upgraded the Academy's image and voting practices. And it all shows in the Oscar nominees and winners—1976–1980.

No Room on the List

Great films that were not nominated for best picture, listed chronologically: *The Crowd, The Jazz Singer, Hallelujah, Anna Christie, Little Caesar, Morocco, Of Human Bondage, Camille, Snow White, The Sea Hawk, Laura, Lifeboat, Meet Me in St. Louis, Body and Soul, The Third Man, Death of a Salesman, Strangers on a Train, Singin' in the Rain, Rear Window, To Catch a Thief, Some Like It Hot, North by Northwest, Inherit the Wind, Psycho, Long Day's Journey Into Night, The Manchurian Candidate, The Miracle Worker, Hud, Cool Hand Luke, In Cold Blood, 2001: A Space Odyssey, Faces, Easy Rider, They Shoot Horses, Don't They?, Women in Love, Ryan's Daughter, Carnal Knowledge, McCabe and Mrs. Miller, Sunday, Bloody Sunday, Alice Doesn't Live Here Anymore, A Woman Under the Influence, Close Encounters of the Third Kind, Manhattan.*

The Winner's Circle

Best Pictures
Wings (award first given 1927–28), *Broadway Melody, All Quiet on the Western Front, Cimarron, Grand Hotel, Cavalcade, It Happened One Night, Mutiny on the Bounty, The Great Ziegfeld, The Life of Emile Zola, You Can't Take It With You, Gone With the Wind, Rebecca, How Green Was My Valley, Mrs. Miniver, Casablanca, Going My Way, The Lost Weekend, The Best Years of Our Lives, Gentleman's Agreement, Hamlet, All the King's Men, All About Eve, An American in Paris, The Greatest Show on Earth, From Here to Eternity, On the Waterfront, Marty, Around the World in 80 Days, The Bridge on the River Kwai, Ben-Hur, The Apartment, West Side Story, Lawrence of Arabia, Tom Jones, My Fair Lady, The Sound of Music, A Man for All Seasons, In the Heat of the Night, Oliver!, Midnight Cowboy, Patton, The French Connection, The Godfather, The Sting, The Godfather, Part II, One Flew Over the Cuckoo's Nest, Rocky, Annie Hall, The Deer Hunter, Kramer vs. Kramer.*

Best Actors
Emil Jannings, (award first given 1927–28), Warner Baxter, George Arliss, Lionel Barrymore, Wallace Beery and Fredric March (a tie), Charles Laughton, Victor McLaglen, Paul Muni, Spencer Tracy, Spencer Tracy, Robert Donat, James Stewart, Gary Cooper, James Cagney, Paul Lukas, Bing Crosby, Ray Milland, Fredric March, Ronald Colman, Laurence Olivier, Broderick Crawford, Jose Ferrer, Humphrey Bogart, Gary Cooper, William Holden, Marlon Brando, Ernest Borgnine, Yul Brynner, Alec Guinness, David Niven, Charlton Heston, Burt Lancaster, Maximilian Schell, Gregory Peck, Sidney Poitier, Rex Harrison, Lee Marvin, Paul Scofield, Rod Steiger, Cliff Robertson, John Wayne, George C. Scott, Gene Hackman, Marlon Brando, Jack Lemmon, Art Carney, Jack Nicholson, Peter Finch, Jon Voight, Dustin Hoffman.

Best Actresses
Janet Gaynor (award first given 1927–28), Mary Pickford, Norma Shearer, Marie Dressler, Helen Hayes, Katharine Hepburn, Claudette Colbert, Bette Davis, Luise Rainer, Luise Rainer, Bette Davis, Vivien Leigh, Ginger Rogers, Joan Fontaine, Greer Garson, Jennifer Jones, Ingrid Bergman, Joan Crawford, Olivia De Havilland, Loretta Young, Jane Wyman, Olivia De Havilland, Judy Holliday, Vivien Leigh, Shirley Booth, Audrey Hepburn, Grace Kelly, Anna Magnani, Ingrid Bergman, Joanne Woodward, Susan Hayward, Simone Signoret, Elizabeth Taylor, Sophia Loren, Anne Bancroft, Patricia Neal, Julie Andrews, Julie Christie, Elizabeth Taylor,

Katharine Hepburn, Katharine Hepburn and Barbra Streisand (a tie), Maggie Smith, Glenda Jackson, Jane Fonda, Liza Minnelli, Glenda Jackson, Ellen Burstyn, Louise Fletcher, Faye Dunaway, Diane Keaton, Jane Fonda, Sally Field.

Best Directors

Frank Borzage (award first given 1927–28), Lewis Milestone, Frank Lloyd, Lewis Milestone, Norman Taurog, Frank Borzage, Frank Lloyd, Frank Capra, John Ford, Frank Capra, Leo McCarey, Frank Capra, Victor Fleming, John Ford, John Ford, William Wyler, Michael Curtiz, Leo McCarey, Billy Wilder, William Wyler, Elia Kazan, John Huston, Joseph L. Mankiewicz, Joseph L. Mankiewicz, George Stevens, John Ford, Fred Zinnemann, Elia Kazan, Delbert Mann, George Stevens, David Lean, Vincente Minnelli, William Wyler, Billy Wilder, Jerome Robbins, Robert Wise (Robbins and Wise co-directors), David Lean, Tony Richardson, George Cukor, Robert Wise, Fred Zinnemann, Mike Nichols, Carol Reed, John Schlesinger, Franklin J. Schaffner, William Friedkin, Bob Fosse, George Roy Hill, Francis Ford Coppola, Milos Forman, John G. Avildsen, Woody Allen, Michael Cimino, Robert Benton.

Best Supporting Actors

Walter Brennan (award first given 1936), Joseph Shildkraut, Walter Brennan, Thomas Mitchell, Walter Brennan, Donald Crisp, Van Heflin, Charles Coburn, Barry Fitzgerald, James Dunn, Harold Russell, Edmund Gwenn, Walter Huston, Dean Jagger, George Sanders, Karl Malden, Anthony Quinn, Frank Sinatra, Edmond O'Brien, Jack Lemmon, Anthony Quinn, Red Buttons, Burl Ives, Hugh Griffith, Peter Ustinov, George Chakiris, Ed Begley, Melvyn Douglas, Peter Ustinov, Martin Balsam, Walter Matthau, George Kennedy, Jack Albertson, Gig Young, John Mills, Ben Johnson, Joel Grey, John Houseman, Robert De Niro, George Burns, Jason Robards, Jason Robards, Christopher Walken, Melvyn Douglas.

Best Supporting Actresses

Gale Sondergaard (award first given 1936), Alice Brady, Fay Bainter, Hattie McDaniel, Jane Darwell, Mary Astor, Teresa Wright, Katina Paxinou, Ethel Barrymore, Anne Revere, Anne Baxter, Celeste Holm, Claire Trevor, Mercedes McCambridge, Josephine Hull, Kim Hunter, Gloria Grahame, Donna Reed, Eva Marie Saint, Jo Van Fleet, Dorothy Malone, Miyoshi Umeki, Wendy Hiller, Shelly Winters, Shirley Jones, Rita Moreno, Patty Duke, Margaret Rutherford, Lila Kedrova, Shelley Winters, Sandy Dennis, Estelle Parsons, Ruth Gordon, Goldie Hawn, Helen Hayes, Cloris Leachman, Eileen Heckart, Tatum O'Neal, Ingrid Bergman,

Melvyn Douglas.

Madelaine Kahn.

Ann-Margret.

Lee Grant, Beatrice Straight, Vanessa Redgrave, Maggie Smith, Meryl Streep.

Best Songs

"The Continental" by Conrad and Herb Magidson (award first given 1934); "Lullabye of Broadway" by Harry Warren and Al Dubin; "The Way You Look Tonight" by Jerome Kern and Dorothy Fields; "Sweet Leilani" by Harry Owens; "Thanks for the Memory" by Ralph Rainger and Leo Robin; "Over the Rainbow" by Harold Arlen and E.Y. Harburg; "When You Wish Upon a Star" by Leigh Harline and Ned Washington; "The Last Time I Saw Paris" by Jerome Kern and Oscar Hammerstein, II; "White Christmas" by Irving Berlin; "You'll Never Know" by Harry Warren and Mack Gordon; "Swinging on a Star" by James Van Heusen and Johnny Burke; "It Might As Well Be Spring" by Richard Rodgers and Oscar Hammerstein, II; "On the Atchison, Topeka and Santa Fe" by Harry Warren and Johnny Mercer; "Zip-A-Dee-Doo-Dah" by Allie Wrubel and Ray Gilbert; "Buttons and Bows" by Jay Livingston and Ray Evans; "Baby, It's Cold Outside" by Frank Loesser; "Mona Lisa" by Ray Evans and Jay Livingston; "In the Cool, Cool, Cool of the Evening" by Hoagy Carmichael and Johnny Mercer; "High Noon" by Dimitri Tiomkin and Ned Washington; "Secret Love" by Sammy Fain and Paul Francis Webster; "Three Coins in the Fountain" by Jule Styne and Sammy Cahn; "Love Is a Many Splendored Thing" by Sammy Fain and Paul Francis Webster; "Whatever Will Be, Will Be" by Jay Livingston and Ray Evans; "All the Way" by James Van Heusen and Sammy Cahn; "Gigi" by Frederick Loewe and Alan Jay Lerner; "High Hopes" by James Van Heusen and Sammy Cahn; "Never on Sunday" by Manos Hadjidakis; "Moon River" by Henry Mancini and Johnny Mercer; "Days of Wine and Roses" by Henry Mancini and Johnny Mercer; "Call Me Irresponsible" by James Van Heusen and Sammy Cahn; "Chim Chim Cher-ee" by Richard M. Sherman and Robert B. Sherman; "The Shadow of Your Smile" by Johnny Mandel and Paul Francis Webster; "Born Free" by John Barry and Don Black; "Talk to the Animals" by Leslie Bricusse; "The Windmills of Your Mind" by Michel Legrand and Alan Bergman-Marilyn Bergman; "Raindrops Keep Fallin' on My Head" by Burt Bacharach and Hal David; "For All We Know" by Fred Karlin, Robb Royer, James Griffin, Rob Wilson, and Arthur James; "Theme from *Shaft*" by Isaac Hayes; "The Morning After" by Al Kasha and Joel Hirschhorn; "The Way We Were" by Marvin Hamlisch and Alan Bergman-Marilyn Bergman; "We May Never Love Like This Again" by Al Kasha and Joel Hirschhorn; "I'm Easy" by Keith Carradine; "Evergreen" by Barbra Streisand and Paul Williams; "You Light Up My Life" by Joseph Brooks.

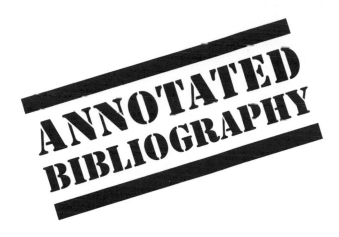

ANNOTATED BIBLIOGRAPHY

The story of the avarice and heartbreak surrounding the Academy Awards comes out in bits and pieces which are scattered through the history of Hollywood. More than 150 books, 500 magazine articles, and hundreds of daily newspaper stories were used in the compilation of this book. The most useful are included in this bibliography. When they are available, I have listed paperback editions.

But two works stand out from the rest:

Osborne, Robert. *Fifty Golden Years of Oscar: The Official History of the Academy of Motion Picture Arts and Sciences.* ESE California Books; La Habra, California; 1979. The full history of the Academy is told by Osborne in a massive work of scholarly nature. Osborne, a film writer for *Daily Variety*, Hollywood's respected trade paper, has also offered a decent actor-by-actor index.

Shale, Richard. *Academy Awards: An Ungar Reference Index.* Frederick Ungar Publishing Company, New York, 1978. Organized so thoroughly that all of the body of Oscar data is available in a few minutes, the book has bridged the gap for writers and scholars.

Books

Baker, Fred and Firestone, Ross. *Movie People.* Lancer Books, New York, 1973. Good interview with Rod Steiger.

Behlmer, Rudy, editor. *MEMO from David O. Selznick.* Viking Press, New York, 1972. Selznick's paranoia about Jennifer Jones' career and the Oscar makes for riveting reading.

Bosworth, Patricia. *Montgomery Clift.* Bantam Books, New York, 1978.

Capra, Frank. *The Name above the Title.* The Macmillan Company, New York, 1971. Invaluable account of the Oscar intrigue during the Academy's decade is spiced throughout the book. And Capra even reveals his own morbid obsession with winning the Oscar.

Carey, Gary. *Brando.* Pocket Books, New York, 1973.

Carpozi, George. *The John Wayne Story.* Dell Books, New York, 1972. Hidden well in these pages is the shameless story of Wayne's attempt to buy an Oscar for his film, *The Alamo.*

Crawford, Christina. *Mommie Dearest.* William Morrow and Company, New York, 1979. Joan Crawford with her Oscar showing—only part of a unique and agonizing book.

Crowther, Bosley. *Hollywood Raja.* Holt, Rinehart and Winston, New York, 1960. Crowther unmasks the greed behind Louis B. Mayer's founding of the Academy of Motion Picture Arts and Sciences.

Davis, Bette. *The Lonely Life.* Lancer Books, New York, 1962.

A whiff of the real thing. Bob Hope, the perrenial everyman who didn't get an Oscar, takes some reflected glory from Brando's first. Oscar and television had just married, Brando didn't know Wounded Knee from tennis elbow, and some stars still used the Oscar as a doorstop.

Dunne, John Gregory. *The Studio.* Bantam Books, New York, 1969. This stylish study of Hollywood studio politics is now a classic—must reading at most film schools. In fact, almost everybody learned from it EXCEPT the studio politicians themselves. It holds up because nothing has changed.

Eels, George. *Hedda and Louella.* Warner Books, New York, 1973. To understand the world of Hedda and Louella is to understand the gamesmanship that created the Oscar. This portrait is essential.

Fowler, Gene. *Good Night, Sweet Prince.* Ballantine Books, New York, 1950. How could Hollywood exclude John Barrymore from the Oscar? This book tells part of the story.

Graham, Sheila. *Confessions of a Hollywood Columnist.* Bantam Books, New York, 1968. Inside stuff on Monroe, etc.

Guiles, Fred Lawrence. *Marion Davies.* McGraw Hill, New York, 1972. This out-of-print book restores Marion to her original place among Hollywood's best comediennes. It also sheds light on the Oscar politics that defeated Orson Welles and his *Citizen Kane.*

Gussow, Mel. *Don't Say Yes Until I Finish Talking.* Doubleday Books, New York, 1971. So-so work on Darryl Zanuck.

Harbison, W.A. *George C. Scott.* Pinnacle Books, New York, 1977. To study Scott's picture career is to follow the Oscar thorugh its trends.

Hopper, Hedda. *The Whole Truth and Nothing But.* Pyramid Books, New York, 1963.
From Under My Hat. MacFadden Books, New York, 1960. "A lot of old rumors and some biting remarks about the Oscar."

Higham, Charles. *Celebrity Circus.* Dell Books, New York, 1980.
The Celluloid Muse. Signet Books, New York, 1969.

Hyams, Joe. *Bogie.* Signet Books, New York, 1966.

Kael, Pauline. *The Citizen Kane Book.* Bantam Books, New York, 1974. Miss Kael follows *Citizen Kane* from its release through its hallowed status as perhaps the best film ever made. On the way she discovers the rotten cesspool of the Oscar voters. This and Guiles' *Marion Davies* nail the Oscars to their deserved infamy for this episode.

Kobler, John. *Damned in Paradise: The Life of John Barrymore.* Atheneum Books, New York, 1977. Too much gossip.

La Guardia, Robert. *Monty.* Avon Books, New York, 1977.

Lambert, Gavin. *On Cukor.* Capricorn Books, New York, 1972.

Likeness, George. *The Oscar People.* Wayside Press; Mendota, Illinois; 1965. This out-of-print and hard-to-find book is an interesting look at the varied fates of Oscar winners. It was written in 1964 when the Oscar was adapting to a "new Hollywood."

Linet, Beverly. *Alan Ladd: A Hollywood Tragedy.* Berkley Books, New York, 1979. Why wasn't Alan Ladd nominated for *Shane*? Linet gives a partial answer.

Marchak, Alice. *The Super Secs.* Bantam Books, New York, 1976. Alice Marchak, Marlon Brando's secretary, writes with humor and insight about life with the great one. And she gives a satirical picture of her boss and his *Godfather* Oscar.

Marion, Frances. *Off with Their Heads.* The Macmillan Company, New York, 1972. The Oscar's first decade, critically viewed by a winner and her friends. Not entirely a happy picture.

Frank Sinatra, the come-back kid. His career as the bobby-sox heart-throb of the forties was in shreds before he landed a role in *From Here to Eternity.* An Oscar resulted, and his popularity has soared ever since.

Oscar goes home for another year. The giant statues that flank the stage for the awards presentations are hauled away after the 1972 ceremonies.

© A.M.P.A.S.

Parish, James Robert. *The MGM Stock Company.* Bonanza Books, New York, 1977. This trail-blazing reference book portrays every MGM contract star and helps explain such people as Luise Rainer.
Lisa. Pocket Books, New York, 1975.

Perry, Louis B. and Perry, Richard S. *A History of the Los Angeles Labor Movement.* University of California Press, Berkeley, 1963. The pitiful attempt by the studio bosses to make a slave of the Academy they created emerges in great detail in these pages. There's no doubt—the Academy was created in Louis B. Mayer's image.

Phillips, Gene. *Stanley Kubrick: A Film Odyssey.* Popular Library, New York, 1977.

Rosenberg, Bernard and Silverstein, Harry. *The Real Tinsel.* The Macmillan Company, 1975.

Russell, Rosalind. *Life Is a Banquet.* Grossett and Dunlap, New York, 1977. "In her own words."

Sands, Pierre Norman. *A Historical Study of the Academy.* Arno Press, New York, 1966. Sands studied the Academy's first three decades for his doctoral thesis at the University of Southern California. He defends the Oscar races, but his statistics unlock the key to the Academy's dark decade—the thirties.

Sarris, Andrew. *Interviews with Film Directors.* Avon Books, New York, 1967.

Sheppard, Dick. *Elizabeth.* Warner Books, New York, 1974. If there ever was any doubt that Liz Taylor got her first Oscar because she nearly died, this book erases it.

Steele, Joseph Henry. *Ingrid Bergman.* Popular Library, New York, 1959.

Steinberg, Cobbett. *Reel Facts: The Movie Book of Records.* Vintage Books, New York, 1978. The best raw reference book ever published on the movies. It gives the results of all top film contests plus salary and profit data.

Swanberg, W.A. *Citizen Hearst.* Bantam Books, New York, 1961. Valuable inside look at the *"Citizen Kane* Affair."

Thomas, Bob. *Selznick.* Doubleday Books, New York, 1970.
Joan Crawford. Bantam Books, New York, 1978.
Thalberg, Life and Legend. Doubleday Books, New York, 1969.
King Cohn. Bantam Books, New York, 1967.
Walt Disney, An American Original. Pocket Books, New York, 1976.
The One and Only Bing. Grosset and Dunlap, New York, 1977.
Bob Thomas, Hollywood reporter for three decades tells thoroughly the story of the Oscar in his many biographies.

Waterbury, Ruth. *Elizabeth Taylor: Her Life, Her Loves.* Popular Library, New York, 1964.

Zolotow, Maurice. *Shooting Star: A Biography of John Wayne.* Simon and Schuster, New York, 1975. Wayne, the good and the bad. But still not an unbiased account of Wayne and *The Alamo* affair.

Articles

Berkowitz, Stan and Lees, David. *"A Race for Fame and Money."* Los Angeles Times. April 8, 1979. A capsulized look at the greed involved in a representative Oscar race. A view you don't get from columnists.

Bogdanovich, Peter. "The Oscar at Fifty." *Esquire.* April, 1978. An insider stands back to look at the Academy Award monster: entertaining, with good views from Cary Grant and James Stewart.

Canby, Vincent. "Hooray, Another Awful Oscar Evening." *New York Times*. April 4, 1974. Criticism from a voice of experience.

"In the Afterglow of the Oscars." *New York Times*. April 16, 1978. Ditto.

Champlin, Charles (Entertainment Editor, the *Los Angeles Times*). "Oscar, the Tail That Wags the Academy." *Los Angeles Times*. February 23, 1980.

"A–Z Rating for Oscar." *Los Angeles Times*. January 3, 1975.

"Oscar Ceremony, Reflection of a Tense Era in Film History." *Los Angeles Times*. April 18, 1971.

"Oscar, Forty Years Old and Still an Adolescent." *Los Angeles Times*. March 2, 1969.

"The Awards, a Rundown of Possible Winners." *Los Angeles Times*. April 7, 1968.

"Craft Over Content, an Oscar Tradition." *Los Angeles Times*. April 2, 1978.

"Brando, and the Offer He Refused." *Los Angeles Times*. March 30, 1973.

"Hollywood's Multi-Million Dollar Question: How Right?" *Los Angeles Times*. January 28, 1971.

"The Oscar Nominations, an Assessment." *Los Angeles Times*. February 28, 1971.

"Signs of Change for the Better in Oscar Nominations." *Los Angeles Times*. February 27, 1972.

"Oscar, '78, It's Business As Usual." *Los Angeles Times*. February 22, 1978.

The versatile Orson Welles as he appeared in a "Hallmark Hall of Fame" production in 1972.

Taken as a whole, Charles Champlin's year-by-year chronicling of the Academy Awards mirrors the Oscar as a troubled institution. His is the closest the Academy has to a voice of conscience, being the only major critic who takes a middle ground between those who crucify the Academy and those who glorify it. Some of his complaints have produced major changes in the process, lessening the greed and manipulation.

Grant, Lee. (film writer, the *Los Angeles Times*). "Redgrave Remarks Arouse Jewish Group." *Los Angeles Times*. April 5, 1978.

"War and Peace at the Awards." *Los Angeles Times*. April 11, 1979.

Virtually the only unbiased reporting of Oscar's backstage. Most others play the glamorous Oscar game.

Harmetz, Aljean. "How to Win an Oscar Nomination." *New York Times*. April 3, 1970. She gets inside a year's worth of Oscar hype and the view is devastating.

Hoberman, J. "Hearst's Lady of Hollywood." *Village Voice*. April 2, 1979. A rare look at Hearst's obsessive quest for the Oscar—which he wanted to present to Marion Davies.

Knight, Arthur. "Assessing the Oscar." *Hollywood Reporter*. March 7, 1980.

Lindsey, Robert. "Oscars Stir Redgrave Dispute." *New York Times*. February 1, 1978.

Mann, Klaus. "Emil Jannings and Life after Hitler." *Los Angeles Times*. June 8, 1945.

Newsweek. "Perils of an Oscar." April 2, 1958.

"Electioneering for Oscars." March 5, 1973.

New York Times. "German Leaders Grew Wealthy on Favoritism." August, 5, 1945. The article depicts Emil Jannings and his connection with Nazi propaganda films which made him wealthy. He won the first Oscar for *The Way of All Flesh*.

Claudette Colbert in David O. Selznick's World War II drama, *Since You Went Away*.

Powers, Charles. "Jack Lemmon: The Long Wait Before Oscar." *Los Angeles Times.* April 7, 1974. An interesting look at the general hysteria surrounding the Oscar.

Royko, Mike. "So Mary Pickford Has Grown Old. So What?" *Los Angeles Times.* April 2, 1976. Exposes the Oscar and its annual trading off the tears and pathos of its aging stars.

San Francisco Chronicle. "Sacheen Littlefeather, a Profile." March 30, 1973. A revealing portrait of the maiden who refused Brando's Oscar for *The Godfather*.

Sarris, Andrew. "The Oscars: Why 'Chinatown' Lost." *Village Voice.* April 21, 1975. Sarris has the voters pegged in this piece which not only focuses on one Oscar year, but flashes back to the skeletons in the Academy Award closet.

Schulberg, Budd. "How My Daddy Won the Oscar." *Los Angeles Times.* April 13, 1969. A clever look at Oscar greed.

Skolsky, Sidney. "Film Flam," *The Hollywood Citizen*, February 11, 1935.

Stumbo, Bella. "Oscar Show Arouses Protest by Deaf." *Los Angeles Times.* April 8, 1978.

Tusher, Will. "Oscar Aftermath Torn by Viet Passions." *Hollywood Reporter.* April 10, 1975.

Warga, Wayne. "A Half Century of Movie Arts and Survival." *Los Angeles Times.* May 8, 1977.
"Academy Spadework, a Long Row." *Los Angeles Times.* February 28, 1971.
Two of the many articles by Wayne Warga, associate arts editor of the *Times*, and an observer of the Oscars for a decade. He's gone to the source with Mary Pickford and King Vidor to separate fact from Oscar hokum.

Yeaman, Elizabeth. "The Awards Puzzle." *Hollywood Citizen.* February 1, 1936.
"Hollywood's Film Prize under Scrutiny." *Hollywood Citizen.* March 2, 1935.

Video Sources

Barrett, Rona. "Good Morning, America." "Rona Comments on Oscar Winners." ABC Television. March 29, 1977.
"Good Morning, America. "Rona Looks at Oscar Winners." ABC Television. April 4, 1978.
These lively spot commentaries catch the flavor of the modern Oscars.

Champlin, Charles. "On the Film Scene with Jane Fonda." Interview on Theta Cable Television. March, 1980.
"On the Film Scene with I.A.L. Diamond." Interview on Theta Cable. Winter, 1979.
"On the Film Scene with Walter Mirisch." Interview on Theta Cable. Summer, 1980.
These shows managed to catch, in capsulized fashion, the feelings of Fonda, Diamond, and former Academy President Mirisch on the current film scene.

LIST OF ILLUSTRATIONS

Eat your heart out, Flash Gordon. This art-moderne lightning-bolt man was featured as entertainment for an Academy Awards ceremony in the 1930s. A film clip of this rather strange production number was aired on the 1979 Oscar show. By then, sad to say, no one was quite sure what it was all about.

Greer Garson, a popular winner.

Yul Brynner—did his shaved head win him an Oscar?

Credits

Academy of Motion Picture Arts and Sciences: *11, 13, 14, 16, 17, 19, 21, 22, 28, 30, 31, 32, 33, 35, 37, 40, 46, 47, 49, 52, 55, 56, 58, 60, 63, 64, 68, 69, 71, 73, 74, 76, 77, 78, 79, 80, 81, 82, 85, 86, 87, 88, 90, 91, 92, 93, 97, 99, 100, 102, 105, 106, 108, 109, 116, 121, 122, 123, 124, 131, 136, 137, 138, 139, 142, 146, 148, 151, 152, 157, 165, 171, 173, 175, 177, 178, 185, 186, 188, 190, 191, 196, 197, 198, 199, 201, 202, 203, 207, 209, 219, 220, 222, 223*
American Broadcasting Company: *133*
Bison Archives, Marc Wanamaker: *2, 6, 8, 11, 12, 25, 27, 29, 36, 38, 41, 43, 44-45, 48, 51, 59, 66, 72, 99, 134, 180, 212, 218*
Brandt's, Eddie, Movie Matinee: *53, 94, 112, 126, 155, 159, 172, 174, 181, 182, 184, 194, 195*
Columbia Broadcasting System: *32, 89, 113*
Columbia Pictures: *114, 139, 160*
Russ Jones: *101, 104*
Lawrence, Kenneth G., Movie Memorabilia Shop of Hollywood: *154*
Los Angeles Times: 128
Paramount Pictures: *115*
Twentieth Century-Fox: *25*
United Artists: *36, 71, 146, 158, 165*

INDEX

Page numbers for illustrations are in *italic* type, those for text references are in roman.

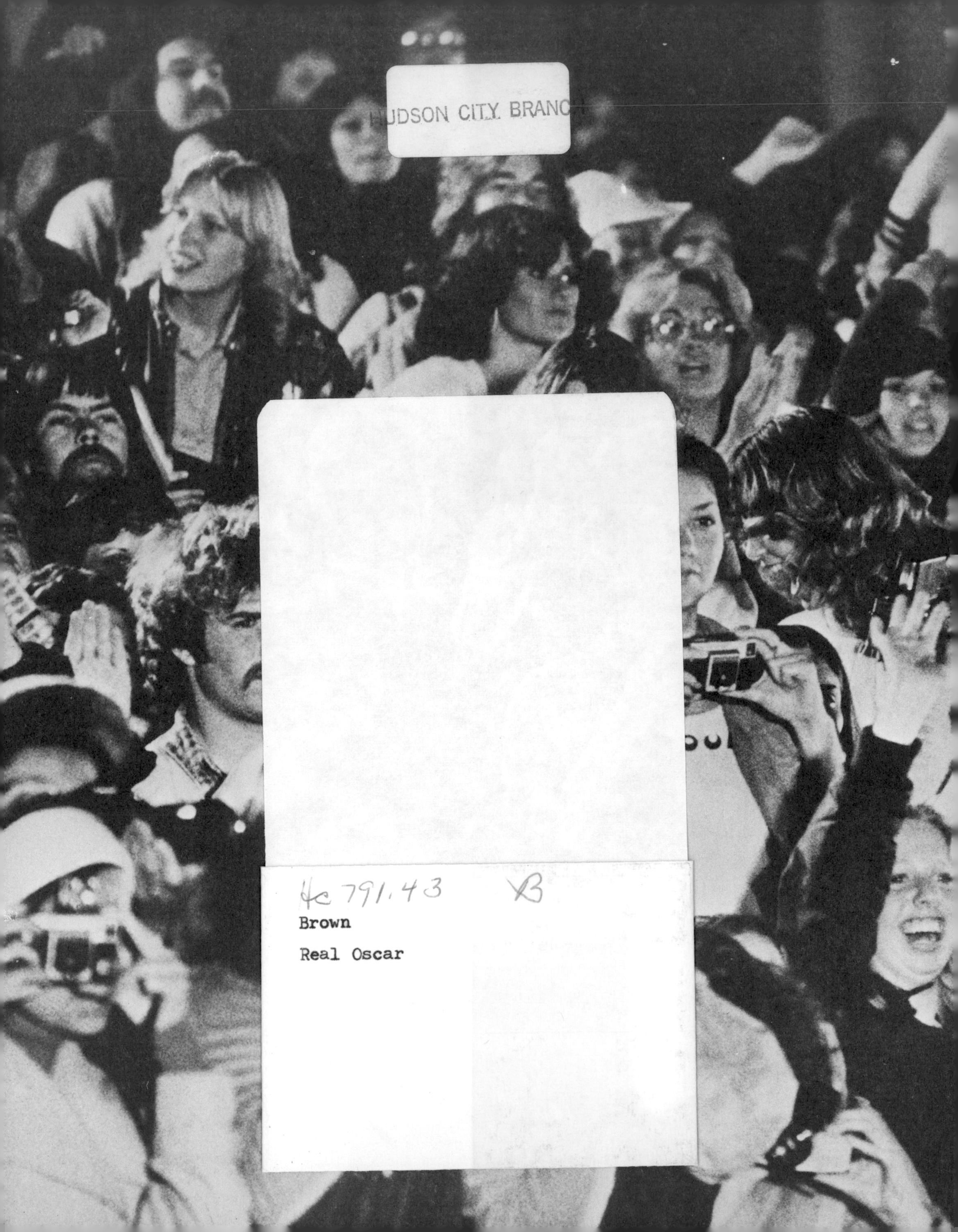